Jesus
the Rabbi Prophet

Jesus
the Rabbi Prophet

A New Light on the Gospel Message

Jacques Baldet

Translated from the French
by Joseph Rowe

Inner Traditions
Rochester, Vermont

Inner Traditions
One Park Street
Rochester, Vermont 05767
www.InnerTraditions.com

Originally published in French under the title *Histoire de Rabbi Jésus* by Éditions Imago,
7 rue Suger, 75006 Paris
First U.S. edition published in 2005 by Inner Traditions

LIBRARY OF CONGRESS CATALOGING-IN-PUBLICATION DATA

Baldet, Jacques.
    [Histoire de rabbi Jésus. English]
  Jesus the rabbi prophet : a new light on the Gospel message / Jacques Baldet ; translated
from the French by Joseph Rowe.—1st U.S. ed.
    p. cm.
  Includes bibliographical references (p.   ) and index.
  ISBN 1-59477-070-0 (pbk.)
  1. Jesus Christ—Teachings. I. Title.
  BS2415.B32713 2005
  232.9'08—dc22

                                                                                2005010421

Printed and bound in Canada by Transcontinental Printing

10   9   8   7   6   5   4   3   2   1

Text design and layout by Virginia L. Scott Bowman
This book was typeset in Sabon with Delphin and Avenir as the display typefaces

For Macéo, Rémi, and Marcus,
my grandchildren

Contents

Preface

And they will not say: "Look, here it is!" or "Look,
there it is!" For the Kingdom of Heaven is within you.

LUKE 17:21*

During the last two thousand years, human beings have killed each other by the millions, sometimes with appalling cruelty, over questions such as whether the God of the Bible exists and whether or not Jesus of Nazareth, crucified by Pontius Pilate, and known as the Christ, was the only begotten Son of God. I am among those who are convinced that such questions (the source of rivers of ink, as well as of blood) are not worth any sort of bloodshed. In any case, they are questions that can be answered only by someone who subscribes to one religious belief or another.

There are many in our time, however, who are convinced that religious leaders, whether theologians, philosophers, or inspired teachers, have been unable to offer satisfactory answers to the question of the meaning of life—a meaning that would have to satisfy our need for both

---

* [The author notes here that he has used the French version of The Jerusalem Bible for biblical quotations. In this English translation, however, we have made use of several Bibles, in addition to the English version of The Jerusalem Bible. For English translations of the Gospel of Thomas, we have used Jean-Yves Leloup, *The Gospel of Thomas* (Rochester, Vt.: Inner Traditions, 2005). —*Trans.*]

freedom and compassion,* both of which are essential for humanity's survival. What strikes me about contemporary Christians who take part in public religious and philosophical debates on the meaning of life is how rarely they discuss the man Jesus of Nazareth—and, even more rarely, his essential teaching.

Raised as a practicing Catholic, I later rejected the Church's religious teaching because I could no longer reconcile the Jesus of Christianity with the Jesus of Nazareth to be found in the gospels. Nevertheless, the hope of someday discovering the "true" historical Jesus never left me. It was in this spirit that I decided, seven years ago, to begin the research that has led to this book. Besides his original teaching, I wanted to understand the motivations behind Jesus' arrest by Jewish religious authorities and his execution by Roman power. He was certainly not the first prophet or religious leader to suffer such a fate in Palestine, where the Romans had dealt harshly with many other agitators. But what was it that he said and did that so upset the Jewish religious establishment?

In researching and writing this book, I have conducted my own kind of "archaeological dig" of the variegated terrain that comprises the surviving gospels and other texts that speak of Jesus. My motivation has been my desire to excavate the original teaching of this man from Nazareth. Naturally, I have not been so presumptuous as to start from scratch and have made use of the great body of contemporary scholarly research on the historical Jesus. My main objective has been to uncover a message that has been repeatedly distorted, and even betrayed, ever since the death of its teacher. I make no pretense of having discovered the authentic teaching, though I do feel that I have at least made some steps in this direction. But that is for the reader to judge.

---

*I have chosen to use the word compassion here for a biblical word that is now often translated as "love." But the word love has become so misused that I have preferred compassion, in spite of the almost condescending nuance that word might seem to have in certain contexts.

Without too much anticipation of my conclusions at the end of this book, I would like to say that, inasmuch as we are able to reconstruct his teaching, the response of Jesus of Nazareth to the great question of the meaning of human life was not so much a set of answers as the showing of a possible way toward these answers. The task of working them out was one that he left to each of his fellow human beings.

Introduction

Whoever drinks from my mouth will become like me,
and I will become like them . . .

THE GOSPEL OF THOMAS, LOGION 108

Whether Christians or not, many people who have questions about the historical Jesus can no longer accept the centuries-old objection that historical curiosity about Jesus is shallow and irrelevant, that it is only the resurrected Christ that truly matters. This traditional position still has its adherents, and though it is often formulated with exquisite subtlety, it can be summed up in the following way: Jesus, whose resurrection from the dead was witnessed by his disciples three days after his crucifixion, was the Messiah and the Christ.[1] His divine parentage was revealed before he ascended to God the Father. Because this divine Jesus Christ has so little in common with the merely historical figure of Jesus of Nazareth, historical research on his life before the resurrection can have virtually no bearing on Christian faith in the resurrected Christ; only theology can properly address it.

This kind of argument seems unconvincing in our age, which tends to see historical time as the fundamental dimension in which the human[2] manifests itself and becomes a thinking subject, or "being that speaks."[3] Many specialists in the historical Jesus now say it is precisely

1

this dimension of time—the development of the man Jesus himself—that provides the basis of the central theme recurring throughout the canonical New Testament scripture.[4] The historical account found within them itself demonstrates that both the words and the deeds of Jesus are inscribed in the time of a story, the narrative of a man who loved, who cared, who was sometimes troubled, who compromised himself by associating with outcasts, who suffered, and who gave his life.

Since the mid-twentieth century, the extraordinary discoveries of manuscripts in the deserts of Upper Egypt and Judaea, as well as the ever-expanding number of interpretive studies of them, have undeniably led to a rebirth of research into Jesus of Nazareth, the founding figure for all denominations of Christianity. A dialogue between Jewish and Christian scholars has also begun, especially regarding the Jewish cultural roots of Jesus. Along with many theological studies, a tremendous number of primarily historical studies have been published during the past two decades. Many of these are based on more sophisticated methods of research that are generally unencumbered by doctrinal or theological presuppositions. To a significant degree, they have brought a new light to bear on both the character and the teaching of Jesus. A number of these studies have largely succeeded in discrediting the tradition of separating the canonical scripture of the New Testament from the more recently discovered apocryphal scriptures on the grounds that only the canonical writings are reliable tools for historical research about Jesus.[5]

It is in the context of this renaissance of research into the historical Jesus that I have undertaken this work. The imperative that has constantly motivated and guided the writing of this book is my desire to understand what meaning we can give to the presence and participation of Jesus in the history of humanity and to show the role of precursor that he has played in the process of the appropriation of the *I* by each one of us. Is it not Jesus who shows us the way, in gospel passages considered the most "authentic," by insisting on the dual necessity of being reborn in ourselves and accepting the difference of the other? We shall have much more to say on this subject in chapter 8.

From the beginning I have been well aware of the possible difficulties involved in selecting and working on a large number of specialized scholarly works, given that I am neither a specialist nor a true believer. Regarding the latter, is it not possible that I have an advantage over those who profess to be true believers? After all, did not Jesus himself often prefer the company of those who were considered infidels? In a more serious vein, I want to assure the reader that I have no ambition of writing a new biography of Jesus, nor is it my intention to repeat the results of research that others have already undertaken with admirable skill. Essentially, the principal aims of this book, based on the largest possible compilation of previous works and conclusions of specialists, are to incite readers to take a fresh look at all texts that speak of Jesus and, I hope, to inspire them toward finding a new vision of him for themselves.

I am struck by the fact that there are still a number of people of my generation who have had a strong Christian upbringing or have experienced a traditional Catholic environment throughout childhood and adolescence who still believe firmly in both the divinity of Jesus Christ and that he came to Earth to redeem the original sin of Adam and Eve.[6] That these beliefs are sometimes inflexible may perhaps be due in part to the positions taken by a number of influential Christian exegetes.[7] They may claim to have nothing to hide regarding the ecclesiastical position from which they speak, yet they also claim to be engaged in scholarly research into the "the man Jesus before the Resurrection."[8] And they do not hesitate to proclaim, *ex cathedra,* that "New Testament historians can never neglect to take into account the inevitability of the Easter drama, a theme that runs throughout the documentary texts."[9]

In this book I have done my best to avoid theological discourse, and make no claim to answer questions that belong to that domain.[10] My goal is to demonstrate that historical research on Jesus will, sooner or later, cause us to ask new religious questions. Perhaps it will ultimately lead us to accept that certain of these questions can never have definite answers. Some might counter this with the charge that there can be no definite answers in the domain of historical research on Jesus, for they would be illusory. I do not agree with this, though of course I accept the principle that historical conclusions must always remain provisional.

It is certainly true that positions have softened over time so that objective historical studies of this subject have lost their former taboo—but a fierce opposition still persists, especially on the part of certain theologians. Their basic argument seems to be that though Jesus of Nazareth is now accepted as a historical person whose existence is no longer seriously disputed, the Christ or Messiah foretold in the Bible, the post-resurrection Jesus Christ, is beyond historical analysis; knowledge of his reality belongs to the domain of faith alone.

Here is a different question raised by this perspective: Is it possible for a Christian to speak objectively of the historical Jesus of Nazareth without the bias of this post-resurrection filter?

Historians' responses to these issues have been evolving along with the acceleration of research over the last half-century or so. Indeed, enormous advances have been made since the pioneering studies of Ernest Renan[11] in the mid-nineteenth century and those of Father Lagrange[12] and Albert Schweitzer[13] in the early twentieth century. John Meier,[14] an American theologian and contemporary writer, has pointed out that many of those who have contributed to the renewal of historical research on Jesus were motivated by a desire to protect the foundation of Christian tradition "by emphasizing the central Christian proclamation of the death and resurrection of Jesus—thereby excluding any role for the historical Jesus as a ground of the content of Christian faith, as a possible place of meeting between the believer and God." Many contemporary scholars would have no problem with Meier's argument. For him, theology "can only act and speak with credibility in a culture, if its methodology incorporates a historical approach."[15] Although Meier does not represent the leading edge of current research, his position is shared by contemporary Christian historical scholars, and shows the remarkable progress they have made in freeing themselves from the straitjackets once imposed by conservative theologians. Also, there is no doubt that many more-recent texts that speak of the historical Jesus have been enriched by the work of authors of Jewish origin and faith, such as Geza Vermès, Robert Aron, Schalom Ben-Chorin, Marie Vidal, and Armand Abécassis.[16] Thanks to them, not only has research been greatly advanced, but we can now hope that this progressive convergence of findings will give rise to an interfaith dialogue that is far less inhibited than before.

Yet we must never forget that historical truth is always provisional. What is accepted as true today may be challenged tomorrow by new evidence or by a new reading of existing documents. Although the literature that deals with the historical Jesus is rich and constantly evolving, the basic documentary materials about the rabbi from Nazareth, whose nucleus consists of the synoptic gospels (which remain our main sources), are extremely tenuous, as we shall see. This is why the question of who Jesus really was may never be settled, in spite of the vast number of books and articles on this subject.

I must emphasize that this essay is not addressed to those who are experts on the subject. It is intended for those who know little or nothing about it. In Mark 4:11, Jesus says, "The mystery of the Kingdom of God has been given to you; but for others, everything must be given in parables." This essay is for those who are familiar with the subject primarily through religiously biased texts they have read or heard, such as: "Believe ye in God Almighty, and in his only begotten Son, who descended from Heaven and took on human form, so as to redeem us through the sacrifice of His own life."[17] For those who are unfamiliar with such language, who are repulsed by it, or who simply don't understand it, however, I offer the following outline, chapter by chapter, explaining how we shall attempt to answer this question: Who was this man called Jesus of Nazareth?

Chapter 1 reviews the historical sources currently available: who their authors were, when they were written, and in what form these claims to knowledge of Jesus have come down to us.

Chapter 2 covers the exegetical treatments of these sources. What credibility do these exegeses have for us today? Are there different methods of interpreting them?

Chapter 3 looks at the person of Jesus, based on our historical knowledge. Where was he from? What was the era like in which he lived? Who were his family, and what was his religion?

Chapter 4 concentrates on Jesus' religious environment, with an overview of Jewish beliefs in the first century, religious factions of the time, and Jesus' own religion.

Chapter 5 examines the question of whether or not the mature Jesus had a mentor, model, or master.

Chapter 6 deals with what has been called the mission of Jesus, covering the last, brief period of his life during which he communicated his message through his deeds and sayings.

Chapter 7 explores what is undoubtedly the most important historical subject: What was the content and meaning of Jesus' message for his own contemporaries? What was the Kingdom of which he spoke so often?

Chapter 8 is devoted to the writing of various authors on the "Passion" of Jesus, as it is called in Christian tradition. We follow this subject step by step, from "treachery" to exaltation. Considering the absence of witnesses to what happened after the Master's arrest, this chapter poses the greatest problems from a historical perspective. It closes with an examination of the most controversial subjects in the history of Jesus: his death and his burial.

The final chapter responds to the major issues that run through the book, and offers my conclusions. Because this book is primarily a historical essay, it seems appropriate that I restrain my eagerness to let the reader know my personal views and first allow other established scholars to speak. As the discussion ends, the final conclusion must be that of the reader.

The Sources

A fundamental criterion of the validity of any historical research is the reliability of its sources. It is thus imperative to begin with a chapter dedicated to this subject. In fact, the multiplicity of available sources dealing with the historical Jesus, which have grown tremendously since the post–World War II discoveries in Egypt and in Palestine, has created a number of problems for scholars, especially those who engage in exegesis. Where was Jesus spoken of? Who wrote about him? Who wrote about him first and in what form was the writing? Is the authenticity of some apocryphal sources equal, or even superior, to that of the canonical sources?[1] What would be the implications if it were convincingly demonstrated that some accepted canonical sources are in fact untrustworthy?[2]

Even though these questions are highly complex and remain controversial, none of them can be glossed over. On the contrary; it is indispensable to examine as fully as possible the responses that scholarly literature has offered regarding these questions. Only then will readers be in a position to develop an informed opinion about them and draw their own conclusions.

THE CANONICAL SOURCES

It is common practice to distinguish among three types of writings that speak of Jesus: the canonical texts, the apocryphal texts, and texts of pagan origin.[3] The first two categories have a common feature, so aptly described by Mordillat and Prieur, that they are "entirely posthumous works which, if not written by Jesus, were at least thought to be inspired by him."[4] Moreover, as regards the four canonical gospels, it is surprising to note that many worthy and educated Christians remain ignorant of the fact that none of the people who wrote these gospels actually witnessed the deeds or Sayings of Jesus.[5] For many of these believers, it seems undeniable that Matthew and John were two of the twelve apostles chosen by Jesus and that Mark and Luke were disciples who followed the Master. These assumptions are not viable, however, as contemporary historical exegesis has amply demonstrated.

The canonical gospels were edited over a long period of time, probably at least fifty years, beginning more than thirty to thirty-five years after the death of Jesus. For the most part, we have no knowledge of the true identities of the redactors. These authors wrote down testimonies collected from different types of informants: those who had known Jesus himself, such as Simon-Peter, one of the Twelve; those who claimed to have known one or more of Jesus' disciples; or other sources judged as trustworthy. The writings were then reworked, corrected, and copied many times by various scribes who were more or less rigorous and scrupulous. Many of the most ancient documents have disappeared over the centuries, either because of their increasing fragility or because they were deliberately destroyed. Texts were added during the first centuries of the early Church as well, either out of concern for protecting the true faith or to facilitate its propagation among the pagans.

All these factors have major implications for assessing the historicity of the documents that have come down to us—texts that, we repeat, were written and edited long after the gospels were first written down. Indeed, we must make a distinction between dating the earliest versions and the supposed date of the texts we have. This does not mean that the latter are mostly falsehoods, even though we are often dealing with copies of copies. The problem is the authenticity of their message. We must bear in mind, as scholars often remind us, that the fictitious attribution of a scripture to a famous and revered teacher, conferring great credibility upon it, was common practice in ancient times. This was not regarded as a "forgery" when the writer was believed to be inspired by the lineage of the Master. The problem has been immensely complicated by a sanctification of the texts that speak of Jesus, especially the four canonical gospels, which has made it almost impossible to question their authenticity.

The "Canonical" Gospels

For more than a century after the death of Jesus, aside from the holy scriptures often designated the Law and Prophets, the first Christians has no texts that contained a coherent narrative of the life and words of the Master. The first to appear were accounts of miracles and small collections of sayings that were transcribed for use in sermons and at communion. More than thirty years would pass before some fairly complete collections of the gospels appeared. As late as 150 C.E., the Samaritan philosopher Justin, a convert to Christianity, first referred to the Memoirs of the Apostles as a sacred scripture, which he considered equal to the Law and the Prophets. From then on, a number of copies began to circulate. During this period, the gnostic philosopher Marcion was excommunicated for advocating the restriction of revealed truth to a small number of texts, including only a part of the Gospel of Luke and a few letters of Paul. Other indications suggest that, around the middle of the second century, most of the texts now considered canonical came into circulation.

The word *canon* comes from the Greek *kanon* (rule, law); thus the documents, produced long after Jesus' death, which the early Roman Church judged to be the only true scriptures, became known as the Canon. Later, they began to be called the New Testament. Tertullian (160–circa 225 C.E.)[6] and Clement of Alexandria (circa 150–circa 215 C.E.) seem to have been the first writers to use this term to refer to the new

Pact of Alliance, which Christian tradition had attributed to Jesus. Agreement as to the complete list of acceptable canonical texts of the Christian faith, however, came much later. It was Athanasius[7] who proposed the twenty-seven books that were finally accepted at the Third Council of Laodicea, in 367 C.E.

Behind the effort to fix a normative list of canonical writings, the motivation of the early Church authorities was, or so they believed, the protection of the faith. One of the key criteria for deciding the orthodoxy of a text considered for inclusion in the Canon was whether it could fit the apostolic tradition. This meant it had to be attributable to one of the twelve apostles, even in those cases when none of them could possibly have authored it personally. This gave tremendous power to those responsible for deciding which texts fit with this apostolic lineage, and were therefore acceptable candidates for the Canon, and which did not, and were therefore heretical.

This was an era, however, when no powerful ecclesiastical center was yet established. Another, looser criterion, therefore, was whether a text had received a more or less "universal acceptance." The aim here was to ensure that the various apostolic texts being disseminated in churches around the Mediterranean, often bringing Christians of Jewish and pagan origins together, could be acceptable to all. This was advocated by Tertullian, who was himself originally from Carthage.

The New Testament canon included the three synoptic gospels (from the Greek word *sunoptikos*, "seeing together"). Attributed to Matthew, Mark, and Luke, these three texts tell roughly the same story, can often be read in parallel, and are based on common sources. The canonical writings also include the Gospel of John; the Acts of the Apostles (attributed to Luke, as a kind of extension of his gospel); the thirteen Letters of Paul (of which seven were probably not written by him); and seven other letters, attributed to the apostles James (one), Peter (two), John (three), and Jude (one). Then there is an anonymous letter, and finally the Book of Revelation, attributed to John.

There is one major fact that we must consider from the start, as André Chouraqui points out in the introduction to his translation of the

Gospel of Matthew: It was not until the fourth century C.E. that four separate gospels were clearly distinguished from each other. Previously, people wrote only of the Gospel of Jesus Christ, also known as the Besorah,[8] comprising four parts that had been redacted *according to* the four apostolic traditions. The four accounts were all written in Greek, even though Aramaic was the native language of three of the Jewish apostles involved. We know very little about Luke (or someone designated by that name) except that he was apparently Syrian, that possibly he was a physician, and that Greek was his primary spoken language.

Dating the Canonical Gospels

When were the gospels written? We have no exact answer to this question, and scholarly opinions differ. What is now well established is that they were all written later than the authentic letters of Paul. The latter are considered to be the earliest Christian documents that were actually dictated by their attributed author, dating from twenty years after the death of Jesus, at least for the first letters. Many efforts have been made to date the canonical gospels and to reconstruct their sources. Most of these studies are based on known historical events of the time or on quotations from ancient authors.

A major historical reference point for studies of early Christianity is the Roman invasion of Jerusalem and the destruction of the Temple in the summer of the year 70 C.E. This was such an important event that it is virtually certain to have influenced the content of documents written later. Vespasian had returned to Rome, and his son, Titus, directed the siege of Jerusalem. After the catastrophe and the massacres that followed, many Jews (at least those who did not remain to become slaves) fled the city, regrouping in Jabneh (now the site of Tel Aviv). From there, they migrated over the next thirty years or so to Galilee. The destruction of the Temple and the consequent Diaspora were such important events that they cannot fail to have deeply affected gospel authors who lived during those times. Hence, one important way of dating texts is the presence, or absence, of any direct or indirect references to these events. For example, in Mark there is no mention of them, yet in Matthew 24:3, the destruction of the Temple appears as a prophecy.

Other historical references consist of the earliest known quotations by Christian authors. This has been useful in the case of an author such as Ignatius of Antioch, who died sometime before 117 C.E. and quoted passages from the Gospel of Matthew. Another example is a papyrus, dated around the early second century, that reproduces a text attributed to John, dealing with the famous interrogation of Jesus by Pontius Pilate (John 18:31–33 and 37–38). These kinds of documents constitute valuable clues that allow us to home in on the possible dates of redaction of the gospel in question. But they are only clues, insufficient for defining a precise chronology.

In any case, a clear consensus has now emerged among scholars that the gospel attributed to Mark is the oldest of the four, probably written before the year 70 C.E. Mark, or whoever wrote this gospel, was probably relying on oral traditions and (according to very recent hypotheses) written sources.[9]

The gospels attributed to Matthew and Luke were likely written independently during the period 70–100 C.E., making use of copies of the Gospel of Mark. This often involved obvious rewriting—inserting a different collection of Sayings attributed to Jesus, for example. These Sayings must have been from an older, common source, now lost, which scholars refer to as Q, or the Gospel of Q (from German *Quelle*, meaning "source").[10] This interpretation, known as the two-source hypothesis, is now accepted by a large number of scholars as the most plausible explanation we have for the structure and origin of these gospels.

Yet many uncertainties remain regarding this interpretation, and some New Testament scholars question the two-source hypothesis. One of the most serious objections is precisely the absence (in those passages presumably written after 70 C.E.) of allusions to the destruction of the Temple. Vermès points out that the existence of Q has never been corroborated by any written or oral tradition. He finds it more plausible that Matthew and Luke copied each other, and that they also relied on oral traditions from the Judeo-Christian communities to which they belonged.

As for the gospel attributed to John, hypotheses abound. A great many authors believe that this text was written around the end of the first century and the beginning of the second by a group of writers, a kind of Johannine school from Asia Minor, based in Ephesus. A minority hypothesis is that the true author was Lazarus. In any case, it is clear that we are dealing with a gospel that (as we shall see later in detail) is far more concerned with theology than are the others. Its author or authors apparently relied on an independent source for the gospel's anecdotal passages, even though some similarities to passages in the synoptic gospels might indicate otherwise.

What is important to bear in mind about efforts to date the canonical gospels is that their composition and transcription were long processes, extending over decades, and that these processes probably did not begin until thirty to thirty-five years after the death of Jesus.

Who Were the Real Authors?

Is a precise answer to this question possible? As we have noted, early Christian tradition referred to the Gospel (Besorah) in the singular, with four versions apparently retained and designated by the expression "according to . . ." (Mark, Matthew, and so on).

Concerning the synoptic gospels, apparently a certain Papias, a second-century bishop of Hieropolis, in Syria, was the first to speak of Matthew and of Mark. According to him, Matthew was the author of a compilation of Sayings of Jesus in Aramaic. But we know virtually nothing else of this Matthew; his identity has never been established. Christian tradition claims that he was a tax collector whom the other apostles called Levi. More recently, scholarship has favored the hypothesis that a team of scribes authored the work. In any case, the gospel attributed to Matthew was written in Greek and contains far more than a collection of sayings.

Papias also provides us with two interesting assertions about Mark: that he wrote down the "memoirs" of Peter, although in a different order than Peter told them; and that Mark was not a direct witness to Jesus. Could the latter be the same man mentioned in the Acts of the

Apostles, and in a letter to Timothy[11] the "John, also called Mark" who accompanied Paul? This remains uncertain.

As for Luke, some authors have claimed that he was a Syrian physician, also identified as a companion of Paul. But here, also, we have only an unproven hypothesis.

As for the "last Evangelist," much uncertainty and confusion remains as to his identity. This mysterious character has long been thought to be the apostle John, known as Jesus' beloved disciple, but modern exegesis now separates the two.[12] Vermès reminds us that the last mention of the apostle John is found in Acts 8:14, where he preaches in Syria accompanied by Peter. He is designated by Paul as one of the three pillars of the Church of Jerusalem, along with Peter himself and James, the brother of the Lord. There is nothing in New Testament writings, however, that permits us to assert that the apostle John ever traveled to Ephesus or to Asia Minor.[13] Vermès notes that several people named John were in this region. By this view, John the Elder (a disciple of Jesus, according to Papias) is not the same John the Elder who authored the second and third letters of John. Vermès also makes the astute observation that it would be quite far-fetched to identify the sophisticated and eloquent author of the fourth gospel with the portrait of John found in Acts 4:13. There, John and Peter appear before the Sanhedrin, who are amazed at their confidence given that both are "uncultured and uneducated persons." Contemporary scholarship now leans toward the hypothesis that the Gospel of John was authored by a sect of Johannine scribes based in Ephesus.

The Composition of the Canonical Gospels

As Meier so aptly said, each of the authors involved in the composition of the canonical gospels "has rearranged the pearls of the rosary along its thread, according to his own personal theology (where pearls = pericopes, and thread = structure of the gospel)."

Mark, the earliest of the gospel transcriptions, is in many respects the one whose narrative fits best with the historical, human Jesus, though Mark the redactor never met him. The author's knowledge of

Aramaic, which he uses several times, gives us a better sense of the man Jesus, his suffering, his doubts, worries, and his affection.[14] Mark does not attempt to gloss over emotional reactions, weaknesses, and even the ignorance of the rabbi, as Vermès notes. In Mark's narrative, Jesus expresses compassion, anger, and irritation at his disciples' obtuseness. The other gospels either ignore or suppress these aspects, probably to avoid projecting a negative image of the Lord.

In Matthew, only after John the Baptist's arrest does Jesus, presumably one of his disciples, take up the slogan "Repent, for the Kingdom of Heaven is at hand!" For Matthew, as for Mark, the Good News is the coming of the Kingdom of God, which is close at hand. With a thorough knowledge of the Torah and the Prophets, Matthew demonstrates great skill in finding events in the life of Jesus that confirm prophecies in the ancient scriptures (*pesher* in Hebrew), using frequent references to the prophets Isaiah, Micah, and Hosea.

Matthew also places far more emphasis on Jesus' opposition to the "scribes and Pharisees," citing, for example, Jesus' arguments with them on detailed points of the Law. This poses two major problems of credibility, however. First, no historical sources speak of the Pharisees exerting any significant influence in the Galilee of Jesus' day; and second, the Jesus of the Sayings shows no such legalistic interest. The scholarly consensus now is that the author of Matthew was not concerned with historicity, and that the practice of introducing anecdotes or reflections relevant to his own time explains the anachronisms. What is more, this helps us to date these passages to the time of the Diaspora, around the end of the first century, when such currents of thought reflected the opposition between Judeo-Christians and Hellenized Christians.

Matthew's Jewishness is far more pronounced than that of Mark, and he initially paints a picture of a Jesus concerned only with preaching to the Jews and avoiding Samaritan towns (Matt. 15:24). Then, in an about-face, he becomes a universalist, emphasizing the resurrected Christ even more than the other Evangelists and insisting that Christ gave Christians the mission to "go and teach all the nations." This current seems to lacks consistency with Matthew's own thought, however, for the gospel becomes intolerant of the children of Israel, going so far as to suggest that they have been disinherited from the Kingdom and replaced by believing Gentiles—a step that even Luke was not willing to take. To illustrate how extreme this current becomes in Matthew, consider the dreadful invective he attributes to the Jewish crowd witnessing Jesus' trial before Pilate: "May his blood fall upon us and upon our children!" This passage was to play a significant role in later Christian hostility toward Jews. It was only near the end of the twentieth century that this teaching was officially renounced by the Catholic Church.

Luke is the only non-Jewish gospel writer. We know almost nothing of him, except that he was supposedly a Syrian, of Semitic origin, perhaps a physician, and that he addressed his writings mainly to the Gentiles. As André Chouraqui emphasizes, however, Luke's gospel shows undeniable Hebraic influence as well as a deep knowledge of the Bible. He begins and ends his gospel by insisting on the universality of Jesus' mission.[15]

Because he was presumably not a Jew, this would explain why he has so little material dealing specifically with Jesus' mission among the Israelites. Also, in contrast to Matthew and Mark, who put so much stress on the eschatological vision, Luke is silent on the subject. He even omits certain key words or expressions that typify the apocalyptic discourse of the other two synoptic gospels.[16]

John, or the Johannine school, has a theological agenda founded on the mission of Jesus. Unlike the synoptic gospels, which tell the story of Jesus in Galilee, John speaks of him as preaching in Judaea and in Jerusalem.[17] John also describes Jesus from the very start as the Word (*logos* in Greek, *dabar* in Hebrew) of God made flesh. Jesus is the Messiah, the source of light, the same that is mentioned five times in the beginning of Genesis. On the subject of John's view, André Chouraqui comments: "Jesus is the witness and the path which leads to perfect obedience to Yahweh and to his Torah . . . He is the source of truth." While openly displaying his deep knowledge of the Hebrew language and culture, John makes a great effort, often enjoying himself in the process, to translate these concepts into Greek, the language of all the gospel's redactions. This gospel is not so much a record of Jesus' ministry as it is a spiritual guide that shows the signs that reveal the presence of Yahweh throughout the life and mission of Jesus, all of which "announce the ultimate and decisive sign: the resurrection of the Crucified Christ."

Many authors now agree that a single, unique, original form in which the Sayings were written down has probably never existed. This is explained partly by the fact that Jesus seems to have repeated his Sayings often, using different wording. Although this hypothesis probably applies to most cases, some go against it. For example, as to Jesus' words about wine and bread during the Last Supper, every gospel gives a markedly different version. Yet this is the only time he ever mentions this subject, a few hours before his death. Perhaps some of these versions are redactions added by the early churches, inserted to address their needs for the celebration of Communion. This question will be further examined in chapter 8, which deals with the Passion and death of Jesus.

This brings us back to a major point that bears repeating: If we wish to gain a correct interpretation of the source materials, we must never lose sight of this divergence in the origins of the four gospels. The result is that the interpretation of Jesus' message as developed by successive redactors was inevitably influenced by events that they experienced after the Master's death. We must also take into account the changes in Christological tradition made by the different churches these redactors belonged to, changes made in response to the difficulties they encountered. In particular, the gospel redactors—perhaps even the copyists—in an effort to answer questions raised by members of the early Christian communities, almost certainly followed their own convictions and interpretations of scripture. These questioners must have experienced great confusion when the early Church found itself confronted with its failure to convert the Jews, on the one hand, and its success among the Gentiles, on the other. In addition, the constantly repeated prophecies of the coming of the Kingdom failed to materialize, and this must have raised many questions. All of these factors must have worked together to produce a growing diversity in interpretations of the teaching of Jesus.

Along with the general diversity found among the four canonical gospels, we might also note significant differences between the three synoptic gospels and that of John, especially regarding the importance of "signs." In the synoptic texts, many of Jesus' miraculous healings are actually exorcisms. When his challengers ask him to reveal the signs of his authority, he refuses to do so (Mark 8:11 and 11:27–33). When Jesus asks his disciples who they think he is and Peter declares that he is the Christ, Jesus enjoins them not to speak of this to anyone (Mark 8:27). In contrast, John gives great importance to signs whose purpose is to demonstrate the divine nature and authority of Jesus Christ.[18]

In the gospel attributed to John, the Kingdom of God is mentioned only twice,[19] whereas it is the central theme of the synoptic gospels, a theme to which Jesus returns repeatedly.[20] In Mark and Luke, the Kingdom of God, or, as Matthew puts it, the Kingdom of Heaven (sometimes simply the Kingdom), is mentioned 108 times.[21] Apart from a reference to the "matters of heaven," the Kingdom of God has no particular importance in Johannine theology, which has apparently replaced it by the annunciation of "eternal Life." In John, the central theme of Jesus' discourse seems to be Jesus himself: his nature, his relation to God, and his identity with God.

In this fourth gospel, the narrative portions are written primarily from a symbolic point of view. For example, when reporting Jesus' Sayings, John reformulates them with a more theological orientation. As Vermès observes, the synoptic gospels and the Gospel of John have very little in common regarding the role of Jesus, whose healings and exorcisms are central in the former and of minor importance in the latter.

A good illustration of these differences in orientation and emphasis is the story of the money changers in the Temple. The synoptic gospels, in a more historical approach, situate the episode only a few days before Jesus' arrest, thus implying that the incident played a causal role in it. John places the Temple incident at the very beginning of Jesus' public ministry, suggesting a kind of theological and prophetic interpretation: a symbol of destruction and reconstruction, of death and resurrection. Another illustration is the divergent accounts of Jesus' meeting with John the Baptist: The synoptic writers see this as an initiation of Jesus' mission whereas John omits the very baptism itself, no doubt because it would suggest an unacceptable deference of the Lord toward John the Baptist.

Finally, there is the striking difference in style between John and the synoptic gospels. In the latter, most of the Sayings are short, even when they deal with several different subjects. In them, the parable is the privileged literary form par excellence: A simple story is made to speak of God and the Kingdom. In contrast, John favors long, metaphorical speeches that often begin with: "I am (the true vine, and so on)." Neither stories nor accounts of deeds are included.

The Acts of the Apostles

Luke is generally considered to be the author of the book of the Acts of the Apostles, which constitutes a kind of continuation of his gospel. We find a unity of vocabulary, style, and vision between the two books. The Acts is a detailed documentary account of the emergence of this early community of Christians. Paul plays a dominant role, and almost all of the second part is devoted to him. Many scholars believe that the author was someone close to Paul who accompanied him on his voyages. In the Acts, Luke tells of Paul's three missions in Asia Minor and Greece, and of his trips to Jerusalem, where he meets with the two major figures of the Church, James (the brother, or perhaps cousin, of Jesus) and Simon-Peter. The thesis that Luke was one of Paul's faithful companions lacks credibility, however, because the Acts never mention Paul's Letters, and also because the Gospel of Luke's own theological vision is quite different from Paul's.

Although it contains limited information that can be directly applied to historical studies, the Acts of the Apostles is nonetheless interesting for the light it sheds on events and teachings that are dealt with in Paul's Letters. Here, we have a post-resurrectional narrative that begins with the ascension of Jesus in the presence of the apostles, who have gathered for a meal in Jerusalem. This miraculous elevation of Jesus to the heavens, already recounted in the Gospel of Mark,[22] is supposed to have occurred forty days after the resurrection. Shortly before Jesus' ascension, the apostles eagerly question him about the coming of the Kingdom, asking him if the time has come when he will restore the throne of Israel. Jesus answers that knowledge of that day is not for them, for only God can know it. He gives them the good news, however, that God is sending them a great strength, the Holy Spirit, so that they may "be its witnesses to the extremities of the earth." Then Luke pictures the apostles left behind, staring up at the sky, when two angels speak to them: "Men of Galilee, why do you stand like this, staring at the sky? He who has been taken away from you, this very same Jesus, will return like that, just as you saw him ascend to the sky."

What is so striking in the text of the Acts is the transformation of the rabbi from Nazareth into Lord and Christ. On the day of Pentecost, when the gathered apostles receive the Holy Spirit promised by Jesus, Luke has Peter say:

Men of Israel, hear these words: Jesus of Nazareth, a man attested to you by God with mighty works and wonders and signs which God did through him in your midst, as you yourselves know this Jesus, delivered up according to the definite plan and foreknowledge of God, you crucified and killed by the hands of lawless men.

But God raised him up, having loosed the pangs of death, because it was not possible for him to be held by it. For David says concerning him, "I saw the Lord always before me, for he is at my right hand that I may not be shaken; therefore my heart was glad, and my tongue rejoiced; moreover my flesh will dwell in hope. For you wilt not abandon my soul to Hades, nor let thy Holy One see corruption. Thou hast made known to me the ways of life; thou wilt make me full of gladness with thy presence."

Brethren, I may say to you confidently of the patriarch David that he both died and was buried, and his tomb is with us to this day. Being therefore a prophet, and knowing that God had sworn with an oath to him that he would set one of his descendants upon his throne, he foresaw and spoke of the resurrection of the Christ, that he was not abandoned to Hades, nor did his flesh see corruption. This Jesus God raised up, and of that we all are witnesses. Being therefore exalted at the right hand of God, and having received from the Father the promise of the Holy Spirit, he has poured out this which you see and hear. For David did not ascend into the heavens; but he himself says, "The Lord said to my Lord, Sit at my right hand, till I make thy enemies a stool for thy feet." Let all the house of Israel therefore know assuredly that God has made him both Lord and Christ, this Jesus whom you crucified.[23]

The Letters of Paul

In his most recent book on the historical Jesus, consisting of the summation of his previous research together with his most recent findings,[24] Vermès writes that many independent researchers consider Paul the true founder of the Christian religion. In this view, Paul is "the creator of the entire doctrine and ecclesiastical system implied in his Letters."[25] In any case, these Letters, if not the most interesting material on Jesus, do constitute the most historically established documents we have, for two reasons: First, Paul wrote them himself;[26] and second, he was a contemporary of Jesus, even though he apparently never met him.[27]

According to Pope Clement, who refers to certain Letters by Paul, the first were written about 50 C.E., but they did not begin to circulate widely until forty-five years later. These Letters are of limited value in historical research about Jesus, however, because their content is essentially theological. In addition, they are so focused on the death and resurrection of the Christ that the events in Jesus' life play just a marginal role. The only material we find there that might be considered "historical" can be summed up in a few words: Jesus was descended from

Abraham through the royal line of David. He was betrayed and died upon the cross, but after three days, he was resurrected from the dead.[28] Moreover, we find no direct quotation of the Sayings of Jesus in any of the Letters.

So what does Paul tell us about Jesus? In Romans, which is considered to be his major work, Paul says that Jesus was "our Lord Jesus Christ, confirmed as the Son of God, empowered by the Spirit of holiness, and by his resurrection from the dead." In the second Letter to the Corinthians (2 Cor. 5:6), we read: "Even if we have known the Christ in the flesh, henceforth it is no longer in this manner that we know him." Thus, it is not in Paul's Letters that we should look for new facts about the historical Jesus. Nevertheless, a thorough knowledge of them is indispensable to understanding the significance of theological teachings in the Christian religion.

We do have some direct knowledge of Paul's life to which his Letters make discreet and sporadic allusion. On the other hand, Luke's Acts of the Apostles go into great detail about Paul's mission, especially regarding his trips and encounters in Jerusalem and the speeches he made in various places. His date of birth is uncertain, but good evidence indicates it was somewhere between 10 and 15 C.E. According to the Acts, he was born in Tarsus, the capital of Cilicia, a Roman province in southeastern Asia Minor. His parents were well-to-do, and Roman citizens as well. There are no direct witnesses to his death. One possible date for the latter is 64 C.E., during Nero's persecutions of the Christians after the burning of Rome. Paul says he is a Jew descended from the tribe of Benjamin and that he formerly belonged to the Pharisees. The Acts claim that he was a student of Gamaliel, a highly respected Pharisee. If so, this would imply that he studied in Jerusalem, but Paul himself does not speak of this. He does have two things in common with the Pharisees: a thorough knowledge of Jewish scriptures, which he often uses in his arguments;[29] and a belief in the resurrection of the body.

Accounts of Paul's career as found in his Letters and in the Acts do not always overlap and often even contradict each other. Reconciling these Letters with the Acts, which was composed thirty to forty years later, is an insoluble problem. Some authors who have written about Paul accord more credibility to his own Letters than to the Acts, in which they perceive an adulatory quality, sometimes to the point of fabrication and legend building. Yet these same authors may conveniently cite the Acts when they need it to support their own point of view, forgetting their previous skepticism.

In any case, the image of Paul that comes through in both the Letters and the Acts is that of an extraordinary man, risking all manner of danger in order to spread the message of Jesus Christ among the pagans. Indeed, Paul says that he was specially chosen by God to be the apostle for the Gentiles, having previously been a persecutor of Christians. Did the famous call he received on the road to Damascus, with its dramatic and quasi-magical aspects, really happen the way it is told in the Acts of the Apostles? Or was it a dreamlike vision? Clearly, Paul underwent a radical change in the direction of his life from that point on. From denouncer and persecutor of Christians, he metamorphosed into an unflagging proselyte. Convinced that he had received a mission directly from the Lord, he sought recognition as an apostle of Christ with a status equal to that of the Twelve. His ambition was to be the equal of Peter, to whom he was violently opposed, accusing him of dissimulation.[30] Indeed, Paul needed such a status if his message and his mission were ever to be accepted by the other Christian communities, and most especially those who were establishing the early Church of Jerusalem.

THE APOCRYPHAL SOURCES

A concise description of the Apocrypha[31] is simply all the New Testament writings that were excluded from the canon. Most were labeled heresies by the early churches that would later become the Church of Rome. These sources are multiple and varied in both form and content, and their number has grown considerably with the major archaeological discoveries since World War II. Much has been said and written about the two most famous apocryphal sources, the papyrus codices found in 1945 near Nag Hammadi in Egypt and the scrolls found at Qumran near the Dead Sea in 1947.[32]

Now that early emotional reactions have calmed down and scholars have had full access to these documents for decades of serious study, it appears that the importance of this new material in regard to our historical knowledge of Jesus himself has been exaggerated. The greatest wealth of information they contain pertains to the history of the early Christian movement, which scholars now often refer to as Judeo-Christianity. They offer no new facts about Jesus' life, at least nothing fundamental of historical interest.

The Dead Sea Scrolls

Over a period of about ten years, approximately a thousand scrolls were collected from the caves at Qumran, the site of an Essene community, a dissident Jewish sect founded sometime around 150 B.C.E. that we shall study in more detail in chapter 4. The religious doctrine and practices of the Essenes had previously been studied in detail by a number of authors, the oldest and most famous of whom were Josephus and Philo of Alexandria. It seems, however, that many of these scrolls are not of Essene origin; at least this is the thesis is put forth by N. Golb[33] in a recent study of the wide variety of styles and techniques of writing in the scrolls.

They contain all books of the canonical Jewish Bible (except for Esther), texts explaining the doctrine of the sect, and other texts. Some of these apocryphal writings, such as the Book of Tobit, the Letter of Jeremiah, and Ecclesiasticus, were accepted by early Christian churches. On the other hand, some scrolls contain books—mostly apocalyptic and eschatological in nature—that were rejected by the Church, including the Testaments of the Twelve Patriarchs and the Books of Levi, Naphtali, and Enoch, and Jubilations.

The content of some of these manuscripts has given rise to intense speculation, especially regarding a supposed link between Jesus and the quasi-monastic Essene community established at Qumran. The rite of purification that this sect practiced in the valley of the Jordan appears similar to the baptizing movement of which John the Baptist was an adept,[34] according to some authors.[35] Given the strong links between Jesus and John, we might conclude that Jesus himself visited Qumran and was strongly influenced by the Essenes. We find neither explicit nor implicit references to Jesus, however, nor to his movements, in any of the Qumran documents. Some scholars also object that it would be extremely difficult to reconcile the relatively liberal attitude of Jesus toward the Law with the strict orthodoxy of the Qumran community, who condemned the Pharisees for their laxity.

The apocryphal gospels are contemporaneous with the canonical gospels, predating them for the most part, that the canon excluded because they originated from churches that were judged either too distant or too heretical.

Among the Judeo-Christian gospels that are very old in form, we might briefly mention the Gospel of the Hebrews, the Gospel of the Egyptians, the Gospel of Peter, the Gospel of the Cross, and the Gospel of the Ebionites. The latter, a product of the Ebionite theological vision, was written in Greek and its author seems to have known the synoptic gospels. In addition, the Gospel of the Nazarenes closely follows that of Matthew, enlarging it and introducing moralizing and legendary elements. The Gospel of the Hebrews, of which only seven fragments remain, is also in Greek. It accords preeminence to James, the brother of Jesus, and apparently contradicts the canonical gospels in this respect. It also amplifies mythic themes already contained in the synoptic gospels and seems to be inspired by gnostic currents. The Gospel of Peter contains an account of the Passion that appears to be inspired by an earlier gospel. The Gospel of the Cross,[36] which dates from the middle of the first century, may have been used by Mark for his own narrative of the Passion, and later by the other gospel writers.[37]

Some of the apocryphal gospels, written after the canonical books, consist of a sort of elaboration on the latter, amplifying the miraculous aspects, especially those that tell of Jesus' childhood. These include the Protogospel of James, the Transitus Mariae, the Story of Joseph the Carpenter, the Infancy Gospel of Thomas, the Arabic Infancy Gospel, the Gospel of Nicodemus (also known as the Acts of Pilate), and the Gospel of Marcion, among others. The latter is by a second-century theologian who rejects Judaism because it worships the creator-God, judged to be a false god by Marcion. In this gospel, the true God sends Jesus to oppose the creator and do away with Mosaic Law. This gospel was edited to omit all references to Jewish scripture that earlier scribes had always included.

The apocryphal Acts, which were probably written between 150 and 200 C.E., are influenced by asceticism. They manifest an archaic, popular type of Christianity. Some of the best-known, oldest, and most important of them are the Acts of John, the Acts of Peter, the Acts of Paul, the Acts of Thomas, and the Acts of Andrew.

The best-known apocryphal Epistles, or Letters, are those attributed to Paul, such as 3 Corinthians. Others worth noting are the Letter to the Laodiceans, which is composed of canonical fragments, and the fourteen letters of correspondence with Seneca. Then there is the supposedly older, legendary correspondence between Jesus Christ himself and Abgar, king of Edessa, probably from the end of the second century.

The apocryphal Apocalypses center on the general theme of eschatology (the end of days) in the form of revelations from Christ, with more or less grim scenarios. The best-known, and certainly the oldest of these, is the Apocalypse of Peter. Only a fragment remains to us, as is the case with the Gospel of Peter. The slightly more recent Apocalypse of Paul seems to have been influenced by it. There is also a sizable and clearly more recent group that includes the Apocalypse of Thomas, that of Stephen, three of John, two of the Virgin, and others attributed to Bartholomew, Zechariah, Daniel, Esdras, and more. Although it does not bear the title of apocalypse, the Letter of the Apostles is usually included in this overall group; its form, theme, and date relate it closely to the Apocalypse of Peter.

The Nag Hammadi Manuscripts

During the winter of 1945–46, near the Arab village of Nag Hammadi, less than forty miles northwest of Luxor, in Upper Egypt, a peasant unearthed an amphora full of papyrus codices that formed the basis of an important gnostic library. The codices contained forty-five works written in Coptic whose principal titles are: the Gospel of Thomas, the Gospel of Truth, the Gospel of Philip, the Apocalypse of Peter, the Apocalypse of Paul, the Apocalypse of James, the Acts of Peter, the Epistle of Peter, and the Secret Book (a.k.a. Apocalypse) of John. The total collection is grouped together in twelve codices (books), plus eight papyrus leaves from a thirteenth codex.[38]

These copies were made in the fourth century for a Christian community, translated from earlier Greek copies that were made sometime in the late second century. Some of these works exist in two or three versions of varying length. They generally consist of gnostic[39] writings, hermetic writings, collections of proverbs, New Testament apocrypha, and Sayings of Jesus. They even include a section from Plato's *Republic*. An in-depth examination of these manuscripts directed by Christopher Tuckett concluded that, with the exception of the Gospel of Thomas, the texts are gnostic manuscripts derived mainly from Matthew, somewhat from Luke, and slightly from Mark, with no evidence of any presynoptic Egyptian tradition.[40]

Most scholars and exegetes consider the Gospel of Thomas the most important of these texts for our knowledge of Jesus' teaching. It consists of 114 logia, or Sayings, simply stated, with no narrative links or commentaries. A number of the logia have close parallels in the synoptic gospels, whereas others are completely different, often displaying a gnostic quality. A few have prophetic traits, and some deal with questions of community rules. Several of these Coptic Sayings of the Gospel of Thomas also exist in an earlier Greek fragment that was discovered previously at the site of Oxyrhynchus. Based on the brevity of the Sayings, their lack of mythic allegory, narrative text, and theological deliberations, a significant number of scholars now believe that the source of this apocryphal gospel is older than the source of any of the canonical gospels, probably dating from 50 to 60 C.E.[41] In contrast, some believe Thomas is derived from the synoptic gospels—but arguments in favor of that thesis still lack substantiation.[42]

In fact, these opposing views reflect an ongoing debate between factions that one might (at the risk of simplification) call the "liberals" and the "conservatives." The latter criticize the former for according too much significance to the Q source and to Thomas, because these sources make no mention of Jesus' divinity, nor of the related themes of his death, resurrection, and redemption.[43] Among the "conservative" scholars, we have E. Linnemann, who dates the Gospel of Thomas to around 150 C.E., arguing that it depends on the synoptic gospels and that it was used to establish a later version of Christianity.[44] Patterson[45] convincingly demonstrates, however, that the linguistic argument used by some scholars to justify the independence of the Q source is entirely secondary, and points out that there is a much stronger primary argument for it. If we accept that Matthew and Luke both used Mark, we still have to explain where the rest of the material common to Matthew and Luke came from, because they are not in Mark. Might not this missing common source be found in Q or in the Gospel of Thomas? After many years of hesitation and suspicion, we see that research is finally beginning to accord the Gospel of Thomas the status it deserves—namely, that its value as a historical document is at the very least equal to that of the canonical gospels.

Rabbinical Documents

Judaic literature,[46] especially the Babylonian Talmud, sheds a useful light on the origins of Christianity. The literature tells of Jesus being hanged on the eve of Passover because no one came forward to defend him against charges brought forty days earlier by the public prosecutor. Jesus was accused of being a magician and an apostate seducer of Israel. Other than this passage, it seems that Talmudic literature contains no information about Jesus of real historical interest, nor any independent references. Its rejections of Jesus as the Messiah, or Son of God, are merely logical reactions to Christianity at a time when Judaism was struggling to survive. In any case, nothing found in Jewish writings from the time of Jesus indicates that the emerging Judeo-Christian movement was regarded as an important phenomenon.

In the rabbinical literature,[47] Joseph Klausner, one of the most respected Jewish scholars in this area,[48] confirms that the few Talmudic references to Jesus are of little historical value.[49] Another specialist, Johann Maier, agrees, adding that mentions of Jesus contained in the Mishna and the Talmud are extrapolations of medieval origin with no historical significance.[50] Their authenticity lies in the fact that they are real reactions to Christian claims, but they teach us nothing new about the historical Jesus.

Other Historical Sources

For independent sources, we must turn to the principal Roman historians writing around the turn of the second century. But these authors left only a few meager passages about Jesus and the early Judeo-Christians. An exception is Josephus, a Romanized Jew and devout Pharisee who wrote an important history of his people and others in the Mediterranean region. Although Roman references are rare and brief, they furnish enough attestations to at least establish the existence of the historical person named Jesus. Before reviewing these authors, we turn to the writings of Philo of Alexandria, a Jewish philosopher who had a decisive intellectual influence both on the Jewish Diaspora and on the emerging Christian movement.

The scion of an aristocratic Jewish family, Philo was born around 20 B.C.E. and died in 45 C.E. He was a contemporary of Jesus but never met him, nor was he in contact with Jesus' disciples or apostles. There is nothing to be learned directly from Philo about Jesus or his teaching. His writings are, however, an extremely important source of knowledge about the culture of Diaspora Jews during the first century. Philo was a renowned scholar and interpreter of the Torah. His exegetical method was allegorical, an original approach that turned out to be essential for his school's understanding of the books of the Hebrew scriptures. His method brings together symbol and fact, teaching and practice, while respecting the literal meaning of the texts. He was deeply influenced by Hellenic thought, which he integrated into his worldview and faith, as well as by his native Jewish culture. His great reputation led to his appointment as a delegate from the Jewish community of Alexandria to Rome to negotiate with the emperor Caligula regarding their imperial status, as well as the delicate question of imperial effigies that Rome wanted to impose in the synagogues.

Philo was deeply convinced that the people of Israel were charged with a unique mission. Through the word transmitted by God to Moses, the Jews were to become a guiding light to all the peoples of the earth. This added a new dimension to the Jewish messianic doctrine: Now Israel's conversion to its true God-given mission would lead all humanity toward a world of wisdom and virtue. In this doctrine, we discern a profound influence of the Stoic school of philosophy. Philo emphasized the transcendence of God, also, as in the Septuagint (the Greek translation of the Torah) version of Exodus 3:14, where God tells Moses, "I am the one who is."[51] The original Hebrew of this is untranslatable. All a human being can know of God is his manifestations, his "powers." But Philo emphasizes God's extreme compassion. Between God and humanity is the Logos, a very complex and difficult concept whose Biblical equivalent is Wisdom, an entity who intercedes on behalf of the Transcendent. Also, Philo considers the central theme of the book of Exodus a symbol of the transformation that God wants for humanity, freeing us from slavery to the senses. The writings of Philo would later exert at least as much influence on the early Church Fathers as did John, especially regarding the trinitary nature of God.

Flavius Josephus was born in Jerusalem in 37 C.E., the first year of Caligula's reign. His father, Mathias, belonged to a high noble and priestly Jewish lineage. At the age of twenty-six, Josephus was charged with a diplomatic mission to Rome, similar to that of Philo, and from Nero he obtained the liberation of some imprisoned Jewish priests. Judaea had lost its independence in the year 6 C.E. and had been governed by Roman procurators ever since. The cruelty, corruption, and sacrilege practiced by the Romans finally pushed the raging inhabitants to revolt against Rome in the year 66. Josephus was in charge of the Galilean army. In July 67, he and his troops were besieged in the citadel of

Jotapata and defeated by the great Roman general Vespasian, to whom Josephus surrendered. The story of this surrender has a dark twist: Having taken refuge in a cave, the top officers discussed their hopeless situation and decided that collective suicide was the only honorable action. Drawing lots, they would kill each other in turn, with the last man committing suicide. Josephus says that he, being the last one, convinced the next-to-last officer that they should spare each other. He then officially surrendered to Vespasian. He subsequently gained great favor with the Roman general by predicting that he would become emperor.

Later, in the power vacuum left by Nero's suicide, various legions proclaimed their own chiefs Princeps Imperator, and Vespasian's prospects suddenly rose high. Two years later, Josephus's prophecy was realized. Freed from the status of captive, he entered Vespasian's service and later served his son and successor, Titus. Both emperors granted Josephus a generous pension. In the year 67, Josephus had accompanied Titus through Judaea, serving as interpreter and witnessing the siege of Jerusalem. The city was taken and the Temple destroyed. Returning to Rome in 72, Josephus spent the last twenty-five years of his life writing. His compositions include two major historical works: *Antiquities* and *The History of the War of the Jews and Romans*. The latter covers a period that embraces a great deal more than the Roman campaigns of Vespasian and Titus. Not only does it provide precise information about the war itself (of which Tacitus left only brief and biased accounts), but it also discusses the reign of the Hasmoneans, as well as that of Herod, during Jesus' time.

Yet in Josephus's other book, the *Antiquities*—also known as the *History of the Jews*—we find two specific references to Jesus. Written in the early nineties, it is his greatest work and is considered one of the major early historical works describing ancient times. In twenty chapters it discusses the entire history of the Jews, from antiquity to Roman times. Volume 18 contains a brief passage about Jesus and is one of the extremely rare "outside" sources that mention him. A number of scholars believe, however, that the copy that has come down to us contains words inserted by an overzealous Christian redactor. Given the importance of the passage in question, some specialists have attempted to reconstruct the "original" text without the Christian interpolation. The version we have is obviously talking about the Jesus of the New Testament, with his great charisma:

> Now there was about this time Jesus, a wise man, if it be lawful to call him a man; for he was a doer of wonderful works, a teacher of such men as receive the truth with pleasure. He drew over to him both many of the Jews and many of the Gentiles. He was [the] Christ. And when Pilate, at the suggestion of the principal men amongst us, had condemned him to the cross, those that loved him at the first did not forsake him; for he appeared to them alive again the third day; as the divine prophets had foretold these and then thousand other wonderful things concerning him. And the tribe of Christians, so named from him, are not extinct at this day.[52]

A recent work by Serge Bardet[53] sheds new light on the source of this text. His study, devoted to the translations and interpretations of this passage from Josephus, draws a provisional conclusion opposed to the hypothesis that the passage is simply a Christian interpolation[54] from as late as the fourth century. Bardet's textual analysis shows that the style is very much that of Josephus. In any case, if it is an insertion, it could not have been made too many years later than the original text. Bardet's argument for the authenticity of the passage is based on Josephus's concern—as he always demonstrated in describing Jewish sects of the first century—for naming this specific Jewish sect and its leader, Jesus. This does not appear to fit well with an agenda of Judeo-Christian proselytism.

There is another indirect reference to Jesus in the *Antiquities,* in chapter 9 of volume 20. It is said that in the time of Albinus, procurator of Judaea, the high priest Ananus, a Sadducee, brought to trial James, "the brother of Jesus, called Christ, as well as others [of his companions], and when he had considered the charges of lawbreaking against them, sentenced them to be stoned."

Some Roman sources are of lesser interest insofar as the Christian influence is obvious on the texts that have come down to us. Tacitus (55–120), however, writes in his *Annals* of the great fire of Rome under Nero. He explains that Nero, suspected of starting the catastrophic fire, instead accused the Christians: "Thus, in order to squelch the rumor, Nero made scapegoats of the 'Christians,' as they were called by the people, a sect detested for its depravities. He imposed terrible tortures upon them. Their name comes from Christ, who had been executed during the reign of Tiberius by Pontius Pilate, procurator of Judaea."[55]

Where did Tacitus get this information? Some believe it came from his close friend Pliny the Younger. Others believe that he had read it in Josephus's *Testimonium*. Still others argue that it might have been found in the Roman archives. If this is true, however, Tacitus did not quote his source directly because it contains an error: Pilate was a prefect, not a procurator. Another possibility is that he simply reported what people of his day were saying. One thing is certain: Tacitus confirms the execution of Jesus under Tiberius and Pilate; and this was an execution by the Romans, not by the Jews, as some Christian churches have claimed.[56]

Pliny the Younger (circa 65–114 C.E.), Tacitus's friend, was proconsul of Bythinia, a province in Asia Minor. During a correspondence with the emperor Trajan, Pliny asked for instructions on how to deal with Christians brought before his court. In these letters, he mentioned the Christians' practice of holding regular meetings at twilight, chanting hymns to the glory of Christ "as to a god." Such a sect must have appeared strange to Pliny, who took pains to add that in their assemblies, the members of this sect took "an ordinary and innocent meal" and committed themselves to "observing moral law, keeping one's word, refraining from theft, adultery, etc." What is striking in these letters is the candor of both authors, who agreed that only those Christians who threatened the public order by persisting in their superstitions should be punished.

Suetonius (70–140), in his *Lives of the Twelve Caesars,* completed around 120 C.E., refers twice to the Christian sect. First, speaking of the expulsion of Jews from Rome under the emperor Claudius, he explains that "they were constantly causing problems at the instigation of *Chrestus*."[57] Some authors believe that *Chrestus* refers to the Christ, with a variant spelling. Later on, when commenting on the many condemnations made by Nero during his reign, Suetonius writes that "they led the Christians to torture, who are a sort of people given to a new and dangerous superstition."[58]

An examination of source documents—gospels, canonical and apocryphal texts, and other sources—demonstrates that they cannot provide satisfactory information about the historical Jesus. The canonical gospels are ultimately dependent on oral traditions that were written down over a period of at least forty years, beginning as late as the year 60 C.E., almost two generations after the death of Jesus. We do not know who their real authors were, but we know that none of them was a direct witness to the life of Jesus.[59]

Besides this, the papyrus or parchment source documents themselves have been recopied, corrected, edited, and redacted by scribes with varying scruples and standards of rigor. Numerous additions were written into the scriptures during the first centuries of the Church, also, whether intended to preserve the true faith or to more effectively propagate the Good News among pagans. Hence, authors who want to sort out reliable historical information regarding deeds and words that may reasonably be attributed to Jesus must follow a rigorous method of interpretation.

2

Exegetical Studies
of the Sources

As we have seen, there are numerous and varied sources that speak of the man Jesus. They vary greatly in their proximity to his life and death. None originates with witnesses who knew him. Many authors and scribes who worked on New Testament texts wrote primarily in Greek.[1] Yet many of them thought and spoke a different native language—sometimes Aramaic, sometimes other Semitic languages; and occasionally they used Hebrew when referring to passages from the Jewish Bible.[2]

We can be sure that none of the four writers of the canonical gospels had direct access to Paul's Letters, even though certain aspects of Paul's theology had begun to spread among Judeo-Christian communities around the Mediterranean. As Perrot said, "Each of them lived at different times, and were members of Christian sects whose views of the Master's teaching and religious practices were not necessarily alike. When the Evangelists borrowed extracts from diverse sources, they frequently introduced their own (or their group's) theological vision into them."[3]

Finally, we must always bear in mind that those texts that have survived the condemnations, accusations of heresy, loss, and the ravages of time are actually copies of copies of versions that have themselves been largely edited. They often come down to us with additions or omissions, whether made voluntarily or not.

What, then, is the best way to study these documents? Based on what we have seen, clearly New Testament writings, canonical and apocryphal, cannot all be interpreted in the same manner. Contemporary exegesis makes use of "reading filters," known as "criteria of historicity," to help readers form an opinion as to the degree of authenticity of a text, and to identify its interpolations or retrojections. They also employ commonsense rules, and sometimes examine the consistency with other sacred texts.

In the following sections, we shall review these various criteria as briefly as possible, given the complexity of hermeneutic tools that certainly deserve a longer discussion than is possible within the scope of this book. It should be clear from the start, however, that these criteria cannot enable us to solve all the problems of interpretation that might arise. Therefore, a primary task is to reestablish the sociohistorical context in which New Testament scriptures were first written and used. This will help us to better understand the concepts, words, and expressions they employ and to avoid misunderstandings or interpretations that are too far removed from the intentions of the authors and from the actions they relate.

THE CRITERIA OF HISTORICITY

A common objection related to the use of linguistic, semiotic, and critical historical approaches in reading the New Testament is that every such exegesis sooner or later runs up against the theological bias inherent in the vision of the Easter drama. In other words, though this approach can be useful for a better understanding of the historical Jesus, how can it simply set aside the "radical transformation implied by the Easter event in the narrative of [the gospel] texts?" Paul's famous remark, cited earlier—"Even if we have known the Christ in the flesh, henceforth it is no longer in this manner that we know him"—stands as a reminder of this.

Such an objection cannot be lightly dismissed. On the other hand, does not "historical" research include possibilities beyond either "a Christian exegesis, be it patristic or critical" or a "fundamentalist [i.e., historicist] reading of the Bible"? Here, we use Perrot's formulation of the question. In his view, historians who avoid dealing with the resurrection of the Christ only encourage it to come back to haunt us in the form of efforts at historical reconstitution that are always illusory, based on the "arbitrary" supposition that some original event must exist that is directly referred to, without intermediation, in the texts themselves.[4] Other authors, well aware of our inability to get at raw facts, believe the essential goal of exegesis is to help identify elements that reflect the theological orientation of a scriptural author. The latter almost always draws its meaning from a faith in the resurrection of Christ as Redeemer.

Therefore, our question is: What criteria can help us distinguish between what we may reasonably attribute to the historical Jesus and material that may have been created by oral traditions of the early Church as well as additions and redactions made by gospel authors and copyists?

The Primary Criteria

1. The *criterion of embarrassment* (Schillebeeckx's thesis), also known as the *criterion of contradiction*. This helps us to identify elements in the Sayings of Jesus that, for the early Church, constitute a likely source of problems, embarrassments, or seeming contradictions with other texts. It also applies to passages that, depending on the context, might have difficulties that could be used as ammunition by adversaries of the Church. To illustrate the use of this criterion, Meier discusses the way Jesus' baptism is treated in the synoptic gospels.[5] It is generally agreed that the criterion of embarrassment is conclusive only when it is supported by other criteria. An example is the Saying "My God, my God, why have you forsaken me?"[6] When compared with the text of

Psalm 22, this statement loses the shocking or scandalous quality that some contemporary critics have attributed to it.

2. The *criterion of discontinuity,* also called the *criterion of double dissimilarity.* This is used to identify words or deeds attributed to Jesus that do not fit the cultural context of Judaism in his day and those that do not fit that of the early churches. This criterion has profited from considerable advances in our understanding of first-century Judaism and of the teachings of the early churches. Two of the many examples that come to mind are Jesus' opposition to his disciples' practice of fasting and his adamant rejection of divorce.[7] In the first example, it is important to note that Jesus himself did not make a practice of fasting. In the second example, we know that Jewish tradition of the time was considerably less simplistic, and more flexible, in dealing with divorce. As with the first criterion, discontinuity should be employed along with other criteria.

3. The *criterion of multiple attestation.* This enables us to attribute greater authenticity to Sayings that have been attested to by at least two independent sources (examples: Mark, Q, John) and/or have been incorporated into more than one literary genre or form. Examples of the latter are parable, debate, history, miracle, and prophecy. This criterion gains credibility when a given theme or thread turns up in different sources and literary forms.

4. The *criterion of coherence,* also called the *criterion of consistency.* This is akin to the criterion of dissimilarity. It helps us to determine whether the nature of reported deeds or Sayings of Jesus are in "harmony" with those found in the "database" of the earliest, best-established deeds and Sayings. A judicious application of this criterion can indicate whether a given account has a reasonable probability of being historical. It should be clear that this criterion can be used only after we have already collected a critical mass of materials whose historicity has been tested by the previous criteria.[8]

Other Criteria

Some exegetes use still other criteria, but their value has not been as well established as the above. Jérémie, for example, considers traces of

Aramaic influence in a text as a criterion of authenticity. The presence or absence of Aramaisms might confirm or cast doubt on the validity of Sayings in Greek according to how easy or difficult it is to perform an Aramaic retro-translation upon them. The use of this criterion can present serious difficulties, however. It could even lead to false conclusions if it turned out that the original translation from Aramaic to Greek was a literal rendering of an inauthentic text, rather than a more liberal translation of an authentic text. Besides this, Greek-speaking Christians could easily imitate the Greek style of the Septuagint, whose built-in Semitisms would then automatically confer this type of "authenticity" on whatever they wrote.

Vermès emphasizes two other criteria that he calls *criteria of verisimilitude*.[9] First, would someone have a vested interest in inventing a given account? If a Saying served the interests of the early Church, yet is in conflict with the overall teaching of Jesus, this criterion would lead us to suspect that the Saying is probably an invention by the Church. On the other hand, if an accepted Saying is incompatible with Church doctrine and/or interests, then the likelihood of its authenticity is greater. For the most part, these criteria can be seen as corollaries of the criterion of embarrassment and should be used only as secondary methods.

THE STYLE OF THE SAYINGS

A number of scholars believe that a close study of content and style in the synoptic Sayings shows that they derive from at least two sources[10] that are very different from each other, both in inspiration and in religious orientation. For our part, the most convincing of such proponents is P. Nautin, who devoted the major part of his career to demonstrating the existence of an "original source" that was drawn upon by the presumed first author of the *Évangile primitif*, or "primitive Gospel."[11] This source, which Nautin qualifies as the earliest, gives us a Jesus wholly "imbued with reverence for the God of Abraham, Isaac, and Jacob, source of all justice, wisdom, and compassion." Thus, his teaching would be clearly "theocentric" in style. The other sources, which several authors posit, would in this view be creations of the synoptic authors. The religious orientation of the sects connected with this movement are highly "Christocentric"; contrary to the first source, they emphasize the exaltation of the person Jesus as Messiah and Son of God, indispensable intermediary of divine revelation. Let us consider a few illustrations of these opposed visions in the canonical Sayings.

Among those considered by scholars to come from the "original source," whose authenticity is therefore judged to be fairly solid[12] and whose orientation is clearly theocentric, we quote the following Sayings:

> At that very hour, he trembled with joy from the working of the Holy Spirit, and said: "I praise you, Father, Lord of heaven and earth, for having hidden this from the wise and intelligent, and having revealed it to small babes. Yes, Father, for thus has been your pleasure." (Matt. 11:25, Luke 10:21)

> And whoever speaks against the Son of Man[13] shall be forgiven, but whoever blasphemes against the Holy Spirit shall not be forgiven. (Matt. 12:32, Luke 12:10)

The redactors of the gospels of Luke and Matthew may well have been perturbed by the self-effacement of Jesus implied in these Sayings, for they juxtaposed two others right after them, which clearly come from one or more "christocentric" sources:

> All things have been delivered to me by my Father; and no one knows who is the Son except the Father, or who is the Father except the Son, or someone to whom the Son chooses to reveal him. (Luke 10:22)

> And I tell you, everyone who acknowledges me before others, the Son of man also will acknowledge them before the angels of God; but whoever denies me before others will be denied before the angels of God. (Luke 12:8–9, Matt. 10:32–33)

Many scholars believe these Sayings are productions of the early Church, for they contradict the previous Sayings. Another oft cited Saying shows Jesus giving an unambiguous reply regarding his view of himself: "And as he was setting out on his journey, a man ran up and knelt before him, and asked him, 'Good Teacher, what must I do to inherit eternal life?' And Jesus said to him, 'Why do you call me good? No one is good but God alone'" (Mark 10:17–18, Luke 18:18–19, Matt. 19:16).

What is so striking, and worth emphasizing, in these synoptic extracts is that in those Sayings that satisfy the criterion of multiple attestation, Jesus never claims a central role for himself in an event or in a teaching.[14] He never presents himself as someone worthy of worship, never as the Son of the Almighty, or as God incarnate. Those themes revolve around the divine origin of the Messiah. This is discussed at great length in the Johannine and Pauline traditions but not in the synoptic. The Good News that Jesus has come to announce to the poor, the marginal, and the disenfranchised is an unmistakably theocentric message—it implies Jesus' own humility as a servant of the Almighty, "Father of us all." In contrast to the Gospel of John, the synoptics offer us a clear picture of a Jesus who refuses to become the center of a personality cult. As he said during his temptation in the desert: "It is written: you shall worship the Lord, your God, and him alone shall you serve" (Luke 4:8, Matt. 4:1).

SCRIPTURAL INTERPRETATION IN SOCIAL, HISTORICAL, AND LINGUISTIC CONTEXT

As we have pointed out, none of the Evangelists was a direct witness to Jesus' life. The gospels are, in a sense, anonymous creations. Did the first followers of Jesus attempt to write a biography of Jesus? Their writings sought to preserve isolated elements—short passages relating words or deeds of Jesus. Later, these elements were rearranged and modified by different redactors and authors. As E. P. Sanders says, "This means that we can never be sure of the immediate context in which these words or acts are taking place. Certain elements have been revised, others created out of whole cloth by the early Church. The gospels have none of the characteristics of biographical works, in the modern sense of the term."[15] The gospel authors' desire was to bear witness, through writing, to their profound faith in Jesus Christ, who died for the salvation of humankind and was resurrected in the glory of God. Consequently, our task is to restore the historical context of these writings while bearing in mind the limitations imposed by the difficulty of translating certain words. This, of course, only further emphasizes what a risky business this kind of exegesis is, imposing humility upon its researchers.

The "Untranslatability" of Certain Words

Edelmann, in his rich and inspired work of research and personal reflections, entitled *Jésus parlait araméen* [Jesus Spoke Aramaic],[16] notes that "Jesus' maternal language is an extremely supple one, for a single word can cover a wide range of meanings." Even though the Evangelists wrote in Greek, they were in effect translating Sayings that Jesus had uttered in Aramaic, also their maternal language.[17] In addition, some of the Greek words used in the gospels pose virtually insurmountable problems of translation.

Without dwelling too long on this subject, let us note two examples that have particular importance in the Sayings of Jesus:[18] the two words that are traditionally translated into English as "sinners" and "the just." We now know that these are imperfect approximations of the Greek words *hamartôloi* and *dikaiois,* which are themselves poor translations from Aramaic or Hebrew.[19]

The Importance of the Historical Context

The work of exegesis goes far beyond compiling and examining the most credible Sayings of Jesus. One of the golden rules of this work is that context gives meaning to what is being related. Indeed, the words alone are not a sufficient foundation for solving the problems that arise. As in any historical reconstruction, we must define a framework of interpretation that enables us to fit the data we have into a well-established sociohistorical context. This requires a reasonable knowledge of Judaism and of Palestine in the first century C.E., as well as of the different currents of Greco-Roman thought that powerfully influenced the Mediterranean world. This will be the subject of the next chapter.

Skepticism Regarding Exegesis of the Sayings of Jesus

Could a thorough, careful, and deep exegesis of the Sayings of the New Testament ever lead us to certainty in judging their degree of authenticity? As we have just seen, in order to be sure of our identification of things Jesus really said, we have to be able to reconstruct the contexts in which they were uttered and compare these to others dealing with the same subject but in a different context. Hence, we can hope to shed light upon only what Jesus probably thought or meant.

But this work of exegesis often deals with anecdotes that are too short and cut off from their original context. Because of this, there is a strong temptation to give too much meaning to passages that, in the form they have come down to us, will probably never reveal their secrets. Pondering the many works dealing with these questions (which often come to diametrically opposed conclusions) has left many readers—both amateur and professional—skeptical, or at least cautious, as to the degree of certainty that is possible given the limits we face in this project.

THE HYPOTHESIS OF A PRIMITIVE GOSPEL

Before concluding this chapter on sources, we must consider the question that a number of researchers have naturally raised. Might there exist an original written source, a proto-gospel that gospel writers made use of? We have seen that a large majority of scholars now agree that Mark came before Matthew and that the latter preceded Luke.[20] By the same token, there is no longer any doubt that both the latter are largely inspired by Mark and generally follow its outlines, notwithstanding their occasional modification of content, rearrangement of events, and introduction of new elements. Also, as we have noted, this mutual borrowing has not prevented the three redactors from being guided by their own theological vision, or those of their time or their sect.

Furthermore, the hypothesis of a common, oldest source for the three synoptics—called the Besorah, or sometimes the Primitive Gospel (*Urevangelium* in German)—is gaining more and more support from new exegetical research. Some go a step further in this gospel genealogy in trying to distinguish which elements of these texts might come from a still older source than the Besorah, a text that would have been written during Jesus' lifetime.

One answer to this question is found in the posthumously published work by Pierre Nautin cited earlier. Even today, in my view, this author has not gained the recognition he deserves.[21] His thesis is that there was indeed a text that preceded the proto-gospel, which he simply refers to (in French) as the Source. According to him, we have lost all traces of it, either because the material itself has been lost or because it existed first as an oral tradition, the original that preceded and inspired all the others.

In general, three points can be made regarding Nautin's description of this earliest Source. First, its relative lack of wondrous accounts, in comparison to the synoptics, suggests that it was composed at a time relatively close to the death of Jesus. Second, when the (presumed) author of the *Évangile primitif* (EP) encounters Sayings of Jesus that are at odds with his own theology, the author scrupulously preserves them, thereby demonstrating a veneration for this Source. Finally, the image of Jesus that emerges from the Source, in contrast to that which emerges via the author of the EP, is of someone who "preaches the reign of God, without making any claims about himself." This strongly suggests that the latter Sayings were produced by the historical Jesus himself, rather than by his followers.

3
Jesus
and His Environment

Now we turn to the sociocultural environment in which Jesus lived. We begin with the overall historical context and focus down to the local level trying to gain a sense of the man in the context of his family, socioeconomic milieu, education, and beliefs. We have not considered the important aspect of his psychology, which would have helped at the very least to understand his personal story and family history. This is not a real possibility, simply because the available sources that speak of his childhood—the first chapters of Matthew and of Luke and a few apocrypha—tell us nothing reliable about the history of this period. Most of these narratives, such as biblical texts like Genesis, are of a mythic nature.[1]

Even the most impatient reader, eager to get to the real questions without getting bogged down in a multitude of contradictions—or simply the uncertainties that characterize all biographies of Jesus—may rest assured: The only biographical data accepted by a consensus of scholars can be summed up in a few lines. Most authors would not disagree with the following brief summary: Jesus, whose full name in

Aramaic was Yeshua ben Yosef, was born of a Jewish mother named Miriam (Mary, in English) sometime between the years 6 and 4 B.C.E., around the time of the death of Herod the Great.[2] His birthplace was undoubtedly Nazareth, a village in Galilee, and not Bethlehem, in Judaea.[3] He spent virtually all of his childhood and probably most of his adulthood in the village of his birth.

Luke 3:23 tells us indirectly that when he was about thirty, Jesus went to receive baptism at the hands of John the Baptist, a popular hermit teacher, who gave baptism by immersion in the Jordan River to all who accepted his teaching of penitence and conversion. Shortly afterward, Jesus chose his disciples and began his mission. This has come to be called his public ministry, in which he preached the Good News of the Kingdom of God in village and rural synagogues around Galilee—but apparently not in the cities. Toward the end of his public ministry, whose duration (according to the sources) was between eighteen months and three years, he went to Jerusalem for Passover. He entered the Temple and apparently caused trouble there. After a last meal with his disciples, he retired alone to a public garden outside the city, where he was arrested. He was brought back into the city, interrogated by the Temple authorities, and turned over to the Roman authorities. He was sentenced to death by the Roman prefect Pontius Pilate.[4] His disciples, who fled at the time of his arrest, reassembled some time later and spread the news that they had seen Jesus after his death.[5] They professed his impending return to found the Kingdom that he had announced during his mission. From this basis of faith, they set out to convert others to believe in Jesus, the Messiah of God.

Given our present knowledge, this is about all one can say about the life of Jesus with any reasonable certainty. Small as it is, it is important to note this point: Except for these few facts that are supported by multiple attestations, other biographical events that have been written have little historical credibility. Also, though we now possess a much greater degree of certainty about his authentic Sayings, they tell us virtually nothing about the man himself. Given the problem of reliability of sources that we have seen previously, we must be extremely cautious when drawing conclusions about the man who presumably uttered these Sayings. Besides, it is amazing how many glaring contradictions about the man would emerge if we accepted all his reported Sayings as authentic. Sometimes they present us with a character who never speaks of himself and other times with one who puts himself at the center of his message. For this reason, we intend to deal only with those facts that have been well established and accepted by most scholars. This will help us to establish a better approach to the person of Jesus of Nazareth, whose actual deeds will be discussed in chapters 6 and 7.

GALILEE, PALESTINE, AND THE ROMAN EMPIRE IN THE TIME OF JESUS[6]

The period that interests us extends from the birth of Jesus to the middle of the second century, the era during which the New Testament writings were, for the most part, composed and redacted. The provinces of Galilee and Judaea experienced alternating periods of calm and troubles during this time, the latter including riots and revolts. This chronic agitation could not help but influence people's minds and further destabilize a political and religious situation that was already relatively precarious. But let us go still further back, to the earlier context.

Palestine under Roman Occupation

In the year 67 B.C.E., faced with serious problems of maritime piracy, especially threatening supplies of Egyptian wheat, the Roman senate accorded Pompey extraordinary powers *(imperium infinitum)* to put an end to the threats. In three months, Pompey restored order to the Mediterranean traffic and then took on the job of pacifying the Asian provinces. The following year, he won decisive victories over Mithridates, king of Pontus, and his son-in-law Tigranes, king of Armenia. From there, he continued his campaign into Syria, then under Seleucid rule.[7] He reached Damascus in the spring of 63 C.E., conquering Syria, which then became a Roman province.

Pompey then marched on Jerusalem to put an end to the instability and chaos caused by a chronic power struggle within the Hasmonean dynasty,[8] between the two brothers, Aristobulus II and Hyrcanus. Meeting a strong popular resistance that lasted for three months, with the people besieged in the Temple, where they had taken refuge, a terrible massacre ensued after which Pompey took control of the holy city. He deposed Aristobulus, who had opposed Rome, and replaced him with Hyrcanus II, who had delivered the city, making him high priest and local ruler of the province of Palestine. Hyrcanus ruled until 40 B.C.E., but Palestine had lost its independence and was forced to pay tribute to Rome. Pompey had imposed an Idumean military commander upon Hyrcanus named Antipater, who then named his two sons, Phasael and Herod, governors of Judaea and Galilee, respectively.[9]

In 40 B.C.E., Antigone, whose father, Aristobulus, was killed by Pompey's men, captured Hyrcanus and Phasael with military aid from the Parthians. Herod fled to exile in Rome, where, bolstered by his friendship with Mark Anthony and Octavius, the other two members of the triumvirate, he succeeded in having himself appointed king of Judaea by the Roman senate. A shrewd man, Herod then went to Palestine and, with military help from the Romans, who saw him as a good client ruler, captured Antigone and sent him to Rome to be executed. Most of the Jews had remained loyal to the Hasmoneans and hated the Idumean Herod, whom they regarded an instrument of Roman power. Nonetheless, he ruled over Palestine for thirty-three years, becoming known to history as Herod the Great, until he died in 4 B.C.E. His cruelty and tyranny were legendary,[10] but he was a grand constructor and an extremely capable administrator who maintained excellent relations with Rome.

After Herod's death, Palestine was divided by the Romans, who had little confidence in the abilities and trustworthiness of his sons. Archelaus, the elder surviving son, inherited Judaea, Samaria, and Idumea. He kept them for ten years and was then deposed and exiled to Gaul by the Romans. Judaea and Samaria then passed over to direct Roman administration, governed by a prefect based in the seaport city of Caesaria, a dependency of the governor of Syria. Philip (4 B.C.E.–34 C.E.), the second of Herod's surviving sons, received territories east of the Jordan and north of Decapolis, an area known as Batanea, including the Golan plateau and Iturea. Antipas, the youngest brother, was given Galilee and Perea, with the title of tetrarch. All three brothers were declared vassals of Rome, subservient to the governor of Syria.

Galilee in the Time of Jesus

During Jesus' life, Galilee was no more than an ethnarchy, a kind of vassal state of Rome. Antipas, who took the dynastic name of Herod, ruled it for almost 43 years. It was a relatively calm period there, in spite of the fact that Galilee had long been a hotbed of rebels whose leaders frequently caused trouble in neighboring countries, especially Judaea. A great constructor like his father, Herod Antipas built the city of Tiberiad on the lake of Genesareth.[11] Having rejected the daughter of the Nabatean king, he married his own niece Herodia, who was divorced from his half brother Philip. The synoptic gospels relate the famous episode where John the Baptist paid with his life for protesting this marriage.

Pressured by Herodia, Herod Antipas pursued intrigues to persuade the emperor Caligula to name him king. But in the end, he was deposed and exiled to Gaul to the town now known as St. Bertrand de Comminges, to which Herodia chose to follow him. His tetrarchy was then given by Caligula to Agrippa, a grandson of Herod the Great. This Herod Agrippa became a favorite of Caligula and had long been a close friend of Claudius, who unexpectedly rose to emperor after Caligula's murder. Herod Agrippa I was then named king of the Jews and had a short and apparently peaceful reign from 41 to 44 C.E.. A passionate Hellenist, he was nonetheless respectful of Jewish religious practices. Probably to curry favor with the dominant Pharisee party, he had James, the brother of Jesus, executed and imprisoned the apostle Peter. It was Agrippa I who began construction of the third Jerusalem rampart.

After Agrippa's death, Claudius judged his son, Herod Agrippa II, too immature and refused him the crown. Instead, Agrippa obtained the kingdom of Chalcis. Claudius named him Temple inspector and, in

49 C.E., Agrippa II obtained the power to appoint the high priest. In the year 50 C.E., Nero finally accorded him the title of king of the Jews. He was not directly involved in the insurrection of 66, which he actually attempted to calm. Agrippa II stood by as a powerless Roman ally during the fall of Jerusalem in 70 C.E.

The Roman system of provincial administration that had been established in Judaea, Samaria, and Idumea in the year 6 C.E. was under the authority of a prefect who himself was attached to the governor of Syria. This system lasted until the first Jewish revolt in 66 C.E. (with the exception of a suspension from 41 to 44 C.E. during Herod Agrippa's brief reign as king). Among the numerous prefects who filled the post during this period, the most famous was Pontius Pilate (26–36 C.E.), spoken of in the gospels, who had Jesus put to death. Pilate's reputation was that of an unscrupulous provincial politician, cruel and indifferent to local customs and religious practices. His brutality and clumsiness caused riots in Jerusalem. Although his tenure in Judaea was apparently of average length for prefects, he was finally recalled to Rome after a massacre of Samaritans that he had ordered.

The physical presence of a Roman prefect in Jerusalem was rare. Normally, he would go there only for Jewish festivals, accompanied by a strong guard in case of trouble. Just a small Roman garrison was maintained within the walls of the holy city, and Rome had exempted Jews from military service. In theory, direct collection of taxes was the responsibility of Roman administrators, but in reality, local intermediaries fulfilled this role. Thus indirect tax collection became a function accorded to private groups called publicans, whom most Jews detested, considering their profession as dishonorable as that of a prostitute. Justice was administered by Jewish tribunals according to Jewish law, except in cases where offenses against Rome were involved. Otherwise, important cases, including criminal charges, were decided by the Jewish high court, called the Sanhedrin.[12] For Sanhedrin death sentences to be carried out, however, they required confirmation and execution by the Roman prefect. As for religious power, the Roman prefect appointed the high priest and could depose him at will.

Until the year 160 B.C.E., the time of the Maccabee revolt, the Jewish population of Palestine was "limited to a zone around Jerusalem whose area was less than 800 square miles."[13] During the next century, following the restoration of peace by the Hasmoneans, non-Jewish areas of Palestine became predominantly Jewish more or less by force. As Baron wrote, "[I]n a very few decades, John Hyrcanus and Alexander Jannaeus, the great Jewish conquerors of the time, annexed, in rapid succession, Samaria, Galilee, Transjordania, Idumea, and part of the coastal plain."[14] In all areas that were considered Israelite in the past, the inhabitants were compelled to adopt the Jewish religion and abandon all idolatry, which was believed to pollute the traditional sanctity of the land. Galilee, which had not been Jewish previously, was also Judaized and became a Jewish enclave surrounded by ten autonomous Greek cities, known as the Decapolis. The best known of these cities were Ptolomeos, Tyre, and Sidon on the Phoenician coast; Caesaria Philippi to the north;[15] and Scythopolis. This last city barred access to the Jordan valley from the south, but Jews preferred to pass through it on their way to Jerusalem to avoid Samaria, a land that traditionally had been inhospitable toward them.

Galilee, though the richest and most densely populated region of Palestine, was geographically heterogeneous. Upper Galilee, in the north, was mostly rural and interspersed with mountainous areas, making access difficult. It became a haven for exiles, rebels, and brigands. There were no towns in the north, only a few large villages such as Gischala and Meron. The region experienced a long period of serious unrest, beginning around 50 B.C.E. and ending with the fall of Jerusalem in 70 C.E. The most famous anti-Roman rebels came from Upper Galilee: Ezechias, executed by Herod in 47 B.C.E., and his son Judas, who laid siege to the arsenal of Sephoris in a revolt that spread into Judaea. Shortly before Herod the Great's death, Judas was defeated by Varus, the Roman governor of Syria, who had him crucified along with two thousand other rebels. At the time of the census decreed by Quirinius, we find a record of this same Judas stirring up rebellion in alliance with the Zealot party, who refused to pay taxes to Caesar and recognized only God as their master. One of Judas's two sons gained a different kind of renown in the latter half of the first century C.E. Known as Tiberius Julius Alexander, he served as procurator of Judaea from 46 to 48 C.E. He was also a nephew of the famous Philo of Alexandria. Tiberius Julius acquired Roman citizenship and became governor of Egypt during the time of the great Jewish revolt stamped out by Vespasian and Titus.

In contrast to the relatively arid highlands of the north, the valleys of Lower Galilee were fertile and well situated as a crossroads for cultural and commercial intercourse between the Mediterranean and the East. Its air was pure and water from springs was abundant, making Lower Galilee a popular place to settle. One of these springs, called Capernaum, gave its name to a small fishing village on the Sea of Galilee, and served as home base for Jesus during his public ministry. Lower Galilee was a producer of vegetables, fruits, olive oil, and wine, with significant fishing and pottery industries as well. Its two most important cities were Sephoris,[16] located halfway between the coast and the Sea of Galilee, and Tiberiad, which bordered the sea. Flavius Josephus considered Sephoris the pearl of Galilee. It was the capital of the province until 17 C.E., when Herod Antipas replaced it with Tiberiad, which he had founded in honor of the emperor Tiberius.

Recent archaeological research suggests that Lower Galilee in the time of Jesus was powerfully influenced by Greco-Roman culture, and that Greek was widely spoken, as well as Aramaic. Digs at Sephoris have revealed the vestiges of a Roman city of high culture. It includes the ruins of a theater, a fortress, and a palace, all dating from the first century C.E. Small statues of pagan gods have been found, as well as mosaics of exquisite aesthetic quality. Some represent Greek divinities, such as Dionysos, son of Zeus, associated with the mystery cults. The proximity of Sephoris to Nazareth,[17] the hometown of Jesus and his family, suggests that Jesus probably visited Sephoris for professional reasons, with or without his father. The gospels say nothing of this, perhaps because Sephoris was resented by Galileans as a foreign city under the political and cultural domination of a hated occupier. Perhaps for the same reason, they do not mention Tiberiad.

Sociocultural Particularities

Baron writes[18] that marked inequalities existed among social and occupational groups in the heart of Galilean society. In particular, the peasants were "exploited by absentee landowners, and oppressed by tax collectors. They were made to feel that their status as Jews brought them permanently under suspicion." Given the relative complexity of the Talmudic prescriptions and customs concerning proper ritual and sacrifice in the Temple, "it was much more difficult for a peasant to observe the Law than it was for artisans and small merchants," Baron writes. Roman fiscal policy and "the Jewish rules concerning agriculture, to say nothing of the laws regarding purity, must have always weighed heavier on peasants, who found themselves caught between Jewish religious obligations, and Roman civil obligations. But the ruthless methods of Roman enforcement left them little choice." As a result, peasants refused more and more often to pay the religious tithe. This crushing financial burden,[19] which inevitably led to widespread impoverishment of the population, was the source of extreme tensions that at times broke out in riots or open revolts.

Bearing on the religious context, Baron reminds us that "the prevalence of new converts in Galilee contrasted violently with the ancient, deep-rooted Jewish culture in Judaea, which had known a true theocracy. Galileans must have resented this difference." Of close ethnic kinship to the Judaeans, they had embraced the rites and dogmas of Judaism with more enthusiasm, and with fewer restrictions than one might expect. . . . Nevertheless, Galileans were mistreated by the political bosses in Jerusalem, "who considered them incapable of understanding the subtleties of the Torah. Galilean rabbis were the object of scorn and discrimination."

Indeed, as Vermès notes, Galilee did not possess a rabbinical school until the middle of the first century C.E. This explains partially its ostracism in religious circles in Jerusalem. However, no credible historical document has shown evidence of the presence of eminent Pharisees in Galilee during Jesus' lifetime. The Pharisees he encountered in gospel accounts were said to be visiting from Jerusalem. In any case, unlike Jesus, the Pharisees gravitated toward cities and were rarely found in villages and rural areas. According to Vermès, this evidence argues strongly against the credibility of gospel claims that Jesus' tragic end was brought about primarily by religious differences.

Other scholars disagree, maintaining that this thesis underestimates the importance of the high priesthood of Jerusalem, as well as this priesthood's deep distrust of the popularity of this man Jesus. Nevertheless, as we shall see later in more detail, these religious squabbles so often referred to in the gospels, especially involving the scribes, were rarely of any social importance. More likely, when the gospels speak of such serious religious conflicts, they are in reality reflections of conflicts encountered at a later date by the early Christian churches and projected by gospel narrators onto the era of Jesus' public mission.

THE FAMILY ENVIRONMENT OF JESUS

His Birth

Was Jesus born just before or just after the beginning of our era? Opinions differ on this question. Most authors lean toward the date of 4 B.C.E. as the most plausible, but recent research suggests the year 7 or 8 C.E., which fits better with other contemporary events mentioned by reliable sources.

The Gospel of Mark, like that of John, says nothing about the birth and childhood of Jesus.[20] On the other hand, Matthew and Luke go into elaborate detail on the subject, each of them based on more or less legendary, but different, sources. Like most of their contemporaries— but especially because they were not trying to be historians—the Evangelists had only a vague notion of historical dates.

Thus they set the childhood of Jesus at a time near the end of the reign of Herod, king of Judaea, some years before the year 4 B.C.E. Both Matthew and Luke write that Jesus was born in Bethlehem, in Judaea.

Why Bethlehem? After all, Luke himself suggests that Jesus' parents were from Nazareth, in Galilee (Luke 1:26). In fact, most scholars now agree that Bethlehem was chosen to give Jesus' birth a scriptural and royal dimension. For Matthew, the choice of Bethlehem fulfills scriptural prophecy.[21] To explain how Jesus' parents came to Galilee, Matthew writes of a return from Egypt, to which they had fled to escape the vengeance of Herod. When they heard that Archelaus had succeeded his father, Herod, they decided not to return to Bethlehem, seeking refuge in Nazareth.[22] This was an odd choice because Galilee, like Judaea, was governed by two sons of Herod. We recall that it was Herod Antipas, in Galilee, who later had John the Baptist put to death, a fact of which Matthew must have been aware.

Luke seems unaware of the legend of a flight to Egypt (or at any rate, it did not devote space to that story). But Luke's main preoccupation was establishing Jesus' descent from David. He used several means to achieve this, including some manipulation of the facts. For example, it was important that Jesus be born in Bethlehem, the birthplace of David, even though Luke had already made it clear that Jesus' family, or at least his mother, Mary, came from Nazareth (Luke 1:26–27). Luke explains this by making use of a historical event: the census of Quirinius, governor of Syria, which he sets during the general time of Jesus' birth.[23] If we accept the chronology of Josephus, however, Quirinius took up his post in the year 6 C.E., ten years after the death of Herod the Great. Josephus also says that the motive for Quirinius's census was a popular uprising led by Judas of Galilee, also mentioned by Luke in the Acts of the Apostles (5:37). On the other hand, Tertullian, a second-century Church theologian, mentions another census under Saturninus, who was governor of Syria from 9 to 6 B.C.E. If we set Jesus' birth shortly before the death of Herod,[24] and accept the census mentioned by Tertullian, the birth would appear to have been around the year 6 B.C.E. These dates fit better with the hypothesis of a census, given the inexact nature of Luke's chronology.

Because we have no civil records nor direct witnesses, we could endlessly debate the problem of dating Jesus' birth. But there is another problem with Luke's claim that Jesus was born during a census, whether ordered by Saturninus or by Quirinius: Luke reports a law that heads of families must return to their birthplace. In fact, we find no trace of such a law in the records of this era. This type of census was undertaken primarily for financial reasons: What mattered was not the geographical origin of families, but rather their current place of residence, whether or not they were property owners, and what profession they practiced. It strains the imagination to suppose that in this part of the Mediterranean, where populations were of such diverse origins, huge numbers of people would be obliged to travel to the place where heads of households were born—to say nothing of proving these origins legally in a land where no system of civil registration existed.

There remains little doubt that this story was motivated by the single goal of having Jesus born in Bethlehem, also said to be the birthplace of his father, Joseph, who was descended from David. It would be of primary importance for both Matthew and Luke that the resurrected Christ, proclaimed a son of David, and Son of God through the power of the Holy Spirit, be born in David's own birthplace of Bethlehem. The contradiction remains, however, between this assertion and the gospel's emphasis that Jesus was a Galilean. The latter will be an important element for understanding his public life.

His Mother

Her name was Miriam, Hellenized as Maria. New Testament writings tell us nothing explicit about who the biological father of Jesus was. As we said before, the chapters of Matthew and of Luke on Jesus' childhood are generally considered to be creations inspired by mythic traditions. They speak of Joseph as the presumed father of Jesus.[25]

J. P. Meier concludes that the historical origins of the traditions concerning Jesus' virgin birth remain obscure.[26] What is more, the debate is ongoing as to the precise meaning of the Greek word *parthenos,* which occurs in the Septuagint and was used in the earliest writings that spoke of Mary's virginity. In fact, *parthenos* can mean either "virgin" or "young woman," but in either case it is associated in

Christian tradition with the notion of a woman who has never had sexual relations. Yet *parthenos* can be translated as single or unmarried, and can apply to a man as well as to a woman. In Judaic tradition, the word *almah,* or virgin, is not without ambiguity.[27] Vermès quotes Rabbi Eliezar ben Hyrcanus (latter first century C.E.), who says that a woman who bears a child without ever having experienced menstruation would still be considered a virgin after giving birth.

Actually, the word *parthenos,* which occurs several times in the synoptic gospels, is used in its original biblical sense, as Matthew uses it in reference to the book of Isaiah: "Therefore the Lord himself will give you a sign. Behold, a young woman shall conceive and bear a son, and shall call his name Immanuel" (Isaiah 7:14).

But we cannot be sure of this unless we compare it with the original Hebrew sources. Vermès, an eminent scholar of Judaic and biblical traditions, points out that Isaiah does not use the word *betulah,* which would have specified an "intact virgin." Instead, he uses the word *almah,* which is correctly translated as "young woman," as in the passage above. In rabbinical terminology, a betulah becomes an almah after puberty. The truth is that the Catholic Church (especially in what is called the Symbol of the Apostles) was first to claim that Jesus was conceived by the Holy Spirit and born of the Virgin Mary.[28] Over the course of time, theologians felt it necessary to clarify the divine conception of Jesus, and Mary herself became a woman exempt from original sin. This is what the Church rather belatedly proclaimed (and not without a certain inner logic) in the dogma of the Immaculate Conception.[29]

Luke shows no hesitation in attributing Jesus' conception to divine intervention when he has the angel Gabriel announce to Mary, in a dream: "The Holy Spirit will come unto you, and the power of the Most High will take you into its protection." The angel adds, as if to reassure Mary, that her aged and sterile cousin will also bear a child, "because for God, nothing is impossible." Vermès notes that divine intervention occurs frequently in the Hebrew scriptures. God can restore fertility to a barren woman, "re-opening her womb," as the

Bible says about the birth of great figures of the sacred story, such as Isaac, Jacob, and Joseph. Luke is thus following established tradition and conferring biblical legitimacy to Jesus' miraculous birth in the story of the annunciation of the angel to Mary.

Matthew's version contents itself (if one may phrase it thus) with a nameless angel appearing in a dream to Joseph—at a time when he was ready to repudiate Mary—to reassure him about his wife's pregnancy, "which has come from the Holy Spirit."

Was Joseph Really the Father of Jesus?

The answer would be in the negative if we accept the following verse: "And he [Joseph] did not know her [Mary], even unto the day she gave birth to a son, whom he gave the name of Jesus" (Matt. 1:25).

The Gospel of Luke also tells us, indirectly, that Joseph was not the father of Jesus: "And Mary said to the angel, 'How shall this be, since I have no husband?' And the angel said to her, 'The Holy Spirit will come upon you, and the power of the Most High will overwhelm you; therefore the child to be born will be called holy, the Son of God'" (Luke 1:34–35). As with all stories of Jesus' childhood, the vast majority of scholars now consider these accounts in Matthew and Luke to be of mythic rather than historical significance.

One thing is certain: Joseph soon disappears from the gospel texts. As soon as Jesus begins his public ministry, there is no further mention of Joseph—perhaps because he had died. The synoptics tell us that Joseph was a *tecton*—a Greek word that can mean "carpenter," "cabinetmaker," or simply "worker." There has been much debate on this question, with some authors deducing that Joseph was a kind of building contractor and others claiming that he was no more than a simple construction worker. The one thing that is certain is that the small village of Nazareth would not have favored much specialization of professions. For lack of detailed information in the source texts, we might assume that Joseph was probably a village carpenter, which would not exclude the possibility that he also framed simple houses.

James and the Other Siblings

This is another subject of which we cannot be certain. Luke specifies that Jesus was Mary's "firstborn son."[30] Does this imply that there were others? Debate is strong on this, but the prevailing opinion is that Jesus had four brothers: James, Joseph (also called Joses), Jude, and Simon. He also may have had at least two sisters, but their names are unknown. The existence of brothers and sisters, for which there seems to be ample evidence in the synoptics,[31] inevitably raises uncomfortable questions about Mary's virginity, especially if any of them were older siblings. Only one apocryphal text, the Story of Joseph the Carpenter, which exists in Arabic and Coptic versions, attributes Jesus' brothers and sisters to a previous marriage of Joseph's. Other contemporary authors, such as Vermès, point out the custom of accepting cousins into a family as brothers and sisters. The Gospel of John speaks of Mary's "sister," also named Mary (Miriam), who was the wife of a certain Clopas. According to Mark, this other Mary was the mother of James and Joses (Mark 15:40). Is there a certain answer to this question? A recent archeological discovery reported in a French daily newspaper article[32] supports the thesis that Jesus had brothers.

As to the family's religious environment, we are on more solid ground, according to the gospels. They affirm that this was a Galilean Jewish family who strictly observed the basic precepts of Mosaic Law, especially the practice of male circumcision, the Sabbath, and the Temple pilgrimage. They apparently did not, however, engage in the complexities of other types of Jewish observance. The synoptics also suggest that Jesus' relations with his family were not particularly amicable. In fact, Matthew and Luke go so far as to say that some family members considered Jesus mentally unbalanced, and that his brothers rejected his message.

Although a close reading of the texts does suggest tension between Jesus and his family, we do not know the reasons for it. It is not unreasonable to suppose that some of his teachings, as reported in the synoptics, may have been unacceptable to his kin simply because the family did not understand the meaning. As to the claim of disbelief on the part of his brothers, this certainly does not seem to apply to James, the best-known brother, who became the leader of Jerusalem's Judeo-Christian community after the death of the Master. In his only Letter, James repeatedly proclaims his faith in "Our Lord Jesus Christ, glorified." On the other hand, this faith may have taken root only after the death of Jesus.

One idea that clearly emerges from the tradition is that Jesus often had a frank and provocative way of speaking. We can see that his words were not always well received by those around him. An illustration of this is his visit to Nazareth, which apparently left bitter feelings in its wake among devout Jews and many others, as suggested by the famous passage from Luke where Jesus says: "Truly, I tell you, no prophet is well-received in his own land." This refers to his speech at the synagogue, when he evoked the great prophets Elijah and Elisha, who had brought aid to foreigners and Gentiles instead of to their own compatriots. This could not fail to arouse indignation among Jesus' listeners, resulting in an attempt by some of them to kill him.[33]

Jesus' Education

In addition to his native Aramaic, Jesus spoke the Hebrew of the synagogue, the language in which the Torah was taught. Possibly (a number of scholars are convinced of this) he spoke some Greek, also. It is well established that Greek was a common language in first-century Galilee, and indispensable for many merchants and travelers to cities such as Jerusalem and Sephoris. The latter was an important, cosmopolitan, Greco-Roman city, only a few miles from Nazareth, and the capital of Galilee until 17 C.E. We need not be historical novelists to find it plausible that Jesus would have made many visits to Sephoris, perhaps related to construction work there, or perhaps to deliver orders. He might have been accompanied by his father on such visits.

The New Testament tells us virtually nothing about Jesus' education, other than the childhood anecdotes that are found only in Luke, and these have little historical credibility. What we do know is that Bible education in Hebrew during the first century was given orally to

Jewish boys. Writing was generally reserved for professionals and was not necessarily associated with learning to read. A few privileged boys, doubtless those who had special talent, were admitted to a more advanced school, the *bet ha-midrash*. There, they studied the deeper meaning of the Torah. Assuming that Jesus was the oldest son, some authors deduce that he may have been encouraged to follow a more advanced religious education, perhaps including learning to read Hebrew. Advocates of this thesis base their argument on gospel passages that evoke Jesus' superior scriptural interpretation, as demonstrated in his debates with devout Pharisees, professional scribes, and Temple authorities in Jerusalem.[34] There is no certain evidence, however, that he did pursue advanced studies. If he did, this would imply that he studied in a city such as Sephoris, Jerusalem, or elsewhere. But nothing in the texts allows us to draw such a conclusion. Other authors take the opposite opinion, referring to a passage in John that says: "Astonished, the Jews wondered: 'How could he read the letters without having studied?'"[35]

Did Jesus Practice a Profession?

The gospels do not speak of this, saying only that he was the son of a carpenter in Nazareth.[36] We might suppose that he learned this trade from his father. Some authors believe that Jesus had a relatively high social status, but there is no solid tradition to back this up. In any case, virtually all agree that his work would have been that of an artisan, like Joseph, rather than that of a peasant or a merchant. What does emerge clearly from the synoptic gospels is that Jesus was at ease among the most humble of people, and is seen to associate with them often, never disdaining to share meals with the most marginal members of society.

Was Jesus Married?

Again, the synoptics tell us nothing of this. Was he a bachelor? A widower? A number of authors point out that in the Judaic culture of his time, being unmarried was unthinkable for a religious Jew such as a preacher or a rabbi. They conclude that the the gospels are silent on this point simply because the oldest traditions presumed that Jesus was married. One might object that the same texts are not silent about his other family ties. If so, then might it be that he had neither wife nor children because he had chosen celibacy for religious reasons? Some authors lean toward this hypothesis. The texts do not support his making such a choice because of any misogynist tendency, however, such as was current among the Essenes. On the contrary, Jesus was surrounded by women friends and admirers. In any case, as Meier says, further speculation on this question risks crossing the boundary between history and historical fiction.[37]

The Judaism of Jesus

*For that which is called the Christian religion today,
existed in Antiquity, and from the beginning of the
human race, until the incarnation of the Christ, and from
him the true religion which had already existed began to
be called Christian.*

SAINT AUGUSTINE, *RETRACTATIONS*, I, XIII, 3

To understand Jesus' message, we must first understand the religion in which he was educated. As we shall see when we discuss his mission (see chapter 6), the available sources clearly demonstrate that Jesus had no intention of founding a new religion, nor a new church. For him, what the Jews customarily called "the Law and the Prophets"—or the teaching of the Torah[1]—was the foundation of his relationship to God.[2] His concern, often found in the Sayings of the gospels, was to bring the "strayed sheep," or the "sheep without a shepherd," back into the way of the Torah.[3]

ESCHATON AND THE NEW
TEMPLE IN JUDAIC THOUGHT

A soteriological tradition that had been developing among the Israelites is critical to understanding Jesus' religion. This has to do with the notion of biblical messianism and the vision of the end of days. Let us recall that the Hebrew word *mashiah* means "anointed by the Lord," hence "consecrated." The Greek translation of this is *christos*. Before the Babylonian exile, ever since the fusion of the Israelite tribes into a unified nation, then during the period inaugurated by David and Solomon and continuing until the end of the sixth century B.C.E., the king was the anointed of the Lord. After the overthrow of Judaea in 587 B.C.E., and for almost four centuries thereafter, until the rise of the Maccabees, there was no king—hence no messiah—for the peoples of Palestine. During this period, there grew an ever more fervent belief in the coming realization of the promise made by Yahweh to David, through the medium of the prophet Samuel, of a royal lineage that "would prevail forever."[4] Faith in this divine promise probably formed the root that grew into the belief in a future messiah, a new King David, who would come to lead the Jewish people.

This eschatological tradition[5] began after the fall of Jerusalem and the destruction of the kingdom of Juda by Nebuchadnezzar in 587. The concept had a profound impact on the faith of Jews in Babylonian exile. It developed into an expectation of the coming of an envoy of the Almighty at the end of the ages: a king who would come to restore, in a concrete and institutional way, the reign of God among a liberated Jewish people.[6] Ezekiel, the prophet of exile and a contemporary of Jeremiah, was no doubt the first to announce the coming of a new David, shepherd of Israel. The prophet experienced a vision of the glory of the God of Israel beneath the porch of the Temple, facing east:

> I heard someone speak to me from the Temple, while the man stood next to me. They said: "Son of Man, this is the place of my throne, the place where I set down my feet. I shall live in the midst

of the Israelites forever; and the house of Israel, they and their kings, will nevermore pollute my Name through their prostitutions and the cadavers of their kings."

This vision of the celestial Temple of Ezekiel serves as the foundation of the apocalyptic tradition. "Its most basic characteristic was that it transformed, or rather transfigured, ancient institutional forms into celestial entities. The mere vision of the latter sufficed, in their own way, to ensure their coming, and also to guarantee its reality. The first of these forms to be transfigured was the Temple."[7] This vision was also associated with the prophet Isaiah's vision of the coming of God, in a chariot of fire, with the sword of judgment: "For behold, YAHWEH will come in fire, and his chariots like the storm wind, to render his anger in fury, and his rebuke with flames of fire. For by fire will YAHWEH execute judgment, and by his sword, upon all flesh; and those slain by YAHWEH shall be many" (Isa. 66:15–16).

The prophet Micah, a contemporary of Isaiah, also sheds interesting light on the eschatological beliefs of this era:

It shall come to pass in the latter days that the mountain of the house of YHWH shall be established as the highest of the mountains, and shall be raised up above the hills; and peoples shall flow to it, and many nations shall come, and say: "Come, let us go up to the mountain of YHWH, to the house of the God of Jacob; that he may teach us his ways and we may walk in his paths." For out of Zion shall go forth the Law, and the word of YHWH from Jerusalem. He shall judge between many peoples, and shall decide for strong nations afar off. (Micah 4:1–3)

But the idea of the restoration of the kingdom of Israel by a messianic messenger developed largely between the Maccabee dynasty and the beginning of the period of the intertestamental literature[8] (so-called because it extends from the middle of the second century B.C.E. to the time of Jesus). The Jewish Pseudepigrapha,[9] as well as the Dead Sea manuscripts and the book of Daniel, all manifest this belief. Jesus and his contemporaries were deeply immersed in such literature, generating an eschatological and apocalyptic atmosphere that was typical of the spirit of the times. Beginning with a strongly political orientation in the exile texts, the messianic concept became more and more transcendental. But, as Meier notes, this messianic concept was probably not entirely clear during the first century C.E. [10] Nevertheless, in Jesus' religious heritage, the importance of faith in the coming messiah deserves careful consideration.

This eschatological hope appears in several places in the Hebrew scriptures, especially in the books of the later prophets and in the intertestamental texts. Although obvious variations in this current appear during Jewish history, we might simplify a bit and sum up the eschatology in the following belief: When God judges the time to be right—a time that will arrive all the sooner if his chosen people truly follow his commandments—he will come, in all his power and glory, to deliver his people definitively from the forces of evil that dominate the world and oppress the righteous. In the minds of the exile prophets, the sufferings and misfortunes from foreign oppression, exile, and slavery were due to the Israelites' disobedience and transgressions against God's law. But over time, as it became clear that this suffering afflicted the righteous as well as the unrighteous, this explanation became less and less credible. Add to this the objection that other nations which existed in a state of defiance and transgression against God were living in prosperity.

The Maccabees revolted against Seleucid oppression, which forbade Jews to follow the laws of the Torah. In so doing, they no longer accepted the teaching of God's continuing punishment of Israel for past sins. In spite of being the chosen people, the Israelites were under the yoke of a foreign oppressor, and one who prevented them from following the Torah. Hence, there had to be some other explanation for the suffering of the Jews. A new belief appeared: For mysterious reasons, God had allowed the forces of Evil to take possession of the world. Of course this state of affairs could not go on forever. In his infinite justice and compassion, God would intervene, probably sooner than anyone expected, to annihilate the forces of evil and establish his people as leaders of the world, reigning over a new age. This divine intervention would happen in an apocalyptic manner involving a great cosmic upheaval.

In intertestamental apocalyptic literature, we find several scenarios of the end of time as revealed by God. The two most prevalent versions can be summarized as follows: (1) a human Messiah is sent to lead the Sons of Light in the final battle against Satan; (2) a cosmic judge of sorts, the Son of Man, arrives to overturn the demonic powers in a cataclysmic intervention. Both these scenarios are followed by a final judgment. The righteous receive eternal happiness; the evil receive eternal damnation. But what about those who have died previously? Are they not subject to the final judgment also? Because God's justice is the same for all, living and dead, the latter are revived, body and soul, to receive their judgment with the others.

What does the literature of Jesus' time have to say about all this? Sanders quotes Tobit, who does not see the full realization of prophecy in the reconstruction of the second Temple, for this realization can occur only at the end of time:

And that again God will have mercy on them, and bring them again into the land, where they shall build a temple, but not like to the first, until the time of that age be fulfilled; and afterward they shall return from all places of their captivity, and build up Jerusalem gloriously, and the house of God shall be built in it for ever with a glorious building, as the prophets have spoken thereof. And all nations shall turn, and fear the Lord God truly, and shall bury their idols. (Tobit 14:5–6)

André and Hadot both quote Enoch 15:8–24, a text that dates from the first half of the second century B.C.E. and offers "the most detailed description of the celestial Temple as a final and systematic transmutation of the Jerusalem Sanctuary. It recalls the first chapter of Ezekiel, with its vision of the celestial chariot . . . it also closely corresponds to the image of the divine 'Ancient of Days,' seated on his throne in the book of Daniel in chapters 7, 9, and 10."[11] But above all, it evokes the passage of 1 Kings, chapter 6, devoted to the "House" of Yahweh.

JEWISH SECTS AND PARTIES IN THE TIME OF JESUS

In his book *Jésus et histoire,* Charles Perrot discusses the remarkable proliferation of Judaic sects and parties. In contrast with the period following the destruction of the Temple, when Judaism began to manifest homogeneity (first in rabbinical Judaism, then in Talmudic), the previous period was characterized by the division of the Jewish people into a number of movements and religious sects. Josephus, who remains the primary source on this, was especially interested in the three major movements of the time: the Pharisees, the Sadducees, and the Essenes. For our purposes, let us consider also the Zealots and Sicarii and the Baptists.

The Sadducees

There is virtually no doubt that this was the most powerful Jewish party in Palestine (subject, of course, to Roman authority) during Jesus' public ministry. Its name derives from the priestly lineage of Zadok,[12] and it attracted the most influential aristocracy and upper social classes of Jerusalem, many of whom belonged to the nucleus of the party. We know the Sadducees only indirectly, since no writings exist that were actually authored by members of this party, unlike the Pharisees (whose members included Josephus himself, as well as Paul of Tarsus). They were, in effect, a party of the elite. They got along well with their Roman overlords, who tossed them a few crumbs of power. They controlled a large majority of the Sanhedrin, a council of prominent Jews who met periodically to deal with local affairs. Apparently the only sacred text they would allow as an authority in these deliberations was the Torah itself, specifically excluding the oral tradition defended by the Pharisees. This same logic led the Sadducees to accord unquestionable sovereignty to the cultural and sacrificial requirements of the Torah, and hence of the Temple. Their rigidity regarding the primacy of this written tradition probably explains their rejection of resurrection beliefs current at the time.

The Pharisees

Paradoxically, the party most often discussed in the New Testament has been the most misunderstood. It is likely that much of this confusion is due to ignorance about the Pharisees on the part of gospel redactors who were writing after the destruction of the Temple. These writings are often hostile, especially in the Gospel of Matthew. They are largely responsible for the pejorative associations that have adhered to the word Pharisee, persisting long after the establishment of the Church. The most common epithet associated with the Pharisees is *hypocrite*. But who were the Pharisees in reality?

Their name *(perushim)* appears to be of Persian origin, meaning "the separate ones." The movement emerged during the Maccabee era. Resistant to Hellenization, the Pharisees were also fervently devoted to the Torah. In order to better adapt to its often vague and contradictory prescriptions, however, they developed a rich oral tradition parallel to the biblical texts that endeavored to interpret those texts in the most minute detail. Among the Pharisees and their leaders, this oral tradition gradually acquired the same level of authority as the Law of Moses, and came to be called the Law as well.

Observance of the Sabbath, purification rites, and dietary rules have a prominent place in this oral law. These were issues of much controversy, as recounted in the gospels. These controversies opposed the scribes and Pharisees to the followers of Jesus, and we shall examine them in detail in this chapter. As to rites of water purity, which certainly were some of the weightiest issues from a sociohistorical point of view, we note that, unlike the Sadducees, who gave little importance to these questions, the Pharisees fought to make the rules applicable to all Jews, not only to the priests who officiated at Temple rituals. This is why the theme of water-related purification rites came to acquire so much importance during the first century C.E. Perrot notes that the growing importance of purification rites in Jewish society actually led to greater social fragmentation, with various groups forming around the degree of purity they were believed to have attained. According to him, we can group them roughly in a descending triad, beginning with the most righteous, pure, or "separated" ones; then the "country people" *(am ha-aretz);* then the lowest, the "sinners." In this last group, one finds professions as diverse as physician, butcher, shepherd, prostitute, customs officer, and others for whom impurity was inherent in their professional activity itself, often because of the contact they might have with peasants, menstruating women, or corpses. Perrot adds that "the Pharisee movement, which had originated in a spirit of generosity (the word of God is for all, and the rites are not just for priests to celebrate), ultimately resulted in the production of insular social groups."

Finally, let us remember that the Pharisees were not the dominant party during the time of Jesus. They did have support among urban dwellers, probably aided by their reputation for uprightness and piety. Not until forty years later was the situation reversed, during the time of the canonical gospel redactions. After the end of the Jewish wars, to use the term of Josephus, the Pharisees were regarded by the Roman victors with more favor than were the other parties. During this period, the oral tradition maintained by the Pharisees took on an importance equal to that of Mosaic Law. But another century would pass before oral law would be written down, to become known as the Mishna, forming the core of the sacred texts of the Talmud.

The Essenes

There is no mention of this sect[13] in the New Testament, yet it also had emerged as an important movement during the time of the Maccabees. The Essenes might be more precisely described as the "fundamentalist" wing of the Sadducees, originally formed as a reaction against the Hasmonean decision to appoint a high priest who did not belong to the priestly lineage of Zadok. The Essene movement grew progressively more radical in its sectarian purism, amplifying its separation from an impure world.[14]

Most of our knowledge of this movement comes from the Dead Sea Scrolls, which are several hundred in number. These were left by a group of Essenes, who were established in Qumran, led by a Sadducee priest from Jerusalem known as the Teacher of Righteousness. In spite of the considerable physical deterioration of these scrolls, they have provided us with an incomparable gold mine of information about this party, and about the religious background of Judeo-Christianity.

The Essenes of Qumran were also breakaway Pharisees who considered their former colleagues in Jerusalem to be deviants. They retired to the west bank of the Dead Sea, where they created an austere, ascetic community that engaged in rigorous observance of Mosaic Law, as well as extremely rigid purification rituals. "They had to take purifying baths several times a day, partly so as to counteract any contact they may have had with a member of a different class of the four which made up the community," Josephus writes. Community rules abounded with such terms as "righteous, perfect, impure, upright, sainthood, humility, iniquity, expiation, sin, etc.," according to Josephus. They did not speak of baptism as such, but they did refer to a ritual purificatory ablution. The latter had to be preceded by a conversion of the heart, which would, as Josephus writes, "permit access to God, and thus to expiation."[15] Social justice, too, was a major preoccupation. Although strict pacifists in principle, they bravely took up arms to defend Jerusalem against the Roman siege.

The Qumran Essenes believed firmly in an imminent, apocalyptic end of days. In expectation of the restoration of the Kingdom of God, the faithful had to maintain their purity by retreating from the impure world to the desert, establishing a sort of monastic community whose entry requirements and lifestyle were subject to rigid rules and discipline, well described by Josephus.[16] In his section on the Essenes, Baron quotes a passage from Pliny the Younger, who speaks of them with the highest praise. He found this sect

... remarkable, more so than all the other tribes of the world: they have no women among them, having renounced all sexual desire;

they possess no money, and have only the palm trees for company. As the days go by, vacancies are filled with an influx of newcomers, and there is no lack of a crowd of adherents, weary of life, whom the waves of fate lead to this place, where they desire to live in the ways of the Essenes.

The Zealots and the Sicarii

We have little information about the so-called Zealot party. The only available sources were written by those who were opposed to it, including Josephus himself. In his *History of the War of the Jews and Romans,* Josephus aimed to convince Romans that the troubles created for them by the Jews were caused by the activities of bands of brigands and other adventurers who led the revolt against Rome. Jesus-Barabbas was one of the best known of these brigands, especially considering his role during the trial of Jesus of Nazareth.

The most formidable of these extremists were the so-called Sicarii (*sica* means "dagger" in Latin), whose name does not appear in historical sources until the mid–first century. These partisans carried daggers under their cloaks and did not hesitate to carry out killings in public places, including attacks on Jewish collaborators and even Roman citizens. However, as Perrot astutely notes, the presence of such armed bands should not lead us to conclude that an organized nationalist movement existed in first-century-C.E. Palestine.

In addition to these political extremists, there were the reformist priests known as the Zealots, whose existence Josephus only mentions in his *History of the War of the Jews and Romans*. He categorizes them among the groups of the "fourth philosophy."[17] In many cases, the Zealots were recruited from the margins of society: These were desperate men who, under the influence of leaders such as Judas of Galilee, had taken up arms to defend an oppressed people against the Roman occupier, the source of all ills. The Zealot faction probably waged a kind of guerrilla campaign against the Romans over several decades. These rebels saw deliverance from Roman occupation only in an armed struggle in the name of God, which would bring ultimate victory and eternal prosperity. Many authors have surmised that there was at least one Zealot among those close to Jesus, in particular a certain Simon—but we have little information about him, and it appears, in any case, that he was not a hard-liner.[18]

The Baptists

As with most Jewish movements of the era, information about the Baptists comes to us primarily from Josephus. He associated with them and lived among them for a time. Other authors, such as Justin Martyr,[19] Hegesippius,[20] and Epiphanes,[21] also speak of Jewish Baptists and their rites of purification by immersion, the same rites practiced by sects in Jordan and Samaria. These Baptist groups were known as the Masbotheans, the Sabeans, and the Nazarites (Nasarioi).[22]

The Qumran Essenes were so insular that they refused to consider making sacrifices in the Temple until the Messiah had come to purify it at the end of time. They rejected the legitimacy of the priestly class. Aware of people's frustrations over the complexity of Temple rites, the Baptists offered a simple rite in their place, a baptism that would confer redemption. Hence, they were notably responsive to the quandaries of ordinary Jewish people—the classes of "country people" and "sinners"—who felt more and more excluded by Essene and Pharisee elites, with their excessive prescriptions that had to be followed to the letter. The message of Baptist welcome toward the modest classes explains the popularity of the movement.

Perrot writes that although water-based rites (whether of passage, of purification, or of initiation) existed almost everywhere around the Mediterranean during Jesus' time, the Baptist immersion as practiced by John and Jesus, and by their disciples, was distinguished by its power to absolve sin. Another advantage, it served as a substitute for rites of pardon dispensed by the Temple, which required elaborate acts of sacrifice and penitence. With the power of this baptism, one could bypass the Temple, for it could be performed anywhere, by anyone. This concept is implicit in Stephen's testimony[23] before the Sanhedrin:

He [David] found favor in the sight of God and asked permission to find a habitation for the God of Jacob. But it was Solomon who built a house for him. Yet the Most High does not dwell in houses made with hands. As the prophet says, "Heaven is my throne, and earth my footstool. What house will you build for me, says the Lord, or what is the place of my rest? Did not my hand make all these things?" (Acts 7:46–50)

THE RELIGION OF JESUS

Jesus Was a Practicing Jew

There is no doubt that Jesus was Jewish, circumcised in his body and in his heart. That he was a devout, practicing Jew is amply demonstrated in many New Testament passages.[24] For him, as for many Jews, prayer was something that should permeate one's day, from sunrise to sunset. Jesus also prayed at the synagogue, which served as a place for reading the Torah and celebrating rituals, probably going there every day of the week. The Sabbath was an especially important day to pray there—*shabbat* in Hebrew means the day of rest, when no work must be done, in memory of the seventh day, when Elohim rested, satisfied with his creation. Jesus also went alone to secluded places in the mountains for prayer and meditation. How did he pray? We know something of this from his own advice to his disciples, as in the following two passages, perhaps the most moving verses in the synoptic gospels:

And when you pray, you must not be like the hypocrites; for they love to stand and pray in the synagogues and at the street corners, that they may be seen by others. Truly, I say to you, they have received their reward. But when you pray, go into your room and shut the door and pray to your Father who is there in secret; and your Father who sees in secret will reward you. And in praying do not heap up empty phrases as the pagans do; for they think that they will be heard for their many words. Do not be like them, for your Father knows what you need before you ask him. Pray then like this:

Our Father who is in heaven, holy be your name.

May your kingdom manifest. May your will be done,
    on earth as it is in heaven.

Give us this day our bread for today;

And forgive us our offenses, as we forgive our
    offenders.

Help us not to lose ourselves in temptation,

And deliver us from evil,

For thine is the Kingdom, the power, and the glory
    of the ages. Amen. (Matt. 6:5–13)

He said to them: "When you pray, say: 'Father, holy be your name. May your kingdom manifest. Give us each day our daily bread; and forgive us our offenses, for we ourselves forgive all those who are in debt to us; and help us not to lose ourselves in temptation'" (Luke 11:2–4).

As we said earlier, Jesus was a true son of Israel[25] from a devout Jewish family. A number of authors have pointed out a common Christian tendency to downplay this fact, recalling it only when it serves their purposes. For Jesus, as for all Jews, the story of salvation was linked to the story of the people of Israel. This is the story that was told and commented upon when he visited the synagogue, where readings of the Torah and other scriptures were held every day.

To offer even a condensed summary of the story of salvation as recounted in the Torah would be beyond the scope of this book. And yet we might note in passing that in the Mediterranean world of Jesus' time, Judaism was the only "monotheistic" religion—"monotheistic" in the sense that it rejected all other gods, acknowledging only Yahweh, who had revealed himself to the Jewish people as the sole and unique God. Yahweh had made a pact, a Covenant, with this chosen people, who had promised to obey him, and he to guide and protect them.

The Torah also contains the Law of Moses, which regulates all human action. The Torah goes well beyond the domain of religion, covering what we now call civil law, commercial law, and criminal law. Leviticus, the third book of the Pentateuch, which lists rules for priests officiating at sacrificial rites, also contains more than a third of the judicial rules and commandments of the Torah. An important point to remember is that under Mosaic Law, a transgressor of these rules must repent and offer sacrifices.[26] Anyone who harms another person physically must make amends, either in kind or in the form of payment.[27] God always forgives an offender who repents, but he punishes the unrepentant—for example, by inflicting illness upon them. The Mosaic Law contains strict prescriptions about Sabbath observations.[28] In certain cases, violation of the Sabbath could lead to trial and condemnation to death by stoning.

Other than discussions related to doctrines of the "scribes and Pharisees" concerning aspects of Mosaic Law, the gospels offer us little information about the prevailing religious views of Jesus' contemporaries. Nevertheless, Stephen's testimony before the Sanhedrin[29] gives us some idea of how Jews of the time viewed their sacred history, especially Jews who belonged to Hellenized sects of the first century. Stephen's frank account is of admirable simplicity and provides a digest of sorts, a candid summary of the history of salvation of the people of Israel up to Solomon's building of the Temple.

The Intimacy of Jesus' Relation to God

If there is one point of unanimity in all sources about Jesus, it is the intense and intimate (if one may describe it thus) nature of the relationship Jesus maintained with the one he called "God the Father." This is made abundantly clear in the canonical gospels. The phrase "God the Father" occurs sixty-two times in the synoptics (five in Mark, forty in Matthew, and seventeen in Luke). At times, Jesus invokes his Father as "he who is in the heavens," other times as "our heavenly Father." We shall cite some of the most characteristic Sayings on this, beginning with one whose meaning and implications seem fundamental to any conception of the message of Jesus:

"Very well! I say to you: Love your enemies and pray for those who persecute you, so that you may be children of your Father who is in heaven; for he makes the sun rise on the evil and on the good, and sends rain on the just and on the unjust" (Matt. 5:44–45).

Though he speaks often of his Father, note that he also speaks of "your Father," the same as his own, as in this passage: "But when you give alms, let not your left hand know what your right hand is doing, so that your alms may be in secret; and your Father, who sees in secret, will reward you" (Matt. 6:3–4).

Jesus claimed to have a direct relationship with God—in other words, with no intermediary of any kind.[30] He maintained this relationship through prayer above all, most often far from the noise of public places, in areas of retreat and meditation. In the following passage from Matthew, Jesus describes how to pray to God, the Father: "And when you pray, go into your room and shut the door and pray to your Father who is there, in secret; and your Father who sees in secret will reward you" (Matt. 6:6).

Jesus' total faith in divine providence is illustrated in this superb analogy: "Look at the birds in the sky: they do not sow, nor do they reap, nor store their grain, and our heavenly Father feeds them. Are you not more worthy than they?" (Matt. 6:26)

Here is another illustration: "Be without fear, little flock, for it pleases your Father to offer you the Kingdom" (Luke 12:53).

Sometimes he speaks to God in the most intimate language, such as his use of the Aramaic word Abba[31] for Father in Mark 14:36.

Jesus Followed the Mosaic Law

Some scholars, especially authors of Jewish origin, have pointed out a number of inconsistencies in Jesus' relation to Mosaic Law as described in gospel and other accounts, raising questions about the meaning of certain Sayings that refer to the Law. This evokes the famous opposition best described as "the spirit rather than the letter." This supposed opposition was the cause of the first schisms between Judeo-Christians and other Jews, divisions that developed during the last half of the first century.

Let us begin with this famous aphorism quoted by Luke: "What you would have others do for you, do it also for them" (6:31).[32] Jesus

was not the first to express this sentiment. In the early second century
B.C.E., Rabbi Yehoshua ben Sira said: "Be as kind to your neighbor as
you are to yourself, and beware of [doing to him] the things you
detest."[33]

Matthew 7:12 adds a crucial phrase to this Saying: "For this is the
Law, and the Prophets!" Like ben Sira, Jesus substitutes a positive affirmation for an ancient precept expressed in the negative in scriptures.

For many authors, this is clear evidence that Jesus had no intention
of abolishing the Law; on the contrary, he intended to reinforce it. They
see no break with Judaic tradition in Jesus' teaching. In their observation, Jesus' preaching is characterized not by rejection of Mosaic Law,
but by an emphasis on precepts that are already in it but lack a sufficiently affirmative expression in Jewish tradition.

It is difficult to see how anyone could construe Jesus' teaching as
opposed to that given by God to Moses, so grandly summarized in
Leviticus:

And YHWH said to Moses, "Say to all the community of the people of Israel: You shall be holy; for I YHWH your God am holy.
Every one of you shall revere his mother and his father, and you
shall keep my sabbaths: I am YHWH your God. Do not turn to
idols or make for yourselves molten gods: I am YHWH your God.
When you offer a sacrifice of peace offerings to YHWH, you shall
offer it so that you may be accepted. . . .

"When you reap the harvest of your land, you shall not reap
your field to its very border, neither shall you gather the leftovers
after your harvest. And you shall not strip your vineyard bare, neither shall you gather the fallen grapes of your vineyard; you shall
leave them for the poor and for the sojourner: I am YHWH your
God. You shall not steal, nor deal falsely, nor lie to one another.
And you shall not swear by my name falsely, and so profane the
name of your God: I am YHWH. You shall not oppress your
neighbor or rob him. The wages of a hired servant shall not be
withheld by you all night until the morning. You shall not curse the

deaf or put a stumbling block before the blind, but you shall fear your God: I am YHWH.

"You shall do no injustice in judgment; you shall not be partial to the poor or defer to the great, but in righteousness shall you judge your neighbor. You shall not behave as a slanderer among your people, and you shall not threaten to shed the blood of your neighbor: I am YHWH. You shall not hate your brother in your heart, but you shall rather admonish your neighbor, lest you bear sin because of him. You shall not take vengeance or bear any grudge against the sons of your own people, but you shall love your neighbor as yourself: I am YHWH." (Lev. 1–5, 9–18)

Hence, the notion that Jesus intended to overturn the Mosaic Law, with its high ethics of life, would appear to be nonsense. For these authors, the historical Jesus, as well as the Jesus of the canonical gospels, never ceased to uphold this teaching, even though he strove to "raise it to a higher level," as Edelmann put it. On the other hand, many authors emphasize that Jesus wanted to unite two commandments, to love God and to love one's neighbor, into one—the latter being a consequence of the former. This unity formed the basis of the new evangelical ethic. The famous Sermon on the Mount contains an unmistakable confirmation of this interpretation: "Do not believe that I have come to abolish the Law, or the Prophets: I come not to abolish, but to fulfill!" (Matt. 5:17)

This is followed by a series of exhortations that his hearers go beyond what has been said, ultimately invoking the perfection of the heavenly Father: "Be perfect, as your heavenly Father is perfect" (Matt. 5:48).

Luke transforms this as: "Be compassionate, as your heavenly Father shows compassion" (Luke 6:36).

In contrast, those who incline toward "the spirit, rather than the letter" have also amassed arguments for Jesus' opposition to tradition. In the Sayings, we find many exhortations that take forms such as: "You have heard what your ancestors said . . . but truly, I say to you . . ." Does this imply a refutation of the Law? Actually, most contemporary historians agree that this rhetorical form was part of Jesus' provocative style, intended to guide the listener's attention to the essential and away from secondary aspects. His way of speaking called for overcoming oneself and movement toward the other: "If you love those who love you, what credit is that to you? For even sinners love those who love them" (Luke 6:32).

According to Vermès, there is no substance to the hypothesis that Jesus was simply unaware of how opposed his teachings were to the Law. He could not have been unmindful of what his contemporaries professed. Vermès writes: "The principle on which the Law was founded was perfectly clear: God had given the Torah to Israel via Moses; obedience to the Torah was the condition for keeping faith in the Covenant; and any intentional and unrepentant disobedience implied a rejection of the Law, a rejection of the Covenant, and a rejection of God, who had given the Law and made the Covenant."

Any remaining doubt about the attitude of Jesus toward the Mosaic Law should be dispelled by this oft quoted Saying: "But it is easier for heaven and earth to pass away, than for one speck of the law to fall away" (Luke 16:17). And Matthew elaborates: "For truly, I say to you, till heaven and earth pass away, not an iota, nor a mark over an iota, will pass from the law until all is accomplished" (Matt. 5:18).[34] These repeated affirmations of the permanence and integrity of the Torah are difficult to reconcile with early Church teachings inspired by Paul, who preached a new covenant that rendered the old one obsolete.

As Vermès says, the foundation of Jesus' teaching is neither observance of the Torah nor self-righteousness in the performance of prayer and worship in the Temple or the synagogue.[35] Nor does it consist in a search for God as a goal in itself. Instead, its essence lies in a total devotion to love of others, according to the ideal of the compassion of the heavenly Father.[36]

Jesus in Relation to Certain Aspects of the Law

Although a strong consensus asserts that Jesus never rejected the Law as a whole, many scholars point out that he was opposed to certain regulations, especially ritual prescriptions. At the very least, he urged his followers to go beyond certain rules. Others go so far as to claim that a well-established Jewish tradition considers the Law one whole, none of whose details can be questioned.

Before going into further detail, let us recall the issues facing the early churches, where Jews and pagans often worshipped together. For them, aspects of the Law such as circumcision, the Sabbath, and ritual and dietary purity posed serious problems. We should therefore not be surprised that the synoptic gospels contain passages where we find Jesus debating with Pharisees about controversies that pertained to later times, yet had no special importance during his own life.

Moreover, some scholars have pointed out that the setting for Jesus' debates on such issues is often implausible. As we noted earlier, many of them take place in Galilee, where the presence of scribes and Pharisees was a rarity. Even if we agreed that these debates did take place, these passages still do not show that Jesus himself broke the Law. For example, his disciples are the accused in the incident about washing of hands.[37] For Mark, the dietary issue follows the washing of hands, with no apparent link between them except as illustrations of transgression.[38] Sanders questions the authenticity of this passage along with most others that depict Jesus advocating transgression of the Law. According to Sanders, Jesus did not believe the Law could be freely transgressed. The fact that his disciples continued to demonstrate respect for the rules of the Torah well after the Master's death indicates that his words and actions could not have encouraged them to reject or transgress the Mosaic Law.

The Sabbath

There is nothing said about Jesus in the synoptics or other sources to indicate that he did not observe the traditional rules of the Sabbath. On the other hand, nothing better illustrates his attitude toward the Sabbath, and toward the whole of the Law, than this famous Saying: "The Sabbath was made for man, and not man for the Sabbath; thus the Son of Man is master even of the Sabbath" (Mark 2:27–28). In other words, the Law was given to serve humanity and not the reverse. There is a shorter version of this in Luke: "The Son of Man is master of the Sabbath" (Luke 6:5). We shall discuss the meaning of the term Son of Man at length in a later chapter. We note in passing that in this context, many exegeses read the expression as equivalent to *human being.*

Divorce

Judaic tradition had no divine decree prohibiting divorce. Jesus appears to have been against it, however, even though Mosaic Law specifically allowed for it. And yet this cannot be considered a transgression: Not allowing what is permitted is very different from allowing what is not permitted. Jesus has gone beyond the requirements of the Law in the matter of divorce.[39]

> And Pharisees came up and in order to test him asked, "Is it lawful for a man to divorce his wife?" He answered them, "What did Moses command you?" They said, "Moses allowed a man to write a certificate of divorce, and be rid of her." But Jesus said to them, "For your hardness of heart he wrote you this commandment. But from the beginning of creation, 'God made them male and female.' For this reason a man shall leave his father and mother and be joined to his wife, and the two shall become one flesh. So they are no longer two but one flesh. What therefore God has united, let not man separate." (Mark 10:2–9)

Here we find Jesus quoting scripture to support his position. The relevant verses from Genesis are: "God created man in his own image, in the image of God he created him; male and female he created them" (Gen. 1:27).[40] "Therefore a man leaves his father and his mother and cleaves to his wife, and they become one flesh." (Gen. 2:24)

Conversely, such use of scripture is precisely what has led to doubts about the authenticity of the passage as well. Jesus, who knew Hebrew and Aramaic, could not have been ignorant of the fact that the texts he quoted have nothing to do with marriage or divorce.

As a kind of concluding commentary on this question, let us again turn to Vermès: ". . . Jesus' overriding preoccupation was a constant didactic effort to return to the essential heart of the Torah's teaching, to make it easier for simple people to read. This required making a clear distinction between the fundamental precepts in Deuteronomy—such as love of God, and of one's neighbor—and the other precepts in Leviticus that regulate daily life, so that the essential teaching did not become buried among the secondary prescriptions." According to Vermès, the difference between Jesus and those scholarly rabbis whose commentaries on the Torah seem more concerned with technical details than with ethics or God was Jesus' priority on clarifying the ultimate purpose of the Law. For him, this purpose was fulfilled by human beings who, rather than following legal rules, were living in a way that demanded more of themselves, so as to respond to God's own compassion.[41] As we have noted, in that era, the Jewish faith was in danger of being distorted by those who would use the Law for their own profit, in a way that excluded "unimportant" people. For Jesus, any rule of life that does not flow from compassion, from an existential conviction of the primacy of God's love, kills the letter of the Law. Salvation does not lie in outer works, but rather in the gift of love from God to humanity, a gift that each human being must reproduce. Without this primary faith in divine love, obedience to the Law and its commandments is a hollow gesture.

Ritual Prescriptions

We have noted the extreme complexity of ritual prescriptions, especially those dealing with purification. Circumstances had reached a point where only the elite classes had the means to practice the legitimate— or what they believed was the legitimate—manner of following these rules. This situation fostered social fragmentation, setting the pure against the impure. Jesus was appalled by this state of affairs, and the radical nature of his response to it is clearly demonstrated in this Saying: "Nothing which goes into a man can pollute him. But what comes out of a man can pollute him" (Mark 7:15).[42]

This aphorism is often misunderstood. Fundamentalists, especially, interpret it as a simple rejection of all dietary and purification rules, which were to be followed to the letter. Yet the tone here is the same as that in other Sayings attributed to this man who so often went beyond commonly accepted ideas. In a passage shortly after the one above, when the disciples seemed troubled by those words, Mark has Jesus add: "And he said to them, 'Do you still not understand that whatever goes into a man from outside cannot defile him, since it does not enter his heart, but his stomach, and is then evacuated?'" [Thus he declared all foods clean] (Mark 7:18–19).

This could hardly be more explicit. The authenticity of the bracketed passage is widely contested as an obvious later redaction, however.[43] If Jesus had actually declared such a thing, how could we explain the conflicts that arose after his death among his followers, many of whom insisted on practicing these very rules of diet?

In any case, Jesus was flexible about traditional rules of purity, since he taught that rules were made to serve human beings, and that observing them strictly had no value in itself:

> The Pharisees and the scribes who had come from Jerusalem gathered around him, and saw that some of his disciples ate with hands defiled, that is, unwashed . . . and they asked him, "Why do your disciples not live according to the tradition of the elders, but eat with hands defiled?" And he said to them, "Well did Isaiah prophesy of you, hypocrites! For it is written: 'This people honor me with their lips, but their heart is far from me; in vain do they worship me, teaching as doctrines the precepts of men.' You put aside the commandment of God, and hold fast to the tradition of men." (Mark 7:1–8)

Jesus and the Temple

In the synoptics, we find numerous accounts of Jesus' presence in the Temple.[44] Although the authenticity of some of these passages is doubtful, Jesus would certainly have made visits to the Temple of Jerusalem, either to pray or to teach.

An occasion that attracts the greatest interest is the scandal he is reported to have caused there. Many specialists consider this incident one of the grounds, and perhaps the only one, that led the Jerusalem authorities to order Jesus' arrest. However it may have been, the symbolism of the incident is at the least integral to an effort to understand Jesus' religious convictions. The interpretation of its meaning has been the source of divergences among his disciples, among early Christians, and among scholars. Let us consider four synoptic passages that deal with this event:

And they came to Jerusalem. And he entered the temple and began to drive out those who bought and sold in the temple, and he overturned the tables of the moneychangers and the stands of those who sold pigeons; and he would not allow anyone to carry anything through the temple. And he began to teach, and said to them: "Is it not written, 'My house shall be called a house of prayer for all the nations'? But you have made it a den of robbers!" And the chief priests and the scribes heard this, and sought a way to destroy him; for they feared him, because all the multitude was impressed by his teaching. (Mark 11:15–19)

And as he came out of the temple, one of his disciples said to him, "Look, Master, what wonderful stones and what wonderful buildings!" And Jesus said to him, "Do you see these great buildings? There will not be left one stone upon another, that will not be thrown down." (Mark 13:1–2)[45]

. . . Finally, two [false witnesses] came forward and said, "This man said, 'I am able to destroy the temple of God, and rebuild it in three days.'" (Matt. 26:60–61)[46]

And those who passed by derided him, wagging their heads, and saying, "Aha! You who would destroy the temple and build it in three days!" (Mark 15:29)

The first quotation from Mark is a detailed description of the Temple incident. Parallel passages in Matthew (21:12–13) and in Luke (9:45–46), derived from the same source, recount the story in fewer words. In contrast with the synoptics, the story in the Gospel of John (provided in the notes for this chapter)[47] takes place not at the end of Jesus' mission, but at the beginning, during his first Passover trip to Jerusalem. In the source used by the synoptics, Jesus uses the term "den of robbers" in opposition to "house of prayer." Yet the Johannine text uses the term "house of merchandise." Though opinions are divided as to the authenticity of the Sayings, many scholars believe that given the multiplicity of testimonies, Jesus almost certainly did something unusual in the Temple, and he said something about its destruction.

Some exegetes have raised doubts about the language that Jesus used in the Temple. They point out that expressions attributed to him are similar to the language used in verses of Isaiah concerning the "house of prayer," as well as verses in Jeremiah. In the presence of the king, Jeremiah accused religious officials of transforming the Temple into a "den of robbers," words that also led to the arrest of the prophet.

> I will bring them to my holy mountain, and make them overjoyed in my house of prayer: their burnt offerings and their sacrifices shall be accepted upon my altar; for my house shall be called a house of prayer for all peoples. (Isa. 56:7)

> Has this house, which bears my name, become a den of robbers in your eyes? Behold, I at least see it clearly, says the oracle of Yahweh. (Jer. 7:11)

As we have noted before, this school of thought holds that it was not Jesus' habit to quote scriptures. Other schools feel that he did on some occasions—for example, when he was dying on the cross, he quoted the beginning of Psalm 22.

Sanders says that the scandal Jesus created at the Temple was a symbol of its destruction and the rebuilding at the end of time. He states, "Jesus had a radical eschatological vision, and hoped that God would act decisively, so as to bring about a fundamental change." Sanders also observes that in our own time, far distant from that of the fall of the Temple and the end of the rites of sacrifice there, the concept of sacrificial rites has disappeared from religious discourse. This is why we find it difficult to understand how powerfully Jesus' warnings must have affected his listeners, given the eschatological climate of the time. Even if we set aside the part of his speech about rebuilding the Temple, "it is likely." writes Sanders, "that a threat of destruction would have been felt by many of his contemporaries as meaning that the end times were coming, and redemption was near."[48]

In any case, scholars remind us that for the Jews, the Temple was the only place where sacrifices were performed, essential practice in the Judaism of that time. In chasing away the moneychangers and pigeon sellers, Jesus was also attacking the practical apparatus necessary to the functioning of sacrificial rites. Indeed, many who came to the Temple, often from other countries, needed to purchase ritually acceptable animals for sacrifice and would also have needed to change their money. In this light, the merchants performed a necessary service for those who wanted to buy a sacrificial sheep or pigeon, according to their means.

Jesus' intervention must therefore have been a deliberate attack by one who knew the system well, since it could not function without the moneychangers and merchants. The action could well have been interpreted as an indirect attack on the Temple itself, one of the main pillars of the Jewish religion. The Jerusalem authorities would naturally see the attacker as a threat to public order, perhaps even a challenge to the existence of the Temple. Sanders points out that even though Jesus' action, supported by his disciples, was hardly sufficient to bring down the system, at the least it had great symbolic power: It suggested the destruction of the Temple and not merely its purification, as some have supposed. Sanders argues that if Jesus had wanted to communicate a message of purification, he would not have resorted to the violence of overturning tables and driving out the merchants. Instead, he would have poured out water, or performed some similar action more in keeping with the notion of purification.

We may well ask why Jesus assailed the Temple in this way, predicting its destruction—was the Temple not the unique place for ritual sacrifice, in keeping with the divine commandments?[49] Citing those gospel verses that deal with predictions or threats of the Temple's destruction, and that speak also of its reconstruction (in three days),[50] Sanders concludes that "destruction" implies "reconstruction." Many exegetes would object that the verses that speak of accusations against Jesus during his trial, like most of the Passion story, are from texts written essentially at the time of the foundation of the early Church, based on Hebrew scripture. Their authenticity would therefore be difficult to establish. Also, the Gospel of Luke does not relate the accusations, and Mark and Matthew consider them unfounded. In the Acts, Luke says that those who dragged Stephen before the Sanhedrin also employed false witnesses.

John, on the other hand, leaves no doubt as to the words of Jesus on this subject; he links the Temple scandal with his prophecy of destruction and restoration. John sees this as an allegory of the resurrection of Christ, whose meaning the disciples began to understand only after his death.

> The Jews then said, "It has taken forty-six years to build this temple, and will you raise it up in three days?" But it was of the temple of his body that he spoke. When therefore he was raised from the dead, his disciples remembered that he had said this; and they believed the scripture and the word which Jesus had spoken. (John 2:20–22)

All of these extracts from John and the synoptics reflect a well-established tradition of provocation that would serve as a basis for accusations against Jesus, and later against the first Christian martyr, Stephen.

5
Was Jesus a Disciple
of John the Baptist?

Like so many other religious people of his time, did not Jesus also have a teacher, one who opened the way for him? Might this teacher have been John the Baptist? In this chapter, we review the conclusions of a number of scholars who have tried to answer these questions. Let us begin with the question of who John the Baptist was. Why "the Baptist"? What was his teaching? How did he and Jesus meet?

The various responses offered to these questions by scholars remain incomplete, for the sources available to us offer little information and are often biased. As P. Johnson says in this work on the history of Christianity: "Our ignorance about the personality of the Baptist obscures our appreciation of the uniqueness of that of Jesus. The problem is that we do not know much about what John taught, very little about his life, and nothing about his education. We do not even know if he taught his own version of theology or cosmology, nor if his eschatology was limited to the simple Messianic message given in the gospels; nor do we know whether on the contrary (which seems more plausible), his teachings were quite elaborate and sophisticated."[1]

WHO WAS JOHN THE BAPTIST?

What the Gospels Say

> And this is the testimony of John,[2] when the Jews sent priests and
> Levites from Jerusalem to ask him, "Who are you?" He confessed,
> he did not deny, but confessed, "I am not the Christ." And they
> asked him, "Then are you Elijah?" He said, "I am not." "Are you
> the Prophet?" And he answered, "No." They said to him then,
> "Who are you? Let us have an answer for those who sent us. What
> do you say about yourself?" He said, "I am the voice of one cry-
> ing in the wilderness, 'Make straight the way of the Lord,' as the
> prophet Isaiah said." Now these people had been sent from the
> Pharisees. They asked him, "Then why are you baptizing, if you
> are neither the Christ, nor Elijah, nor the Prophet?" John answered
> them, "I baptize with water; but among you stands one whom you
> do not know: it is he who comes after me, and the thong of whose
> sandal I am not worthy to untie." This took place in Bethany
> beyond the Jordan, where John was baptizing. (John 19–28)

For once, we begin with the fourth gospel, as John furnishes the only
detailed answer to the first question. In fact, from the beginning of his
gospel, he speaks of the investigation by the priests, at the behest of the
Jerusalem authorities,[3] concerning this desert hermit who was attracting such crowds and who offered them baptism in the waters of the
Jordan in return for their repentance. The questions they ask seem
naive, though they are perhaps part of a ruse. They ask him if he is the
Christ, or Elijah returned to earth, or the Prophet—a term for the
Messiah awaited by the Jews, like a new Moses. He answers that he is
none of these. We will recall that according to the book of Kings, Elijah,
prophet of Yahweh, never died. He was taken up to heaven from the
banks of the Jordan on a chariot of fire, as had been prophesied by the
angel of Yahweh.[4] The author of the book of Malachi,[5] written around
450 B.C.E., had announced the return of Elijah at the end of days and
the last judgment.[6] So if John is none of these, who is he? John the

Evangelist has the Baptist quote (still without giving his own name) the prophet Isaiah: "I am a voice crying in the wilderness. Make straight the ways of the Lord."[7] Thus all four canonical gospels see John the Baptist as the precursor of Jesus, the Messiah.

But was he Jesus' precursor or his teacher? The most striking point is that three of the four canonical gospels (Mark, Luke, and John) begin their story with John the Baptist.[8] Many scholars see this as clear proof of the importance the gospel writers accorded to John as they set out to write down, each in his own way, the story of the life and teaching of Jesus. This indicates that they all wanted to portray John as a predecessor to Jesus, though each gospel writer has a different interpretation of that relationship.

Mark already speaks of John, and the baptism of Jesus, in the opening verses of his book.[9] He devotes no fewer than twelve verses, as well (6:14–26), to explain why Herod had John beheaded. Matthew devotes his entire third chapter to the Baptist. Before reading a description of John's baptism of Jesus, we find a surprising description of the life of the desert hermit, dressed in camel hide, a leather cinch around his waist, and feeding himself on locusts and wild honey. John the Evangelist's accounts are rarely of equal historical interest to the synoptics because of his teleological preoccupation,[10] centered on the incarnated Logos of God. Yet even he speaks of the Baptist in the early part of the prologue: "There was a man sent from God, whose name was John. He came to witness, to bear witness to the Light, so that all might believe in him." Here we see the Christocentric view of this man called the Baptist (along with the status of Jesus as Messiah and Incarnate Word) already well established in these opening verses by all the gospel writers. But whereas the synoptics have Jesus explicitly (Matt. 11:14, 17:12–13) or implicitly (Matt. 3:13) recognizing John the Baptist, the fourth gospel does not even mention a meeting between them, as if nothing of the sort had ever occurred. As we have seen, John ignores the personality of John the Baptist, as if it were of no importance to the story. Yet this is not the case.

Luke is the most forthcoming about the Baptist's personality.[11] His account is also a strange one. We first learn (to our surprise, given the silence of the other gospel writers on this subject) that Jesus and the Baptist were cousins through their maternal lines. Yet, as Meier points out, Luke never has Jesus and John meet each other.[12] This could be explained by Luke's erroneous chronology, which has John imprisoned before Jesus' baptism. In any case, Luke does not mention who baptized Jesus. Also, the tone of his account of the Baptist's birth is a curious echo of other birth stories in the Bible, where angels are sent by God to announce to sterile women (often in menopause)—or to their hus-bands—that they are to give birth to a child of exalted destiny. Examples are Sarah, wife of Abraham; Rebecca, wife of Isaac; and Rachel, second wife of Jacob. Gabriel himself, the highest of the Almighty's angelic hierarchy, announces John's birth to Zechariah: "But the angel said to him, 'Do not be afraid, Zechariah, for your prayer is heard, and your wife Elizabeth will bear you a son, and you shall name him John'" (Luke 1:13). Compare this with the annunciation to Mary:

> In the sixth month the angel Gabriel was sent from God to a town
> of Galilee named Nazareth, to a virgin betrothed to a man whose
> name was Joseph, of the house of David; and the virgin's name was
> Mary. And he came to her and said, "Hail, O favored one, the
> Lord is with you. . . . For behold, you will conceive in your womb
> and bear a son, and you shall name him Jesus."[13]

Such apparitions are part of the synoptic mythos, inserted to imbue the annunciation with a supernatural dimension, referring back to the prophets of old. In the first case, an old woman long past menopause regains her fertility; in the second, a young virgin is fertilized by the action of the Holy Spirit. In the apparition to Zechariah, who was a Temple priest married to an elderly woman, Gabriel tells him that his son John will be a source of joy and cheer for many:

> For he will be great before the Lord, and he shall drink no wine
> nor strong drink, and he will be filled with the Holy Spirit, even

from his mother's womb. And he will turn many of the sons of Israel to the Lord their God, and he will go before him in the spirit and power of Elijah, to turn the hearts of the fathers to the children, and the disobedient to the wisdom of the just, to make ready for the Lord a people prepared.[14] (Luke 1:15–17)

John the Baptist According to Josephus

Other than the gospels, we have another valuable source of information about the person known as the Baptist. In Josephus's *Antiquities*,[15] we find a substantial digression about this man:

A certain number of Jews felt that the defeat of Herod's army[16] was the will of God in his infinite justice, as punishment for what he had done against John, called the Baptist. Indeed, Herod had him executed, this good man who admonished the Jews to practice virtue, both through righteousness toward others and piety toward God, so that they could be baptized; for this immersion would have no value for God unless it was undertaken, not so as to obtain remission of certain sins [only], but for the purification of the body. This required that the person had previously purified his soul through the practice of righteousness. Because [many] other crowds came to John because his words moved them, Herod, fearing that John's great influence with the people would lead him to use it for fomenting rebellion (for the people seemed ready to do whatever he advised), had judged it best to put him to death, so as to prevent any trouble he might cause, and not make the error of sparing a man who could make him regret his inaction when it was too late. This is why Herod, with his mistrustful nature, had John imprisoned in the fortress of Macheras mentioned earlier, where he was then executed. This is why the Jews felt that the destruction of his army was a punishment inflicted upon Herod, and a sign of divine discontent with him.[17]

It is interesting to note that Josephus, an orthodox Pharisee, manages to convey his high admiration for the Baptist in this short description. This might be explained by Josephus's story, in his autobiographical work, of his own retreat to the desert in the company of an ascetic named Bannus. The latter's way of life was similar to that of John, including his way of dressing and eating, and his practice of purification in the waters of a river, which likely was the Jordan.

What emerges clearly from this passage is that John had tremendous popularity, provoking Herod Antipas to extreme measures.[18] John's arrest and death were not so much due to the content of his teachings (they could have been offensive only to certain groups, including some Sadducees) as to his influence on the mass of the people of Israel. Antipas judged this excessive, and a potential danger to his own relationship with the occupier.

If we read this passage carefully, we cannot avoid noticing a striking similarity to the circumstances of the arrest and condemnation of Jesus. That, too, was a dangerous and potentially subversive situation: A man who was revered by the lower classes could spell trouble for the local authorities in their relationship with Rome. As with John, it was not so much the content of his message that was dangerous, but rather his influence itself. In his preaching, which had a markedly eschatological tone, the Baptist accompanied his exhortations to virtue with an apocalyptic prophecy of an imminent, direct, and stormy intervention by God to save Israel, as ordained by the holy scriptures.

WHAT DID THIS PROPHET REALLY PREACH?

Mark and Matthew write that the Baptist proclaimed "a baptism of repentance, for the remission of sins," for "the Kingdom of Heaven is at hand."[19] The Greek text reads *metanoias eis agesin amarton,* which could be translated as "conversion, so as to obtain liberation from one's errors." Some commentators have pointed out that the originality of John's teaching lay in the demand of a prior "conversion," which he required of everyone who came to see him before he would offer them baptism by immersion. The mere act of baptism had no purifying power in itself—it was a symbolic rite of passage that marked the point of return to the way of righteousness by someone who had been living in the ways of error. In other words, these authors see John's preaching as essentially that a change in one's life is a prior condition for admission to this Kingdom that was soon to come. How soon? The texts say nothing specific. We find this same "enigma" as to the time of arrival of the Kingdom in the teaching of Jesus, as well.[20]

The synoptics tell us that many Pharisees and Sadducees were among the crowds who came to John to be baptized. Even so, John reviled these sects as a "generation of vipers." The gospels also make it clear that he did not fear speaking the truth to the most powerful. Thus he spoke frankly in front of the cruel tyrant, Herod, who had violated Hebrew law in marrying his niece and sister-in-law, Herodia. John reproached the king to his face, saying "It is not permitted for you to marry the wife of your brother!" This of course cost him his life.[21] His diatribe against the Sadducees and Pharisees was in fact directed toward people who claimed to inherit righteousness because they were descended from Abraham. His reply to this claim is implacable: "So, then, produce some fruits which are worthy of repentance; and do not begin to say to yourselves, 'We have Abraham as our father'; for I tell you, God is able from these stones to raise up children to Abraham. Even now, the axe is being laid to the roots of the trees; and every tree that does not bear good fruit will be cut down and thrown into the fire" (Luke 3:8–9).

Certainly these were hard words that must have elicited strong reactions from some of those who believed themselves to be "apart" (the literal meaning of *Pharisee*). Jesus would speak in similar terms. It would be difficult not to recognize an echo of the preaching of his mentor, the Baptist, in this response to the crowds who asked him:

> "What, then, should we do?" He answered, "He who has two coats, let him share with him who has none; and he who has food, let him do likewise." Tax collectors also came to be baptized, and

> said to him, "Teacher, what shall we do?" And he said to them, "Collect no more than is appointed you." Soldiers also asked him, "And we, what shall we do?" And he said to them, "Rob no one by violence or by false accusation, and be content with your wages." (Luke 3:10–14)

As Perrot[22] points out, the Baptist's teaching, like that of Jesus (and even the original teaching of the Pharisees themselves, for that matter), was addressed to everyone—no one was excluded, from the smallest to the most powerful. It was a universalist teaching. Both John and his disciples wanted to reach the small people, the sinners and others who felt themselves excluded from the complexities of the religion of the purists and the righteous (cf. Mark 1:6, 11:32; Luke 7:29).

In Acts 13:24, we find Luke setting limitations to this: "John, the precursor, had prepared the way for Jesus in proclaiming a baptism of repentance for all the people *of Israel*." It seems likely that the last, italicized qualification was inserted by Luke. In any case, John's language, which was totally new to many people among the huge crowds he attracted, made some wonder if he were not the long-awaited Messiah. According to Luke, John categorically denied this. However, Luke also adds: "And by many other exhortations, he announced the good news to the people" (Luke 3:18).

Was Jesus Continuing the Teaching of the Baptist?

This is a natural question, which can be rephrased: Was there an unbroken continuity of teaching passed directly from master to disciple? The response to this can be only mixed. According to Mark and Matthew, Jesus, like the Baptist, spoke from the beginning of his mission of the imminence of the Kingdom of God and of the need for repentance. It appears that he was also offering his version of the eschatological vision of his "master": "Now after John was arrested, Jesus came into Galilee, preaching the gospel of God, and saying, 'The time is fulfilled, and the kingdom of God is at hand; repent, and believe in the good news'" (Mark 1:14–15). "From that time Jesus began to preach, saying,

'Repent, for the Kingdom of Heaven is at hand'" (Matt. 4:17).

However, a number of exegetes are of the opinion that the language of these admonitions is more typical of Mark and his community, and is not that of Jesus himself.[23] According to Matthew (3:2), John the Baptist and Jesus both spoke of the Kingdom of Heaven. But none of the other gospels contain passages where the Baptist speaks of the Kingdom. Even in Matthew, he only speaks of it once without saying what it means, although one might deduce its significance from the eschatology that was current at the time. In spite of this, some authors still strongly support the hypothesis that Jesus, as a good disciple of John the Baptist, preached the same eschatology, and even that it was the central theme of his preaching. Later, we shall examine the implications of this thesis, propounded both by these authors and by most clerics, for the meaning of the Kingdom of which Jesus so often speaks.

For now, let us briefly return to our remarks in the section about eschatological beliefs. According to the authors, these beliefs arise from a vision founded upon the divine promise that the Messiah would return at the end of time to restore the Kingdom of God, in a visible and institutional way, for all the Jews who were liberated from the yoke of the occupier. The fulfillment of this promise would come all the sooner, inasmuch as the people of Israel manifested great ardor in following the divine commandments. To this was added a belief that the last times would see the coming of the Son of Man, in a cataclysmic, apocalyptic intervention, to consummate the final judgment.

With this in mind, we might again rephrase our question: Were Jesus and the Baptist speaking of the same Kingdom? Was it the same as the apocalyptic-style Kingdom, whose coming was referred to in eschatological beliefs? Or was it something entirely different? As we have seen, Matthew tells us nothing about the meaning of the Kingdom John speaks of—only that it is "at hand," and that one must prepare oneself for it by repentance and baptism.

Was the Kingdom of which Jesus was always speaking something that would arrive in the future? This, of course, is the pivotal question about its meaning, and the meaning of the Good News itself and different authors continue to have radically different interpretations of it. This serious divergence of opinion among scholars is not surprising, given that we can find no real definition of the Kingdom in the Sayings of Jesus (at least not in those whose authenticity is least in doubt). To put it more correctly, the passages in the gospel Sayings that speak of the Kingdom sometimes appear to contradict each other, or to be in disharmony with some of the analogies illustrated by parables.

We can at the least establish that the discourses of Jesus reported in the synoptics—at least those attributed to the beginning of his public ministry—link the concept of repentance with the arrival of the Kingdom. As we have seen, this is also a central linkage in John the Baptist's preaching. In both cases, the Greek word *metanoia* is used. The Jerusalem Bible, like most others, translates this as "repentance," yet it has also been translated as "change of mind" or "change of heart" (Funk), "return, turnaround" (Chouraqui), and "conversion" (Soeur Jeanne d'Arc). However, *metanoia* occurs only four times[24] in the Sayings attributed to Jesus, and its authenticity has been questioned by many authors, with the possible exception of this passage: "I have not come to call the just, but the sinners, to repentance" (Luke 5:32).

In light of our previous observations about the meaning of the words *sin* and *repentance,* these words by Luke seem to fall well in line with the message of Jesus, as when he says he has come for the sick who want to be healed rather than those who are well. Afterward, *repentance* appears no more. The Gospel of John never attributes this word to Jesus himself. There does not seem to be any possible collection of authentic Sayings that lead to the conclusion that Jesus called for some sort of collective repentance.[25] A belief in judgment, however, and punishment linked to the justice of God was still widespread during Jesus' time.[26] Sanders and Bultmann cite a number of passages in the canonical gospels where Jesus speaks of judgment.[27] Two of these appear to have some degree of authenticity.[28] But serious doubts remain even about these because the content of the Sayings does not correlate with the concept of the Kingdom that Jesus appeared to teach, especially in the parables. Which is not to say that liberation from a life of error and going astray (i.e., *metanoia,* also translatable as "turnaround") does not involve both pain and hope.[29]

Were John and Jesus Essenes?

Both men seem to have emerged from a desert experience where they found visionary inspiration. Only later would this be spoken of as receiving the breath of the Holy Spirit. Is there not a clear kinship—and even more, a possible relationship of lineage—between this and the practices and values of the Essenes? If we focus on certain common points, the relationship becomes striking. For example, the systematic rejection of a worldly way of life, whether urban or rural; a hostility toward the priestly hierarchy that had taken total control of the Temple and the sacrificial rites; and a belief in the imminence of God's intervention in human history. For the Essenes, their mission of living in the desert to prepare for divine intervention was derived from the words of Yahweh as spoken through the prophet Isaiah.[30] Like the Baptist, the Essenes called sincere Jews to repent to be ready for the approaching end of days. Their salvation or their condemnation would depend on their response to the call for repentance. The Essenes also practiced the water ritual, or other rituals symbolic of inner purification.

True, there are significant differences between the Qumran Essenes and John the Baptist.[31] First, nothing indicates that John ever settled down to a community lifestyle similar to that of the Qumran sect. Whereas he was solitary, his disciples returned to their previous occupations, even those who were part of his inner circle. Also, in contrast with the Qumran group, the Baptist apparently did not accord such importance to rites of purification, nor was he obsessed by the impurity of the Temple. As his surname indicates, he was an adept of baptism by immersion, which he administered himself to those who came to him, once and for all.

This fits the picture of a "moderate radical," as conveyed by the gospels. There is nothing in him of the fundamentalist rigidity found among the Essenes. Perrot writes: "Whereas the people of Qumran were known for the intransigence of their interpretation and observance of Mosaic Law, so that even the Pharisees were considered lax by them, the words and actions of the Baptist, as reported in the gospels and by Josephus, demonstrate a total lack of preoccupation with such secondary questions of observance."[32]

Yet the person of John the Baptist remains an enigma for many scholars. As one of them said, if we believe the texts, then "if John believed that another messenger of God was coming to fulfill his eschatological promise, he had no really clear idea about how it would happen."[33] Others have correctly noted that the four Evangelists must have encountered thorny problems fitting the figure of John the Baptist into a Christocentric story. For example, the first verses of Mark reveal a major paradox when Jesus is going to be baptized by John. Invoking a Hebrew scriptures prophecy, Mark writes:

> As it is written in Isaiah the prophet, "Behold, I send my messenger before your face, who will prepare your way. His is the voice of one crying in the wilderness: Prepare the way of the Lord, make his paths straight." So John the Baptist appeared in the wilderness, preaching a baptism of repentance for the forgiveness of sins . . . And he preached, saying, "After me comes he who is mightier than I, the thong of whose sandals I am not worthy to stoop down and untie. I have baptized you with water; but he will baptize you with the Holy Spirit."[34] And it happened that in those days Jesus came from Nazareth of Galilee and was baptized by John in the Jordan. (Mark 1:2–4, 6–9)

But other gospel passages cast doubt on this picture: According to them, the Baptist never understood the mystery of Jesus' true identity, even when he administered the rite of immersion to him. "Thus," says Meier, "the Messianic secret has been well kept, even from the one who opened the way for him. In Matthew's text, John the Baptist recognizes the stature of Jesus, and publicly admits his own inferiority to the one who is coming to be baptized": "Then Jesus came from Galilee to the Jordan to John, to be baptized by him. John would have prevented him, saying, 'I need to be baptized by you, so why do you come to me?' But Jesus answered him, 'Let it be so for now; for thus it is fitting for us to accomplish all that is righteous.' Then he consented" (Matt. 3:13–15).

In the Gospel of John, on the other hand, this rite of immersion—clearly linked in the synoptics to repentance and the remission of sins (Mark 1:4)—does not have the same meaning. The fourth gospel describes John the Baptist as primarily an instrument of Christological revelation:

> The next day he saw Jesus coming toward him, and said, "Behold, the Lamb of God, who takes away the sin of the world! This is he of whom I said, 'After me comes a man who ranks before me, for he was before me.' I myself did not know him; but for this I came to baptize with water, that he might be revealed to Israel." (John 1:29–31)

Was Jesus a Baptist?

Did Jesus himself become a part of the Baptist movement; and/or, did he belong to a group led by John? The answer to these questions is still under debate both by historians and theologians. Recent research points toward an affirmative answer to the second question.[35] In any case, one point on which little doubt remains is that Jesus was baptized by John: "And it came to pass in those days that Jesus came from Nazareth in Galilee, and was baptized in the Jordan by John" (Mark 1:9). "So Jesus arrived at the Jordan from Galilee, and came to John to be baptized by him" (Matt. 3:13). "Now, it happened that when all the people had been baptized, and at the moment when Jesus had also been baptized, and was praying, the heavens opened" (Luke 3:21).

The fact that the Gospel of John does not mention this baptism is evidence, according to some scholars, of the "hierarchical" problem it raised for the gospel's redactors.[36] However this may be, the text does state that Jesus performed baptisms concurrently with John, and did even more of them. Curiously, a little further on, the gospel specifies that it was not Jesus who did the baptism, but his disciples:

> After this Jesus and his disciples went into the land of Judaea; there
> he remained with them and baptized. John also was baptizing at
> Aenon near Salim, because there was much water there; and peo-
> ple came and were baptized. (John 3:22–23)

> Now when the Lord knew that the Pharisees had heard that Jesus
> was making and baptizing more disciples than John (although
> Jesus himself did not baptize, but only his disciples), he left Judaea
> and returned to Galilee. (John 4:1–3)

When Jesus began his mission, he was joined by disciples of the
Baptist. These included Andrew, and probably his brother, Simon-Peter.
But the synoptics say nothing about Jesus performing baptisms.

In Paul's writings there is no mention of the Baptist. For Paul, it was
the baptism of the Cross that brought salvation, not the purification rite
of immersion in water. "We were buried therefore with him by baptism
into death, so that as Christ was raised from the dead by the glory of
the Father, we too might walk in a new life" (Rom. 6:4).

This post-Easter vision of baptism of the Spirit in the resurrected
Christ became the doctrine of the dominant churches, including the
non-Pauline churches. Nevertheless, the disciples continued to practice
both baptism and the laying-on of hands. Luke affirms this on several
occasions in the Acts, especially when he relates the extraordinary
encounter between Philip and a high-ranking eunuch in the service of
the queen of Ethiopia, on the road from Jerusalem to Gaza. The royal
official, seated in his palanquin, is reading the book of Isaiah, where it
tells of the sheep that will be sacrificed.

> And the eunuch said to Philip, "Tell me, about whom does the
> prophet say this: about himself or about some one else?" Then
> Philip began to speak, and beginning with this scripture he told
> him the good news of Jesus. And as they went along the road they

came to some water, and the eunuch said, "See, here is water! What is to prevent my being baptized?" And he commanded the chariot to stop, and they both went down into the water, Philip and the eunuch, and he baptized him. (Acts 8:34–38)

The Baptism of Jesus

As we have seen, the fourth gospel ignores Jesus' baptism. According to the Johannine school, the Baptist's principal mission was not to baptize, but to bear witness to Jesus, the Lord, who "was before [himself]." Meier attributes this contradiction with the synoptics to an unavoidable historical situation. Even before the beginning of Jesus' ministry, another popular Jewish ministry existed: that of the Baptist. And he preached a message of repentance and remission of sins through a rite of immersion. The fact that Jesus accepted this teaching, repenting and receiving baptism at the hands of this man in a gesture of deliberate humility, was almost certainly troubling for the authors of the canonical gospels and their churches. And even after Jesus left it, the Baptist movement continued to exist separately from the early Christian churches.[37]

As many scholars emphasize, this embarrassing situation was especially revealed in issues of hierarchy evoked in gospel passages previously quoted. Although the Johannine text makes it clear that the Baptist recognized Jesus' superiority, this is not the case in Matthew, where it says John the Baptist sent messengers to Jesus to ask who he was:[38] "And you, are you the one who has come, or should we wait for another?" (Matt. 11:3)

According to many scholars, this dance of equivocation, whose contradictions have been preserved by generations of scribes, furnishes the best proof of John the Baptist's importance. If we follow Sanders, we may draw an important conclusion for understanding the figure of Jesus as well. The latter appears to have accepted John's teachings about God's wrath and the need to repent and about an imminent divine intervention to establish the Kingdom.[39] Also, the Baptist's themes of repentance and conversion (or turnaround, the meaning of *repentance*)[40] also enter Jesus' preaching, though less frequently and with less importance. At the start of his public ministry, Jesus speaks of repentance in a clearly eschatological tone; subsequently, the idea of repentance appears alone, no longer linked to the coming of the Kingdom: In those days came John the Baptist, preaching in the wilderness of Judaea:

Repent, for the kingdom of heaven is at hand. (Matt. 3:1–2)

From that time Jesus began to preach, saying, "Repent, for the kingdom of heaven is at hand." (Matt. 4:17)[41]

Then he began to upbraid the cities where most of his miracles had been done, because they did not repent. (Matt. 11:20)

Later, a concern with justice, or righteousness, takes precedence over repentance when speaking of the Kingdom and as a condition for access to it:

If your justice is no better than that of the scribes and Pharisees, you will not enter the Kingdom of Heaven. (Matt. 5:20)

But seek first the Kingdom and its righteousness, and all the rest shall be given you as well. (Matt. 6:33)

Excluding the Book of Revelation (probably wrongly attributed to John), which is in a category separate from the rest of the New Testament,[42] the theme of repentance appears most often in Luke (both the Gospel and the Acts). It is seen less in Matthew, still less in Mark, and not at all in the Gospel of John.[43]

But it was clearly John the Baptist, the eschatological prophet, whom Jesus followed when he accepted baptism in the valley of the Jordan before beginning his own ministry. This is why many believe

Jesus was the Baptist's disciple, at least in a general sense. Some gospel passages, especially in John, allude to an extended period that Jesus spent with the Baptist, further reinforcing this hypothesis. In any event, we know a time came when Jesus left the Baptist, apparently taking some of John's disciples with him.

> The next day John was again standing with two of his disciples. He looked at Jesus as he walked, and said, "Behold, the Lamb of God!" The two disciples heard him say this, and they followed Jesus. Jesus turned, and saw them following, and said to them, "What do you seek?" And they said to him, "Rabbi" (which means Teacher), "where are you staying?" He said to them, "Come and see." They came and saw where he was staying; and they stayed with him that day, for it was about the tenth hour. (John 1:35–39)

To this day, considerable controversy remains about the relationship of Jesus to John the Baptist, especially concerning the degree of Jesus' commitment to John before beginning his own ministry. Some scholars take rather extremist positions, proposing a continuous relation of disciple to master, broken only by Jesus' "apostasy" and rejection of John's teaching and vice versa. Guyénot believes they were divided by rival interpretations of the return of Elijah, each man seeing himself in this role. Such a schism would deprived Jesus of the important support of the Baptist in his effort to succeed as a self-proclaimed Messiah.[44]

Taking a more moderate position, Meier cites the Gospel of John to illustrate that the baptism Jesus learned from John, which they both practiced, was an important indication of fellowship between the prophets. This point is often overlooked, and even omitted, in the synoptics. Let us return to a passage from John, quoted earlier: "After this, Jesus and his disciples went into the land of Judaea, where he remained with them and baptized. John was also baptizing at Aenon near Salim, because there was much water there; and people came and were baptized" (John 3:22–23).

For Meier and others, the most important point that emerges is that we find "no evidence that Jesus ever abandoned this practice of Baptism, once he adopted it. On the contrary, it seems to have been practiced by Jesus and his disciples, in an unbroken tradition which was incorporated into the ritual of the early Church, even though its meaning changed over the course of time." Jesus moved away from the focus on a last, wrathful judgment of God toward an offer of forgiveness. Nonetheless, baptism did not disappear, though it ceased to hold primary importance as a vivid symbol of water dampening the fire of wrath. In emphasizing God's compassion—symbolized by the many healings and sharing food with everyone—Jesus never abandoned (at least according to Meier) the Baptist's proclamation of the imminent judgment of God: "Such a rejection would have immediately made a suspect figure of Jesus."

Whatever date of his death might be, veneration of John the Baptist did not die with him.[45] As implied in the canonical gospels and the Acts, a certain rivalry persisted between Jesus' disciples and those of John after the Baptist's death. As Meier writes, "In his death, as in his life, John stands as an independent figure, one whom the Evangelists were not entirely able to 'tame,' so as to fit him into the Christian mold."[46]

6

The Mission of Jesus

In chapter 1, we saw that the first thirty years of Jesus' life remain obscure; the texts that speak of them offer little of historical value. By contrast, when Jesus apparently passed the age of thirty, we have a relative abundance of documents, both canonical and apocryphal, from which he emerges as a historical personage.

He left his village of Nazareth, making his first public appearance on the banks of the Jordan, in Galilee. This is of course the renowned meeting with the desert preacher John the Baptist, as described in the preceding chapter. All scholars agree that this public mission constituted a brief period in Jesus' life, ending in a violent death. Exactly how long was it? Some scholars lean toward eighteen months, others toward three years.[1]

In this chapter, we review the historians' findings on Jesus' career as a public teacher, including the geographical scope of his mission, his companions, his audiences, and finally *the means* through which he expressed his message (that is, healings, miracles, sermons, parables). A study of the content of his message, and what various authors have said about it, will be the subject of the following chapter.

THE MISSION

During the last period of his life (from eighteen months to three years, depending on which scholar we follow), Jesus worked continuously and tirelessly as an itinerant, homeless preacher. He was not a great traveler, for his voyages were mostly limited to Galilee, with occasional trips to Judaea, including several pilgrimages to Jerusalem and elsewhere. This implies short trips—the longest being a few dozen miles at most. The geographical scope of Jesus' public ministry thus is small in comparison with that of many apostles and disciples, such as Peter, Paul, and Barnaby.

Disagreement remains, however, as to the precise scope of Jesus' mission, both among historians and among gospel authors. One school of thought, which includes Sanders, considers it plausible that Jesus' entire career, with the exception of the last two or three weeks of his life, was limited to Galilee. Another school believes that Jesus probably made at least four voyages to Jerusalem (counting the incident of the palm branches[2] preceding the week of his arrest). It may be that he did not go often into Judaea because of the death threats made against him by the Jerusalem priests.[3] Luke has him preaching in Judaean synagogues (Luke 4:44), and the accusers at his trial denounce him for his preaching all over Judaea (Luke 23:5). Perrot, basing his argument on the Gospel of John, argues that Jesus did not go to Jerusalem "only during the last week of his life, as suggested by Mark," but that he actually began his mission there. Mark is not alone, however, in speaking of Jerusalem as the last step of Jesus' ministry—the other two synoptics mention Jerusalem only at the end of his ministry, a few days before his death.[4]

If we consider the diversity of sources and opinions, we might conclude that Jesus also made trips to Samaria, to the Decapolis, to Tyre, and to Sidon, in Phoenicia. However, his trips to the latter cities would have been short. Whatever the case may be, there is no doubt that Jesus was an itinerant teacher and, as he said in a famous reply, that he had "no place to lay his head."[5]

For many scholars, Jesus' motive in traveling the roads of Palestine was not to preach to as many people as possible. If that had been his objective, why would he systematically avoid the larger cities? In all the New Testament writings, there is no mention of visits or organized appearances in cities such as Sephoris, former capital of Galilee, and Caesaria, the seat of the Roman representative. The impression the canonical gospels give is that of a preacher whose reputation inspired people to travel in order to hear him. Many scholars emphasize the importance Jesus gave to personal contact. And even though Jesus visited places where people expected him, he also sought out places where he felt at peace, such as Capernaum, where he spoke at the beginning of his public mission (Matt. 4:12–13). In this sizable town, his friend Simon-Peter had a house, on the shore of Lake Capernaum, that he shared with his brother Andrew (Mark 2:1, 15).

Jesus' Selection of His Companions

Jesus was neither a hermit nor a solitary, as the Baptist may have been. One of the first known acts of his public career was the choice of his fellow travelers. Multiple testimonies deal with this.[6] In the Mediterranean world, philosophers, prophets, and rabbis were commonly accompanied by disciples.[7] What made Jesus' disciples unusual is that they were chosen by him and in order to follow him, they had to abandon home, family, friends, and possessions, with no hope of return.

What sort of people did he choose? Apparently Galileans of different social classes. The first were fishermen he encountered on the road, near Lake Tiberiad, an abundant source of fish. Others included a tax collector, people of modest means, and sons of higher-ranking families. These disciples, impressed by the charisma of this man, became so attached to him that they left everything to follow his call. Apparently some of them had already heard about him, especially those who were disciples of the Baptist, such as Andrew, who brought Peter to Jesus, and James and John, the sons of Zebedee. The gospels emphasize the force of Jesus' personality, which was so powerful that some disciples were immediately ready to follow him.

Within this inner circle (which also included women, of whom we shall speak later), Jesus singled out twelve special companions (the first disciples, sometimes known as the apostles). The tradition of the Twelve is well established, even though gospel writers disagree on the exact list of names. Scholars now believe that the number twelve should not be taken literally; it had a symbolic significance, like the twelve tribes of Israel, that would have evoked the prophecy of the restoration of the kingdom of Israel in the eschatological atmosphere of that era.[8]

Sanders quotes a series of scriptural passages indicating that "eschatological expectation and the restoration of the twelve tribes of Israel are practically synonymous expressions."[9] One of the last New Testament texts is this passage from Acts, where Jesus, after his resurrection, had this exchange with his disciples: "So when they had gathered together, they asked him, 'Lord, will you now restore the kingdom of Israel?' He answered, 'It is not for you to know the times or seasons which the Father has fixed by his own authority'" (Acts 1:6–7).

Sanders maintains that the symbolism of the Twelve must be understood in this context. Historically, the first mention of the Twelve is in the Letters by Paul to the Corinthians (1 Cor. 15:5); we then find them eight times in Matthew, seven times in Luke, and four times in John. Matthew's first mention of the Twelve says: "Having called his twelve disciples to him, Jesus gave them power over unclean spirits, so as to expel them and cure all sickness and infirmity" (Matt. 10:1).

Then the Twelve are named. But the key verse in Matthew is the one that links them to the twelve tribes of Israel: "Jesus said to them, 'Truly, I say to you, in the new world, when the Son of man shall sit on his throne of glory, you who have followed me will also sit on twelve thrones, judging the twelve tribes of Israel'" (Matt. 19:28). Luke repeats this theme, but without mentioning the twelve disciples—perhaps because he didn't want to include Judas (Luke 22:30). In the Acts, Peter speaks of the need to replace Judas, the traitor, and Matthew was selected through a drawing of lots (Acts 1:12–16).

Although Sanders does not doubt that Jesus spoke of the twelve disciples, he acknowledges that not all scholars agree with this. To be sure, twelve must have been a significant figure for Jesus, as well as for scripture. But, as we have noted, their names differ among the gospels, although the differences do not involve major figures. Some scholars believe that the concept of the Twelve was invented by gospel redactors, or even by the early Church, and that Judas' treachery was also invented by them. But for Sanders, the evidence indicates that a restricted group of disciples was close to the Master, considering the multiple accounts of this in the sources. Whether or not they were actually twelve in number is not ultimately important, nor is the disagreement about the names of less significant disciples. Sanders also notes a confusing distinction in the New Testament between the original twelve disciples and the post-resurrectional apostles—who probably acknowledged James, "the brother of the Lord," as their leader: ". . . and [the Christ] appeared to Kephas [Peter], then to the twelve. Then he appeared to over five hundred brothers at once, most of whom remain until now, but some have also fallen asleep. Then he appeared to James, then to all the apostles" (1 Cor. 15:5–7).

The Gospel of Mark offers this list of twelve:

He appointed twelve, that they might be with him, and that he might send them out to preach, and to have authority to heal sicknesses and to cast out demons: Simon, to whom he gave the name Peter; James the son of Zebedee; John, the brother of James, and he surnamed them Boanerges, which means, Sons of Thunder; Andrew; Philip; Bartholomew; Matthew; Thomas; James, the son of Alphaeus; Thaddaeus; Simon the Zealot; and Judas Iscariot, who also betrayed him. (Mark 3:14–19)

In the Acts of the Apostles, during the last appearance of Jesus before his Ascension, Luke lists eleven disciples present: Peter, John, James, Andrew, Philip, Thomas, Bartholomew, Matthew, James, son of Alphaeus, Simon the Zealot, and Jude, son of James (Acts 1:13).[10] As we see, the list is not constant, for Thaddeus no longer appears. On the other hand, Luke's list names Jude, son of James—but is this James the brother of Jesus?[11] The Gospel of John mentions Nathaniel, from Cana in Galilee, a friend of Philip, the "unwavering Israelite" whom Jesus met under the fig tree. Besides these, Luke tells us that Jesus had many other disciples, which he numbers at seventy (Luke10:1–20).

Were women close to Jesus? There is no doubt. Jesus was no misogynist. Among the women who followed him, the canonical gospels mention the mother of Zebedee's children;[12] Mary, mother of James the younger; Joanna, wife of Chuza, the treasurer of Herod Antipas; Susanna;[13] Salome; Mary Magdalene;[14] and Martha and Mary, sisters of Lazarus. These women were close friends of Jesus,[15] and still others are mentioned. Indeed, the women proved most faithful to him, especially during his crucifixion on Calvary. Also, according to Matthew, Luke, and John, after his death, he first appeared to women, who witnessed his apparition before the male disciples.

Jesus' Congregation

The People of the Earth. The synoptics make it clear that Jesus had a fondness for simple people, the *am ha-eretz,* or "people of the earth,"[16] also known as peasants or "country people." Baron defines them as "that part of the population whose Jewish education was inferior, and whose orthodoxy in religious matters was judged harshly by the stricter Pharisees." Among these country people, he preferred speaking to the sinners, the poor, and the excluded. What was the reason for this preference, which brought him much reproach, especially from the elite, including the Pharisees?

Volumes have been written on this subject, often manifesting a misunderstanding that seriously distorts Jesus' teaching, so we have placed major emphasis on how we interpret certain words used in the gospels. When Jesus urges his listeners to be like God—a recurrent theme in the gospels—Vermès notes that Jesus is advocating compassion, not only for the unfortunate, the sick, and the defenseless, as commanded by biblical prophets of old, but also for those excluded from respectable society.[17] Perrot defines the category of a "socio-religious" underclass called the "sinners." (As we noted previously, this might include people as diverse as physicians, butchers, shepherds, prostitutes, and publicans—members of groups denounced because of their impurity, either due to a pollution inherent in their profession or because of their contact with unclean peasants.) During a dinner at the home of Simon, a Pharisee, Jesus befriended a "prostitute" who had washed his feet with her tears.[18] One of the most serious reproaches against him was that he associated with publicans. But what did these labels really mean and what were the reasons for the ostracism of these people by conventional Jewish society?

Publicans and Sinners. Speaking of the scandal that Jesus created by visiting a publican, Luke recounts:

> He entered and was passing through Jericho. There was a man named Zacchaeus. He was a chief tax collector, and he was rich. He was trying to see who Jesus was, and couldn't because of the crowd, because he was short. He ran on ahead, and climbed up into a sycamore tree to see him, for he was to pass that way. When Jesus came to the place, he looked up and saw him, and said to him, "Zacchaeus, hurry and come down, for today I must stay at your house." He hurried, came down, and received him joyfully. When they saw it, they all murmured, saying, "He has gone to stay with a man who is a sinner." (Luke 19:2–7)

Matthew tells of another scandal involving Jesus and publicans:

> And as he sat at table in the house, behold, many tax collectors and sinners came and sat down with Jesus and his disciples. And when the Pharisees saw this, they said to his disciples, "Why does your teacher eat with tax collectors and sinners?" But when he heard it, he said, "Those who are well have no need of a physician, but those who are sick do."[19] (Matt. 9:10–12)

To these passages on sinners and publicans, we add another that associates the two categories while distinguishing them: "However, all the publicans and the sinners came close to him, so as to hear him. And the Pharisees and scribes muttered: "This man offers good welcome to sinners, and eats with them" (Luke 15:1).

In these extracts, as elsewhere, the task is to determine the original meaning of the vocabulary in the Sayings as reported in the gospels.

Let us first note that, for respectable Jews, publicans were sinners. To them this was self-evident—this socio-professional class of people were the object of the most violent ostracism. What did *publicans* mean? What did the populace hold against them? In fact, they were collectors of taxes, customs duties, and other tariffs.[20] As Philo of Alexandria wrote around 40 C.E., they "steal systematically from others, and live as if God did not exist." In Jesus' time, Baron explains, "when the country was fully incorporated into the Roman Empire, in 6 C.E., the many in-kind contributions and hard labor exacted by administrators, as well as the indirect taxes, including many tolls and customs duties, had made life extremely difficult for the peasants." It is not surprising that the publican, an intermediary charged with collecting the taxes *(mokhes),* often an independent entrepreneur, was a despised fiscal agent. His entire family was reviled. According to a rabbinical saying, "There is no family containing one publican that will not sooner or later consist only of publicans."[21] The synoptics place publicans, sinners, and prostitutes in the same category.

But let us consider the semantic question more closely, for it has been the source of many misunderstandings about Jesus' teaching. The Sayings that we have just quoted contain two key words that persist in the canonical gospels: the *sinners,* and the *poor.* Authoritative commentaries on the differing translations of these two words show that they are rarely acceptable. Their original sense in Aramaic has undergone two reductive translations by the time it reaches us. This problem is typical when moving from a spoken, native language to an intercultural literary language, especially when considerable cultural differences are involved. The first distortion happens when the gospel scribe must translate the Saying from Hebrew or Aramaic into Greek, his working language. He may encounter a concept that he does not understand in his own language. A second distortion often occurs when the Greek is translated into Latin or into a modern tongue.

Let us first return to the Greek in which the gospels were written. In the Sayings on pages 113–14, the word *sinners* is a translation of the Greek *hamartaloi*. Now, when Luke tells the three "parables of compassion"[22] in chapter 15, he sometimes uses the substantive *hamartôloi* and other times the verb *hémarton,* translated as "I have sinned." In fact, in the first two of these parables, the word *hamartôloi* appears in the concluding passages, which—according to a majority of scholars— are not Jesus' words but instead were added by Luke. However this may be, except for the prodigal son whom Jesus describes as "living wrongly," neither the shepherd nor the woman is presented as a sinner or a publican. As for the prodigal son, his father's words about him, according to Jesus in verse 24, have little to do with sin in its traditional sense: "For behold, my son, who was dead, has returned to life: he was lost, and now he is found."

Now our task is to seek the original meaning of the Hebrew word *khatahayn,* found so often in the Bible. The word was translated into Greek as *hamartaloi* in the Septuagint and is rendered as "sinners" in most English Bibles. We can already begin to see that the latter term is misleading. Indeed, since everyone is said to be a sinner, the term means little. Other words proposed in older English translations are *wicked,* and *lost.*[23] In French, some translators have tried alternatives to the word *pécheur* (sinner), proposing *insoumi* (insubordinate), while others have made the translation still heavier with words such as *mécréant* and *impie,* implying an unrepentant sinner.

We might shed more light on the subject by considering the parable of the Pharisee and the publican, to see who is (or, rather, is not) a sinner:

Two men went up into the temple to pray, one a Pharisee and the other a tax collector. The Pharisee stood and prayed thus by himself, "God, I thank thee that I am not like other men, extortioners, unjust, adulterers, or even like this tax collector. I fast twice a week, I give tithes of all that I get." But the tax collector, standing far off, would not even lift up his eyes to heaven, but beat his breast, saying, "God, be merciful to me a sinner!" I tell you, that man went down to his house justified rather than the other; for every one who exalts himself will be humbled, but he who humbles himself will be exalted. (Luke 18:10–14)

This parable has been the source of much controversy. Scholarly opinion is divided on its authenticity. Some argue for it, invoking the criterion of embarrassment,[24] according to which (as in the parable of the good Samaritan) the conclusion goes against conventional expectations. Others doubt it simply because a Pharisee was unlikely to be praying in Galilee during the time of Jesus.[25] For our purposes, we must remember that according to Jesus' adversaries—including particularly intolerant priests, scribes, and some Pharisees—he was a man who had "publicans, *sinners,* and licentious women" for disciples.

With the notion of *sinner* (whose meaning, we repeat, remains unclear), the idea of "impurity" is often associated. In fact, this association in New Testament texts causes confusion between the two concepts, which are, however, quite distinct. Thus it becomes vital to see what Jesus said about the notion of purity, so important in traditional Judaism.

According to Hebrew law, to be impure denotes a failure to observe the rules of purity; it does not necessarily imply that the person is a sinner. Sanders says that impure people become sinners only when they try to enter the Temple in an impure state or attempt to eat the sacrificial food. Such actions represent serious sin and require repentance. By the same token, keeping company with impure people is not a sin in itself, but doing so repeatedly risks exposing oneself to impurity by contact and may become a sin over time. Even more, someone who systematically disobeys the elementary biblical prescriptions of purity is considered an outright sinner, in the sense of an impious person who has no intention of respecting the law. Intention determines whether sin is present.

Some Pharisees accused Jesus not only of cultivating the company of people considered "sinners" by conventional criteria, but also of offering them access to the Kingdom of God. No one would question that these people were impure, but that fact alone did not make them sinners.[26] According to Perrot,[27] the literature of Jesus' time shows that rules concerning water and food had assumed excessive importance in Jewish traditional life. These rules, often complicated in practice, contributed to an increased fragmentation of society.[28] The degree to which these rites were observed formed a social grouping in itself.[29] "The righteous, the pure, or the 'separated ones' (i.e., Pharisees) were distinguished from the 'country people' and the sinners. The Pharisees . . . tended to form small 'purity groups' influenced by scribes of their particular movement.[30] They took care to guard themselves from the constant impurity in which country people lived—those poor people who were unable to follow the minutiae of all the rules . . . The rite of purity always leads to increased separation and isolation. It was this exclusion that Jesus opposed, for it was making the country people suffer." Note the important distinction Perrot makes between involuntary sinners and the impious, or wicked, who deliberately refuse to follow ritual prescriptions of purity.

Other scholars have markedly different views on this question. They stress that rabbinical literature shows more flexibility than this, even a tolerance that considers the country people's level of education in the Law. This flexibility is founded on the principle that sin applies only to the degree that the person is conscious of his sin.

What emerges from this is that we must take care not to confuse the term *sinners* with the term *country people* or *peasants,* whom even the most orthodox Pharisees did not consider to be sinners. Second, impurity does not necessarily imply sin. We would be wrong to conclude that Jesus' affection for sinners implied a plan to do away with the rules and rituals of purity. We are equally mistaken to conclude that the dispute between Jesus and the Pharisees involved rules of purity and diet, and that they reproached him for advocating that sinners be re-admitted into Judaism. What Jesus actually offered sinners was admission into his group of faith (the Kingdom) if they accepted his teaching. Surely this could not have been perceived as an offense.

The Poor. A translation problem also exists, with possibly serious distortions, regarding the Greek word *ptôkoï,* which is systematically translated in most versions of the New Testament as "the poor" regardless of the context. The Greek root actually has several meanings: "to crouch, or huddle"; "to seek protection"; and "to beg, to be a mendicant."[31] Here, it is very important to note that Jesus describes his own disciples as among the poor: "And, raising his eyes to look upon his disciples, he said: 'Blessed are you, the poor, for the Kingdom of God is yours.'"

THE MIRACLES

Different types of signs appear in the gospels. Some announce the Kingdom; others are miracles for those who lack faith and need signs. Healing the mentally ill, exorcising the possessed by ridding them of demons, curing those who have pain in body or soul, reinfusing hope and dignity in the poor—these are signs that signify the compassion of Jesus' love.

> And he went all around Galilee, teaching in their synagogues and preaching the gospel of the kingdom and healing every disease and every infirmity among the people. So his fame spread throughout all Syria, and they brought him all the sick, those afflicted with various diseases and pains: demoniacs, epileptics, and paralytics; and he healed them. (Matt. 4:23–24)

But when people asked Jesus for signs, it was a different matter. Only those who lacked faith demanded signs, tangible proof from this messenger of God. They did not seek inspiring words or acts of compassion, but rather extraordinary, supernatural signs. Jesus' response to this was different: "The Pharisees came and began to argue with him, seeking from him a sign from heaven, to test him. And he sighed deeply in his spirit, and said, "Why does this generation seek a sign? Truly, I say to you, no sign shall be given to this generation" (Mark 8:11–12).

The Greek word *dunamis*, translated as "miracle," actually means "power" or "act of power." From a historical perspective, our task is to determine not whether miracles actually happened (or could happen), but whether witnesses believed miracles took place, whatever the true nature of the phenomenon. We must recall that reports of miracles were widespread in ancient times. Those who performed them were by definition out of the ordinary, such as magicians, prophets, and holy hermits. In first-century Mediterranean society, few doubted the possibility of miracles, or that some had a gift for accomplishing such wonders, which were signs of their supernatural power. The vast majority of people in those times would never think to invoke the inviolability of "natural laws." Few such laws had been formulated by scientists of the era, and they were not cited to refute reports of miracles.

We must remember that in Greco-Roman culture, the prevailing view of the cosmos was a vast hierarchy, with inanimate objects at the low end, then plants, animals, human beings, and finally the realm of the divine. Even the highest level had its own elaborate hierarchy. The borders between these levels were very thin, and gods could sometimes take on human form, establishing relationships with humans, even to the point of sexual relations leading to pregnancy and childbirth. In addition, a widespread belief held that certain exceptional people could escape death. The Bible gives an example in the prophet Elijah, who was taken up to heaven in a chariot of fire (2 Kings 2:11). Certain kings and emperors also attained divine status after their death.

But Jesus' contemporaries were concerned about a different problem. Their question was not merely whether Jesus had such powers, but where they originated. What was the nature of the power, the *dunamis*, that manifested through him? In the long chapter that Meier devotes to Jesus' miracles, he argues that whether or not one accepts the possibility of miracles is irrelevant to historical analysis—that question belongs to the domains of philosophy, psychology, and theology. We can assert therefore, that from a historical point of view, Jesus never denied performing miracles during his public ministry, and we can also state that his followers, admirers, friends, and partisans were convinced he had accomplished extraordinary acts that manifested the power of the Almighty—powers his adversaries attributed to an alliance with demons.

Jesus' own position in the synoptic gospels, with regard both to miracles and to what he called "signs," differs from that in the Gospel of John. According to the synoptics (which have primacy over John as historical sources), when Jesus accomplished what people call "miracles," he did so modestly—even in secret—deliberately avoiding all self-glorification.[32] In contrast, the miracles reported in John, such as water being changed to wine and the multiplication of the loaves, take place in full public view, furnishing proof of Jesus Christ as messenger of the Most High. Some modern scholars hypothesize that the entire miraculous tradition was invented by the early Church as propaganda, but Meier and others find this argument specious. The attempt to rid Jesus of this aspect smacks of an effort to create a first-century Jewish prophet whose personality and worldview fit those of modern intellectuals.

Nevertheless, a careful application of historical criteria enables us to filter out stories that were almost certainly created by the early Church, separating them from those that have a greater chance of taking us back to the historical Jesus, even though they may have been altered along the way. The application of historical criteria can at times yield startling results. The most surprising for our present subject is that one of the most solidly established traditions speaks of "miraculous" healings. This stands on more solid historical ground than other notable and often well-accepted traditions about Jesus' life, such as his working as a carpenter, his use of the word Abba in referring to God, and his prayer in the Garden of Gethsemane before his arrest. On the other hand, these same criteria show that, unlike healings, most of the extraordinary events suggesting divine control of natural phenomena are probably creations of the early Church. The purpose of these inventions was to bring the story of Jesus' ministry into accord with ancient prophecies, such as those of Elijah, to reinforce belief in his divine nature.

Healing the Ill and the Possessed

> That evening they brought him many who were possessed with demons. He cast out the spirits with a word, and healed all who were sick. This was to fulfill what was spoken by the prophet Isaiah, "He took our infirmities and bore our diseases." (Matt. 8:16–17)

In the canonical gospels, we find no clear distinction between healing mental illness and physical illness. Jesus' central intent, and the purpose of his mission, was to minister to the sick and to call to them: "It is not the healthy who need a physician, but the sick. I have not come to call the righteous, but the sinners"[33] (Mark 2:17).

Note that in this one verse, Mark makes a parallel of two Sayings: one opposing health with sickness, the other opposing righteousness (or justice) with sin. Of course this is not accidental. For Jesus, they were the same. A sinner is someone who has "missed the mark," who has committed a mistake, or a fault, and who knows it. A sinner is the same as someone who is ill and wants to be healed. A righteous man, who believes he knows the truth, and therefore believes himself whole, has no need of a physician. The physician (in Greek *iatèr*) provides a cure, an action that brings salvation and liberation (in Greek *sautérios*).[34] To be liberated from wrongness, from error, is to be healed—this is what Jesus urged people to ask of God.

In this context, we recall this was the first good news that Jesus announced after his desert retreat at the beginning of his public ministry. Entering a synagogue in Nazareth and opening the Bible, he fell upon a passage from Isaiah, which he read aloud: "The Spirit of the Lord Yahweh is upon me, because Yahweh has anointed me; he has sent me to bring good news to the afflicted; he has sent me to mend broken hearts, to proclaim liberation to the captives, and deliverance to those who are in prison" (Isa. 61:1 and Luke 4:18).

In a sense, this quotation says it all. We shall return to this message in more detail in chapter 7. What impresses Jesus' listeners here is mending broken hearts and delivering captives. Jesus has come to heal the wounds of the body and to free the mind by exorcising its alienation.

Jesus as Exorcist

Exorcism is not an important theme of the Hebrew Bible. Sanders writes that the practice had become widespread in the first century. The gospels contain a number of passages that show Jesus driving out demons. Here are two of the most characteristic:

> And he healed many who were sick with various diseases, and cast out many demons; and he would not permit the demons to speak, because they knew him. (Mark 1:34)

> Now, when the sun was setting, all those with companions that were sick with various diseases brought them to him; and he laid his hands on every one of them and healed them. And demons also came out of many, crying, "You are the Son of God!" But he rebuked them, and would not allow them to speak, because they knew that he was the Christ. (Luke 4:40–41)

Luke has Jesus say that his God-given power to drive out demons is a sign that the Kingdom has come:[35] "If it is through God's finger that I drive out demons, then it is because the Kingdom of God has come unto you" (Luke 11:14–20).

The Gospels of Matthew and Luke present five specific cases of exorcism Jesus performed on people who were possessed by demons: (1) the two men in the Gadarene country,[36] (2) the man in the synagogue,[37] (3) the only child of a man in the crowd,[38] (4) the mute man, and (5) the daughter of the Canaanite woman.[39]

Although scholars have good reason to suspect some of these stories as significant redactions, the existence of multiple testimonies for several of them indicate a high probability of authenticity. This was an era when physicians had virtually no recourse for dealing with serious psychological stress resulting from family, social, religious, and political pressures. Illnesses such as schizophrenia and multiple-personality syndrome were diagnosed by social custom as forms of demonic possession. Since there existed nothing analogous to a psychiatrist, people turned to exorcists, people of varying degrees of competence. Jesus' first fame came from his reputation as an exorcist.[40]

Other Healings

Other than exorcisms, the gospels contain fifteen accounts of healing the sick and crippled. Five of these[41] involve paralysis or deformation (the sources are Mark, Luke,[42] John, and Q);[43] three of them involve healing the blind (Q); two are cases of leprosy (Mark and Luke); and five involve diverse illnesses.

Even though these accounts are supported by multiple attestations, other historical criteria give them mediocre ratings. The main reason for doubt is that all of these miracle stories were orally preserved and transmitted for a generation or two, expressed in stylized formulas belonging to a well-defined narrative genre.[44]

Funk points out that Jesus himself attached little or no importance to healing methods, for he wanted to demonstrate that everyone has the power of forgiveness of sins, which breaks the chain of cause and effect between illness and fault.[45] In Funk's view, Jesus taught that the power of forgiveness is available to all human beings according to divine will. This represented a threat to the monopoly of such power claimed by the priesthood.

The Resurrection Miracles

Now we come to the difficult problem of the resurrection narratives. According to Sanders, a number of Christology scholars see these narratives as a direct expression of the doctrine of the Church, based on Paul's teaching, that Jesus was resurrected from the dead, thereby conquering the power of the devil, for death represented the ultimate evil.[46]

Three accounts of resurrection miracles appear in the canonical gospels. Actually, the two miracles that occur in the synoptics are not precisely resurrections in the sense of reviving a dead person. There is no doubt that many people in the Mediterranean world at that time would have found it believable, or at least plausible, that someone of divine stature could resurrect the dead. The three accounts of Jesus resurrecting the dead derive from a significant number of literary sources, including Mark, the special L tradition, and the Johannine tradition. This tends to support a hypothesis that these accounts were not created by gospel redactors, but rather go back to an earlier tradition.

But we must ask this question: Are these Christological specialists themselves operating under the conviction that gospel accounts of miracles, and especially of resurrections, are based on historical events? As we have noted earlier, our only historical concern must be for events that Jesus, his disciples, and other witnesses *believed* to be miracles. If we can determine with a reasonable degree of probability that these resurrection narratives date back to the ministry of Jesus, this would support the thesis that people believed, during Jesus' lifetime, that he performed resurrections.[47]

The case of Lazarus is particularly interesting. According to the gospels, this close friend of Jesus showed all the symptoms of physical death. His resurrection would obviously represent a spectacular occurrence whose meaning has been the source of much controversy. Meier's thorough study of this question reflects prevailing opinion today. For him, even though the resurrection of Lazarus occurs only in the Gospel of John that does not mean John invented it. The narrative is constructed around a central tale that most scholars believe dates to a tradition older than the canonical gospels. In contrast, the "mini-speeches," or dialogues about theological issues important to John, probably originate with the gospel writer. These include metaphors of light and darkness and statements such as: "I am the Resurrection and the Life," "Whoever believes in me will live, even if they die," and "Yes, you are the Messiah, the Son of God."[48] Contradictory currents are also found in this text, displays of tension and awkward repetitions, that may be signs of redaction and rewriting of tradition. But Meier considers the Lazarus incident satisfactory in criteria for a narrative that goes back to a real event in the life of Jesus.

He is convinced that Jesus' disciples believed, while he was still alive, that some sort of miraculous resurrection had taken place. The synoptic gospels' silence on the subject of Lazarus's resurrection is insufficient to establish that the narrative did not originate in a historical event.[49]

Thus a significant number of scholars conclude that the accounts of exorcisms and healings, in the context of first-century culture, at least establish the historical existence of a Palestinian Jew who had a reputation of power and authority, and who was said to have accomplished wondrous acts—acts that he himself saw as affirming the Kingdom of God, as announced by the prophets. There can be no single, privileged theory to explain these miracles. But studies based on history show that Jesus' healings of physical handicaps and illnesses stand on even firmer historical ground than accounts of his exorcisms. The signs and miracles offered by Jesus certainly must have played an important role in attracting crowds, for better and for worse. As Meier says, "These miracles not only supported, but dramatized his eschatological message; they probably played at least some role in alarming the authorities, who finally had him put to death." Meier deduces from this that "any historian who tries to produce a portrait of Jesus without giving due weight to his reputation as a miracle-worker will not be able to produce a true likeness of this strange and complex Jew. Instead, he will wind up with a tame Jesus, recalling the pale, moralist picture of him created by Thomas Jefferson."

On the other hand, a majority of scholars have agreed to suspend judgment about the historical authenticity of the resurrection traditions as they have come down to us—there is sufficient reason neither to accord nor to deny them authenticity. Although there are good reasons to believe that the story of the resurrection of Jairus's daughter is based on an older tradition that reflects a real event in the life of Jesus, evidence remains insufficient to assign the same degree of authenticity to the resurrection story of the son of the widow of Nain, nor to that of Lazarus. In the resurrection miracles related by Luke and Matthew, we cannot even be sure that the people had died. Matthew has Jesus say: "She is not dead, this girl, but sleeping." Even in the account of

Lazarus's resurrection, John has Jesus say, "Our friend Lazarus has fallen asleep, but I will go and awaken him."[50]

To be sure, having only one source for a story does pose a problem. The text probably contains at least some older material, but it is filled with words and phrases attributed to Jesus that are typically of the Johannine school. This does not correlate well with the style and teaching of the synoptic Jesus. Besides, Jesus' apparent assent to a public promotion of the Lazarus event as a sign is in marked contradiction to his discretion about such things in the synoptic gospels. As we noted earlier, in the latter scriptures, Jesus typically intervenes alone, or with a small group of disciples. We find this same discretion in most of the other miracles mentioned above.

Miraculous Intervention in Natural Phenomena

In addition to resurrection miracles, presented as supernatural phenomena (notwithstanding the possibility that they were revivals of comatose people), the gospels contain a series of miraculous events that involve natural phenomena. I am in full agreement with Meier's strong arguments on this subject: With the exception of the multiplication of loaves, which occurs in several versions,[51] all the accounts of supernatural events—the wedding at Cana,[52] calming the storm, and walking on water—are most likely creations of the early Church, done for its own theological purposes. But an argument for an older source for the story of the joyous meal shared by Jesus after the multiplication of loaves is supported by the consistency of accounts, as well as by their number. This may have eschatological implications. Even if no "multiplication" occurred, a number of scholars agree with Meier that the miracle story at least reflects a highly memorable and symbolic meal Jesus shared with a large group of people on the shores of the Sea of Galilee.

JESUS AS PREACHER

We recall that Jesus spent his childhood, and probably most of his adult life, in Nazareth. It is unlikely that, during all those years, he never left this small village to go to a large town—for example, nearby Sephoris, an important cosmopolitan center and the capital of Galilee during Jesus' youth. A few scholars hypothesize that Jesus went there, possibly accompanied by his father, to deliver orders or even to work on construction sites. Plausibly, as well, the adult Jesus, like any other open-minded and curious young man, would have been attracted by Sephoris.[53] In this Greco-Roman center, people of different cultures crossed paths, probably including voyagers from the East, perhaps from as far away as the banks of the Indus River.[54]

Whether accurate or not, a number of careful readers note a resemblance between Jesus' teachings and those of the Buddha. Their common theme harmonizes with those of other wisdom teachers, proclaiming a new way, a radical turnaround, a renaissance.[55]

Some authors even discern a Stoic influence in the wisdom teachings of the gospels. One example among many is a passage from Seneca, who probably wrote some years before the death of Jesus, that offers a useful summary of the Stoic philosophy of that century: The spirit of the wise person should be a likeness of the spirit of God.[56] Can we deny the kinship between this and Jesus' words: "Be perfect, as your heavenly Father is perfect"?[57]

We should also remember that religious teaching in Jesus' time took on various traditional forms corresponding to the source being interpreted. Thus, for Bible interpretation, they included the Targum, the Midrash,[58] and homily; when discussing laws and customs, the Mishnah and the Halakah.[59] The teachings were offered in schools, academies, and synagogues. Also, preachers and mystics spoke daily to crowds around the Temple of Jerusalem (perhaps not unlike Hyde Park in London) promulgating their messages and religious views.

Jesus also taught, preached, and gave speeches. This practice was not *ex cathedra* teaching, to use later Church language. In fact, Jesus spoke to disciples and others who asked questions, and to crowds gathered to listen or to see him perform miracles. He taught in synagogues, in the streets and public places, and in the Temple area. He also spoke to people gathered on a mountain and on the shores of Lake Genesareth; he even spoke standing in a boat.

Jesus had studied the scriptures. He certainly knew powerful texts like this passage attributed to the prophet Isaiah:

Yet they seek me daily, and desire to know my ways, as if they were a nation that practiced justice and did not forsake the law of their God; they ask me for righteous judgments, they desire to draw near to God. "Why have we fasted, and you do not see it? Why have we mortified ourselves, and you do not recognize it?" Behold, in the day of your fast you seek your own pleasure, and oppress all your workers . . . Is it the fast that pleases me, or the day for a man to mortify himself? Is this not rather the fast I prefer: to loose the bonds of injustice, to untie the yoke, to let the oppressed go free, and to break every yoke? Is it not to share your bread with the hungry, and bring the homeless poor into your house? Is it not to clothe the naked when you see them, and not to hide yourself from your own flesh? (Isa. 58:2–7)

In biblical and post-biblical texts, we find a systematic use of analogy or of metaphor, which is characteristic of traditional Jewish thinking—especially parables, proverbs, and aphorisms. Jesus makes frequent use of the proverb, although some attributed to him by early Church or gospel redactors were known prior to his time through traditional wisdom or from religious texts. Consider a few of his best-known metaphors, beginning with the narrow gate, or door:

Enter by the narrow gate; for the gate is wide and the way is easy, that leads to destruction, and those who enter by it are many. For the gate is narrow and the way is hard, that leads to life, and those who find it are few. (Matt. 7:13–14)

Strive to enter by the narrow door; for many, I tell you, will seek to enter and will not be able. (Luke 13:24)

Then there is the analogy of the speck and the log: "Why do you see the speck that is in your brother's eye, but do not notice the log that is in your own eye?" (Matt. 7:3)

Or that of the lamp: "The eye is the lamp of the body, and if your eye is wholesome, your entire body will be radiant. But if your eye is unwholesome, your entire body will be in darkness. Truly, if the light within you is darkness, what a darkness it is!" (Matt. 6:22)

Note the famous proverb of the prophet in his own land: "And Jesus said to them: 'A prophet is only despised in his own country, by his own kin, and in his own home'" (Mark 6:4).

The Parables of Jesus

And he spoke to them of many things in the form of parables. (Mark 4:2, Matt. 13:3)

This is why I speak to them in parables: because they see without seeing, and hear without hearing or understanding. (Matt. 13:3)

Jesus told all of this to the crowds in the form of parables, and he said nothing to them that was not a parable. (Matt. 13:34)

Apart from certain doubtful interpretations, conclusive evidence exists that Jesus made systematic use of parables to communicate the deeper meaning of his teaching. The parable is an oratory technique that compares two things or two situations that are essentially different. It often uses the phrase "is like" in order to clarify a concept without abstract explanations. A major example is: "The Kingdom of Heaven is like . . ." In contrast to the synoptics, the Gospel of John does use parables, in the strict sense of the term, though it includes long speeches full of implied metaphors without the phrase *is like*.

The synoptics contain thirty-eight parables: six in Mark, nine from the Q source common to Matthew and Luke,[60] nine that are particular to Matthew, and fourteen particular to Luke. In his in-depth study of the forms of parables attributed to Jesus,[61] Vermès distinguishes five categories: (1) rural parables, (2) parables of everyday life, (3) socially significant parables, (4) parables about judges and tribunals, and (5) parables of wedding celebrations. He concludes that six of these are probably not Jesus' own, either because they express a position that does not agree with his teaching or because the narrative has a context foreign to that of Jesus and his time.[62] In addition, Vermès identifies seven parables whose redactions, or whose original form, have been fundamentally modified by the early Church.[63]

As with the proverbs, historical research shows that the use of parables was not unique to Jesus. Called *mashal* in Hebrew, the parable was often used in oral and written Jewish tradition. Contrary to what some scholars have claimed,[64] most historians agree that the parable was not an original literary genre invented by Jesus or his disciples, nor was it a didactic technique that arose after the fall of the Temple. Indeed, the parable form frequently appeared not only in biblical texts, but also in the Jewish Pseudepigrapha and in the Qumran texts.[65] Accompanied by a key for interpretation, they were used to illustrate biblical quotations, typically during a sermon at the synagogue. The art of telling parable stories was indispensable to communication in a culture of rich oral tradition when addressing simple people. Jesus had an extraordinary gift for this expression, enabling him to use the parable as an essential and effective vehicle for the propagation of his message.

Jesus' parables differ in form from those in rabbinical writings. Unlike the latter, they are not accompanied by detailed explanations,[66] nor are they composed to illustrate Bible verses.[67] This difference is often explained as Jesus' concern for communicating succinctly to crowds for whom elaborate sermons would have been less accessible. But for this argument to hold, the parables would have to be understandable in themselves, needing no external explanation. This is not the case, and the objection is raised that Jesus used parables not to make himself understood by simple people, but quite the reverse. This argument finds support in the words that Mark attributes to Jesus, speaking to his disciples about his parable of the sower:

And he said, "Whoever has ears, let them hear!" And when he turned away, the twelve and others who were accompanying him asked him about the parables. And he said to them, "To you has been given the secret of the kingdom of God, but for those outside everything is in parables, lest they see but not perceive, and lest they hear but not understand; and lest they should turn away, and not be forgiven." And he said to them, "Do you not understand this parable? How then will you understand the other parables? The sower sows the word. And these are the people along the path, where the word is sown: when they hear, Satan immediately comes and removes the word which is sown in them. And these are like the seeds sown upon rocky ground: when they hear the word, they immediately receive it with joy, but they have no root in themselves, and keep it only for a while. Then, when tribulation or persecution comes on account of the word, they quickly fall away. And others are those sown among thorns: they are people who hear the word—but the cares of the world, and the delight in riches, and the desire for other things, enter in and choke the word, and it proves unfruitful. But those that were sown upon the good soil are the ones who hear the word and accept it and bear fruit, thirtyfold and sixtyfold and a hundredfold." (Mark 4:9–20)

This passage makes sense only if the word *parable* has an enigmatic or esoteric connotation, which is absent from the Hebrew word *mashal*. One might object, with Vermès, that this conclusion implies that Jesus is presenting himself as a deliberately esoteric teacher, like those of the gnostics or the Essenes.[68] But neither the synoptic nor the mainstream tradition supports this hypothesis. If it were true, it would present a picture of Jesus that is radically different from that seen elsewhere in the synoptic gospels. Vermès' explanation is that the synoptics, anticipating the disbelief of the Jews, wanted to show a Jesus who would not make access to understanding easy for his co-religionists who rejected the annunciation of the Kingdom. This explanation appears a bit far-fetched. Indeed, a majority of scholars believe that

Jesus wanted his parables to make the meaning of the Kingdom more, not less, understandable.[69]

Whatever the Master's true intentions may have been, one thing is certain: To read the parables of Jesus is often to encounter a shock that borders on religious provocation. On many occasions, the images he used must have shocked religious Jews of the time. A frequently cited example is his comparison of the Kingdom with yeast—a substance considered impure in rabbinical literature[70]—or his famous metaphor of the mustard seed growing into a tree—another plant considered impure. Moreover, some parables seem to violate common sense or flout conventional morality (the parables of the hidden treasure, the dishonest steward, and the worthless servant, among others). In general, recent studies conclude that Jesus' principal aim in using parables was to get his audience's attention, beginning with apparently simple stories with images from ordinary life, then leading them to provocative conclusions that defied common sense, like the ethical vision of the Kingdom, which was a liberating vision rather than a moralizing one.

The Charisma of Jesus

The gospel writers often speak of how impressed Jesus' listeners were by the originality of his teaching and by the authority with which he expressed it. Mark uses the Greek word *exousia,* which has no equivalent in English but contains connotations of "faculty," "power," "authority," "majesty," and so forth. "And they were astonished by his teaching, for he spoke as a man of authority, and not like the scribes" (Mark 1:22).

One impression of Jesus emerges clearly from the synoptics: He is a man who speaks with authority, who is unlike the Galilean scribes or experts in biblical interpretation. But where did his authority come from? If we can answer this question, we may better understand how his message was received and appreciated and to what extent his method was derived, or was a departure, from accepted practices of the era. Above all, we will better understand who this man was and how he was distinguished from other prophets and preachers.

As we have noted, Judaic tradition comprises three types of teachings. The first are of divine origin, often directly proclaimed by God, such as the commandments graven in stone and given to Moses. Next we find the words of the prophets, who are declared to be channels of divine communication—either directly from God or through a vision of supernatural meaning. Finally, we have the "wisdom teachings,"[71] whose prototype is the Wisdom of Solomon: To these, we may add writings attributed to canonical or non-canonical prophets, inspired by visions or revelations.[72] Both the Hebrew scriptures and the New Testament abound in teachings that take this form. A few examples are: Zechariah in the Temple (Luke 1:11); Mary and Joseph visited by angels (Luke 1:26, Matt. 1:20); Peter hearing a heavenly voice while in an ecstatic state; and Paul overwhelmed by a voice from heaven while on the road to Damascus.

Most scholars now agree that Jesus' speeches do not fit into these categories. Whether considering the authority invoked by their content, or the authority of the speaker's membership in a lineage transmitted from master to disciple, his words do not conform to the traditional categories, with the exception of two parallel passages in Matthew and Luke, whose Christocentric bias casts doubt on their authenticity: "All things have been delivered to me by my Father; and no one knows who is the Son except the Father, or who is the Father except the Son, or someone to whom the Son chooses to reveal him.[73] (Luke 10:22, Matt. 11:27)

Other than this, the synoptic gospels contain no allusion to a divine transmission of words to Jesus of Nazareth.

Essentially, Jesus is never presented as a person endowed with spiritual gifts of this type. When he speaks about the Law, or about ethics in general, he does so not as a messenger divinely commanded to do so, but by his own authority. As Sanders emphasizes, Jesus considered himself fully invested with the authority to forgive and act in the name of God.[74] Regarding those narratives or Sayings that contain implicit or explicit references to biblical passages, most specialists now believe most of these were inserted by the redactors for literary or stylistic reasons. Consequently, considerable doubt is raised that Jesus made systematic use of scripture to support his teaching. None of the best-authenticated Sayings shows him quoting scripture to give authority to his message. When he does occasionally make use of the Bible, he does so in simple, illustrative ways. In any case, though the possibility remains that Jesus would have characterized his teaching as primarily a fulfillment of biblical scripture, we can be sure that he rarely expressed this intention.[75] As we shall see in greater depth in the next chapter, when gospel writers allude to scriptural fulfillment, this almost always introduces an event for which there are no firsthand witnesses. The Passion narrative, for example, is laden with predictive biblical allusions.

The Pharisees, and especially the scribes, who felt their monopoly on religious interpretation threatened by Jesus' characteristic authority, forever ask him: "By what authority do you do this? Who has given you the authority to do it?" (Mark 11:28)

Mark never has Jesus reply directly to such a question. Elsewhere, he tells this story:

> And there was a man in their synagogue possessed by an unclean spirit; and he cried out, "What have you to do with us, Jesus of Nazareth? Have you come to destroy us? I know who you are, the Holy One of God." But Jesus rebuked him, saying, "Be silent, and come out of him!" And the unclean spirit, convulsing the man and crying with a loud voice, came out of him. And they were all amazed, so that they questioned among themselves, saying, "What is this? A new teaching! With authority he commands even the unclean spirits, and they obey him." And at once his fame spread everywhere throughout all the surrounding region of Galilee. (Mark 1:23–28)

In a number of passages of the synoptics, we find phrases such as "astonished," "full of wonder," and "full of admiration":

> . . . [A]nd coming to his own country he taught them in their synagogue, so that they were astonished, and said, "Where did this

man get this wisdom and these mighty works? Is not this the carpenter's son? Is not his mother named Mary? And are not his brothers James and Joseph and Simon and Judas? And are not all his sisters with us? Where then did this man get all this?" And they were offended by him. But Jesus said to them, "A prophet is only despised in his own country and in his own house." And he did not perform many great works there, because of their lack of faith. (Matt. 13:54–58)

And they were on the road, going up to Jerusalem, and Jesus was walking ahead of them; and they were amazed, and those who followed were afraid. (Mark 10:32)

To the same question about the authority of his words, John has Jesus reply: "My teaching is not from me, but from him who sent me. If a man's will is to do his will, he will know whether the teaching is from God or whether I am speaking on my own authority. He who speaks on his own authority seeks his own glory; but he who seeks the glory of him who sent him is true, and there is no falseness in him." (John 7:16–18).

The word *charisma* is somewhat anachronistic in this context, derived from a Greek word that, though often used in later writings of the New Testament, is not found in the canonical gospels. Matthew uses the word *prophet*—that is, someone whose authority lies not only in his words, but also in his deeds, his healings, his power of exorcism, and his vision of the world to come. Like John the Baptist, Jesus is seen as a prophet who does not need to justify his Good News with scriptural references. The crowds and his disciples believed in the man Jesus as a prophet of God, whose authority was self-evident. As Perrot says, "It is the exegetical tradition of the scribes that is being challenged." Jesus often has recourse to his well-known formula: "You have learned . . . but I tell you, . . . " He does not need an intermediary authority. As we shall see later, his authority derives from the intimacy he maintains with the heavenly Father.

Jesus as a Nonconformist Teacher

> "Truly, I say to you, the tax collectors and the prostitutes will enter
> the kingdom of God before you. For John came to you in the way
> of righteousness, and you did not believe him, but the tax collec-
> tors and the prostitutes believed him; and even when you saw it,
> you did not afterward repent and believe him. (Matt. 21:31–32)

> The Son of man has come eating and drinking; and you say,
> "Behold, a glutton and a drunkard, a friend of tax collectors and
> sinners!" (Luke 7:34)

Contemporary literature brings out the nonconformist and the non-
normative character of Jesus' teaching. As the above passages well illustrate, Jesus did not censure, but rather restored confidence in the
capacity of each person to find the way. He was not judgmental; he was
compassionate. Far from being a puritan, he was a provocateur. He
enjoyed banquets and was even accused of being a glutton and a
drinker. But at the same time, Jesus often "took a position opposite to
the most deeply rooted and tenacious ideas."[76]

His Sayings do not contain commandments as such, in spite of certain language attributed to him that does not conform to his message.[77]
Certainly some Sayings can be read as precepts (Greek: *entolè*), and
have been translated as "orders," to use military language. One of the
most noted and original should be mentioned here: "You have heard
that it was said, 'You shall love your neighbor and hate your enemy.'
But I say to you, Love your enemies and pray for those who persecute
you, so that you may be sons of your Father who is in heaven; for he
makes his sun rise on the evil and on the good, and sends rain on the
just and on the unjust" (Matt. 5:43–45).

And he adds: "For then you will be perfect, as your heavenly Father
is perfect."[78]

In the first of these Sayings, the prescription to love in the first part
is founded to a degree on the last part. It is because God treats all peo-

ple as equal that human beings should treat each other as equal.

Many scholars emphasize that Jesus' words dissolve the boundary between the sacred and the profane. He questioned the validity of "common sense." As Sanders explains, his particular brand of perfectionism (compassion and humility) is in harmony with his vision of the Kingdom of God as "upside-down," a reversal of many conventional values. His fraternization with heretics, prostitutes, and tax collectors demonstrated the freedom and independence of a highly unusual mind. Jesus appeared at banquets and enjoyed eating and drinking. He did not fast, as did the disciples of John the Baptist. He sat at the same table with tax collectors, prostitutes, and sinners.

The Sabbath is the day of the Lord in Jewish religion, a day of rest that involves several prohibitions. As we noted in an earlier chapter, Jesus had a different view of this holy day.

Another synoptic passage illustrates his nonconformity on a similar subject: "Another disciple asked him: 'Lord, allow me to first go and bury my father.' But Jesus said to him: 'Follow me, and let the dead bury their dead' "[79] (Matt. 8:21). The obligation to bury the dead, especially one's own parent, was held strictly by Jesus' Jewish contemporaries. In his answer, we find two prescriptions: "Follow me" and "Let the dead bury their dead."

We must be careful to understand the meaning of the expression "Follow me." As explained by the translators of the Ecumenical Bible [*La Bible oecuménique* (Paris: Le Cerf, 2004) —*Trans.*], "In first-century Judaism, the verb 'to follow' normally referred to the respect, obedience, and various services which disciples of rabbis owed to their teacher." According to Edelmann, the verb "to follow" (Greek: *akoloutheô*) can be translated as "to accompany," in the sense of a servant accompanying a master.[80] The second prescription evokes the idea that the coming of the Kingdom is not to be put off. It could be seen as an invitation to disobey divinely given Law. Although some scholars go to great lengths to minimize this aspect, there is no denying that this Saying must have been shocking in the context of Jewish religion of that time. Sanders concludes that "at least in this instance, Jesus meant to say that 'following' him was more important than the ritual prescriptions of the Torah."

The Remission of Sins

This notion has often been misinterpreted through errors in translation. First, we recall that Jesus was accused of blasphemy[81] by the Galilean scribes, on the pretext that he had claimed to have the power of remission of sins.[82] At the other extreme, Christian theologians consider this power as proof of his divinity. Take note that the narrative about healing the paralytic at Capernaum, involving the remission of sins, uses passive language with regard to both the healing and the remission of sins: "Your sins have been forgiven!" In Semitic thought, this less active expression implies that God has been the one who has done the forgiving. The systematic use of this form in the synoptics clearly demonstrates that Jesus made no claim to divine status, nor for authority given him by God. The use of this language indicates that the healing and remission of the paralyzed man's sins have their source in the faith of everyone involved.[83]

The healing here is not so much of paralysis as of the state of sin. But this brings us back to the crucial problem of how to understand Jesus' teaching about "sin." As we have seen, going back beyond the English word, and even farther back than the Septuagint Greek *hamartôloi*, we arrive at the Hebrew word *khatahayn*, which is typically translated as "sin," even in the Jerusalem Bible. But the literal meaning of this word is closer to "error," "missing the mark," or "missing the target." As Edelmann explains clearly, the meaning here is that one has strayed from the goal, or the truth. One has made a mistake, an error. He adds: "The consequences that then result from this are indeed serious, because once the goal has been missed, thought continues to pursue its mistaken direction, and the distortion of the truth can only be further aggravated . . . Sin is certainly a mistake, but in the same sense as a mistake in writing or in arithmetical calculation."[84] Indeed, the gospel writers were correct to choose the Greek word *hamartia*, whose meaning is practically the same as *khatahayn*.

Thus Jesus urges us not to miss the goal, to return to the path toward truth. As Edelmann says, "*Sin* is no longer seen in the perspective of Good and Evil, but in that of *true* and *false*." For some authors, the redemption of sins is foreign to the gospels. But what Jesus appears to preach, according to many, is the forgiveness of error. After all, he himself is quoted while on the cross: "Father, forgive them, for they know not what they do" (Luke 23:34).

If those who crucified Jesus knew not what they did, then this must have been an error on their part, though admittedly a monumental one. In reality, it appears that Paul of Tarsus reintroduced the notion of redemption, or deliverance, in his Letters.[85] This reestablishes the concept of Hebrew scriptures prophets, especially of second Isaiah,[86] Jeremiah,[87] and Micah,[88] or as found in the prayer of David[89] and in Psalms 49 and 130. According to some, this concept arises from a translation of the Greek word *aphésis*, which means "acquittal," "release," or "deliverance." Although people have often associated *remission* with the word *ransom*, the concept of paying for others' sins is not actually in the gospels. One mention of "ransom" for sins does occur in Mark 10:45, which is repeated in Matthew 20:28, but the authenticity of these verses is doubtful, and scholars attribute its insertion to the early Church.[90] As Edelmann points out, a better translation than "redemption of sins" would be "deliverance from error." The latter has no moralizing connotation. What is at stake, and what Jesus is offering, is freedom from our error, from the delusion that holds us in a state of slavery. No ransom is necessary for this!

7

The Good News

The Kingdom of Heaven is a state of the heart—it is not something which happens beyond Earth or after death.

NIETZSCHE, *BEYOND GOOD AND EVIL*

DID JESUS INTEND TO LEAVE A MESSAGE?

Was it Jesus' aim to leave behind a message like the prophets of old, one that he believed had been revealed to him from On High? Some scholars do not believe Jesus saw himself as a part of this traditional pattern. Rather, he wanted to shake people out of a sleep that was leading them inexorably toward a spiritual death. For these scholars, Jesus did not want to convey a message as such, but rather a proclamation of the "Good News" to anyone ready to listen to it. In Greek, the word is *euanggélion,* of which "good news" is a literal translation.

Before beginning our study of what this might mean—based on Sayings with a high probability of historical authenticity—let us first pursue a sense of the historical background of this debate and what

140

is at stake in it. As Armand Abécassis writes: "During the two centuries before Jesus, the very core of the Jewish community in Palestine was involved in the many rival interpretations of biblical writings which had arisen. These often conflicted seriously with each other, to the point of violence. Each of these interpretations of the same Torah claimed supremacy over all the others; yet none of them spoke of creating a 'new religion' which would replace the old one, nor of a 'new testament' in the place of the Old Testament."[1] Any attempt to interpet the Sayings of Jesus must be considered in the context of this spiritual fermentation that characterized Judaic society before and during his lifetime.

The principal difficulty for scholars attempting to reinterpret these texts is the abundance of sources, along with the impression of patchwork in many of them. In our first chapter, we mentioned the existence of a major "neglected" gospel—the Gospel of Thomas—in addition to the four canonical gospels.[2] This document, found among the papyrus codices at Nag Hammadi in Egypt, is more and more recognized by scholars as a text at least equal in authenticity to the canonical gospels. These scholars remind us that this gospel was used in early Christian rites as often as the canonical gospels. A majority consider the Gospel of Thomas the most significant discovery at Nag Hammadi.[3] This intact gospel contains no narrative passages, consisting entirely of 114 Sayings attributed to Jesus. These are intended to transmit wisdom and eternal life to the reader, as proclaimed by Didymus Judas Thomas in the introductory lines: "Whoever finds the meaning of these Sayings will never taste death."[4]

If we have rarely referred to this Gospel of Thomas, that is because its non-narrative text contains no biographical or other material that would further a historical study of the social environment, the life, and the deeds of Jesus of Nazareth. On the other hand, it has crucial value in efforts to understand his message, and we shall refer to its Sayings whenever they offer an alternate perspective or when they shed light on his teaching.

We must recall that all the gospels were written or transcribed by people or groups of people whose identity has never been firmly established. The writers did not witnesses the events related. They wrote in a second language, one that was not Jesus' native language. We must bear in mind, also, that the process of transcribing the gospels began about thirty years after the death of the Master. The process continued over the next forty years, which saw the fall of Jerusalem. During those traumatic times, interpretations of Jesus' message were bound to reflect the different currents of thought in the emergent Judeo-Christian churches. Finally, we must never forget that the gospel authors' or transcribers' understanding of Jesus' teaching was influenced by their own religious convictions, as well as by the theological vision of the particular Judeo-Christian movement they belonged to.

FOR WHOM WAS THE GOOD NEWS INTENDED?

The Lost Sheep of Israel

To what type of audience did Jesus address his message? Did he intend to reach as wide a public as that of the Baptist, including pagans and foreigners? Reading the canonical gospels reveals that he was convinced he had been sent to minister to the lost sheep of Israel. Thus Jesus' message was intended for Jews, even though he had contact with non-Jews, including Samaritans and soldiers of the Roman occupation[5]: "I was sent only to the lost sheep of the house of Israel" (Matt. 15:24).

However, the majority of scholars agree that his teaching was also intended for *all* Jews, including those of the Diaspora. Partisans of the universality of Jesus' teaching often cite the following Sayings extracts, where the expression "all the nations" recurs. There are two in Mark:

And he taught, and said to them, "Is it not written, My house shall be called a house of prayer for all the nations? But you have made it a den of robbers." (Mark 11:17)

And the gospel must first be preached to all nations." (Mark 13:10)

There are also these four passages from Matthew:

Behold, my servant whom I have chosen, my beloved with whom my soul is well pleased. I will put my Spirit upon him, and he shall proclaim justice to the Gentiles. (Matt. 12:18)

And this gospel of the kingdom will be preached throughout the whole world, as a testimony to all nations; and then the end will come. (Matt. 24:14)

When the Son of man comes in his glory, and all the angels with him, then he will sit on his glorious throne. Before him will be gathered all the nations, and he will separate them one from another as a shepherd separates the sheep from the goats. (Matt. 25:31–32)

Go therefore and make disciples of all nations, baptizing them in the name of the Father and of the Son and of the Holy Spirit. (Matt. 28:19)

And, finally, one in Luke:

. . . [A]nd that repentance and forgiveness of sins should be preached in his name to all nations, beginning from Jerusalem. (Luke 24:47)

However, the authenticity of these Sayings is far from accepted by all scholars. Their form indicates that they did not come from Jesus, but rather from homilies preached in the early Church. But an even more important objection is that if Jesus clearly intended his teaching "for all the nations," why was the early Judeo-Christian community divided over whether its mission was also to preach to the Gentiles? The Acts of the Apostles contain many references to such disputes. Paul remained opposed to the Jerusalem church on this issue virtually all his life.

Might Jesus have intended his message at first for Jews, with conversion of the rest of the world to come afterward? This is what Luke appears to suggest in the phrase at the end of verse 47 of his twenty-fourth chapter: "beginning with Jerusalem." Perrot was probably correct to say that "Israel was the primary preoccupation of Jesus." But "primary" does not imply "exclusive." Without accepting it as true, we might consider that Jesus felt if he could reach the simple Jewish people of Galilee with his message, and if it took root and grew among them, it would naturally expand beyond Galilee and even Palestine. This is a convincing explanation, at least in harmony with the universality of Jesus' teachings, which are adamantly opposed to social exclusion.

Nowhere in the "core" of the gospels—that is to say, the parts considered the most "archaic," which have not undergone redaction by ardent proselytes—do we find anything that provides us with strong enough evidence to conclude that Jesus was aware he was engaged in founding a church of universal dimensions. Those who see Jesus as an eschatological visionary claim that founding a durable church would make no sense because the end of the world was at hand. If true, the view would add to the argument, now accepted by many scholars, that the extracts cited above were created by redactors or scribes faced with the apostles' failure to convert the Jewish community and wanting to justify the new direction of their growing success in the pagan world.

The Question of the "Gentiles"

There is little direct information in the Judaic literature of Jesus' time dealing with the accessibility of the Kingdom for pagans or their participation in it. The most widespread belief was that they would be admitted to the Kingdom of God at the end of time, under certain conditions. Sanders cites the prophets who announce that "the wealth of the gentiles will flow towards Jerusalem; the gentile kings will bow down, and their nations will serve Israel, which will be their guiding light." Isaiah specifically says that Yahweh will welcome foreigners. Zechariah predicts that the nations will come to Yahweh, and does not say they will be rejected. And Tobit speaks of mass conversions.

And the foreigners who join Yahweh, to worship him, to love the name of Yahweh, and to be his servants—every one who keeps the Sabbath, and does not profane it, and holds fast my covenant—these I will bring to my holy mountain, and make them joyful in my house of prayer; their burnt offerings and their sacrifices will be accepted on my altar; for my house shall be called a house of prayer for all peoples. (Isa. 56:6–7)

Thus says Yahweh, Lord of the Sabaoth: Peoples shall come, even the inhabitants of many cities; the inhabitants of one city shall go to other cities, saying, "Let us go at once to implore the face of Yahweh, and to implore the face of the Lord of the Sabaoth. I am going!" Many peoples and great nations shall come to seek the Lord of the Sabaoth in Jerusalem, and to implore the face of Yahweh. (Zech. 8:20–23)

Then all the peoples of the earth will turn to fear the Lord God in truth. And they will repudiate their false gods, which have led them into error. . . . And they will bless the God of the ages in righteousness. (Tobit 14:6–7)

But the question remains: What did Jesus think of the Gentiles? Some scholars answer this by quoting the end of the parable of the feast: "[And the king said] 'Go therefore to the thoroughfares, and invite to the marriage feast as many as you find.' And those servants went out into the streets and gathered all whom they found, both bad and good; so the wedding hall was filled with guests" (Matt. 22:9–10).

However, other exegetes point out that different interpretations of this parable might lead to varying conclusions. For them, Jesus' views about pagan access to the Kingdom are clearly expressed in this: "I tell you, many will come from east and west to attend the feast of Abraham, Isaac, and Jacob in the kingdom of heaven, yet the sons of the Kingdom will be thrown into the outer darkness; and there will be weeping, and gnashing of teeth" (Matt. 8:11–12).

Indeed, this content seems more in harmony with Judaic tradition.

Nevertheless, it has an apocalyptic tone, which many scholars consider alien to Jesus' vision of the Kingdom.

Still other scholars find their answer to the question in this Saying from Matthew:

"And this gospel of the Kingdom will be preached throughout the whole world, as a testimony for all nations. And then the end will come" (Matt. 24:14).

But again, the authenticity of most of these verses is generally considered to doubtful. Their eschatology suggests they were probably added by redactors or by the early Church. Several scholars note that these Sayings disagree with the following: "These twelve Jesus sent out, charging them, 'Go nowhere among the Gentiles, and enter no town of the Samaritans, but go rather to the lost sheep of the house of Israel'" (Matt. 10:5–6). He answered, "I was sent only to the lost sheep of the house of Israel" (Matt. 15:24).

Outside of the Sayings and the parables, the canonical gospels mention only two cases when foreigners are healed: the healing of the son of the centurion[6] and the healing of the daughter of the Canaanite woman.[7] These are the only testimonies that tell of healing non-Jews.

In fact, the New Testament texts offer no historical certainty as to Jesus' intentions regarding the Gentiles. What we know from the canonical gospels is that his own ministry was limited to the world of the Israelites. Again, it is possible—even quite plausible—that Jesus shared the conviction of some of his disciples that, in an indeterminate future (perhaps not far off), the Good News would be announced to the whole world. Paul may have based his vocation to preach to the Gentiles on this conviction.

Whatever one might believe about Jesus' intended audience, one important issue goes well beyond the debate: the language that he used. Many scholars are convinced it was a popular form of language, accessible to all. This simplicity contributes to the impression of a universal teaching. But here, too, there is no unanimity among scholars. We have noted the same disagreement about the meaning of the parables. Some exegetes say that in these simple stories and metaphors there is a hidden message, understood only by a small, enlightened number. This ancient tradition regarding the New Testament was in a sense the source of the gnostic teachings.

As we have seen, when Jesus spoke to those he encountered on his way—individuals, small groups, and large crowds—he typically expressed himself through parables, proverbs, and aphorisms. Elaborate speeches, such as the Sermon on the Mount,[8] were rare occurrences. Some exegetes agree with Vermès that this speech shows little of Jesus' usual style, and that it is a collage of Sayings or small pronouncements taken from different contexts and put together by gospel redactors. A major argument supporting this thesis is that the Sayings of Jesus are characterized by a succinct and pithy quality. The parables, too, are (with few exceptions)[9] stories that have been formulated in such a way that they can easily be memorized.

However this may be, when we consider the concern Jesus showed for the lower social classes, we cannot doubt the priority he gave to making his message understandable to illiterate people "for whom the Torah was a complicated text, and whose interpretation was reserved for an elite monopoly."

THE KINGDOM OF GOD

The Good News Is Primarily the Annunciation of the Kingdom

Let us begin this subject by quoting verses 30–34 from chapter 12 of the Gospel of Mark, whose language is close to that used by Matthew and Luke:

> Jesus answered, "The first is, 'Hear, O Israel: The Lord our God, the Lord is one; and you shall love the Lord your God with all your heart, and with all your soul, and with all your mind, and with all your strength.' The second is this, 'You shall love your neighbor as yourself.' There is no other commandment greater than these." And the scribe said to him, "You are right, Teacher; you have truly said that he is one, and there is no other but he; and to love him with all

the heart, and with all the understanding, and with all the strength, and to love one's neighbor as oneself, is much more than all whole burnt offerings and sacrifices." And when Jesus saw that he answered wisely, he said to him, "You are not far from the Kingdom of God." And after that no one dared to ask him any question.

This passage follows some Sayings about the nature of those who are resurrected (neither male nor female, but like angels) that are of doubtful authenticity.[10] Here, however, Jesus answers a scribe's question about which of the Mosaic precepts has primacy.[11] These verses are often quoted as proof that Jesus' central teaching was love of one's neighbor. But as we shall see, this central teaching may well have another aspect—one that is neglected when people quote this passage, leaving out the conclusion: "You are not far from the Kingdom of God."

Virtually all scholars now agree that the annunciation of the Kingdom is at the core of Jesus' teaching, and he gives it his own special meaning. It is the Good News of the Kingdom.[12] We have already noted that the word *kingdom* occurs 107 times in the synoptic gospels. Sometimes it is the Kingdom of God, sometimes the Kingdom of Heaven, and more rarely the Kingdom of the Father.[13] By contrast, the Kingdom of God is mentioned only twice in the Gospel of John.[14] (Interestingly, the latter gospel is the only place where Jesus speaks of the Kingdom as his own.) This language of the Kingdom is virtually absent from the Hebrew scriptures,[15] and occurs rarely in texts written later than the canonical gospels.[16] Thus it was a new expression for those who came to hear Jesus speak.[17]

This does not imply, however, that the concept of the royalty, or reign, of God was foreign to biblical thought—quite the contrary. The relevant Hebrew word *melukah,* or the Aramaic word *malkutha,* is found a number of times in the Bible.[18] The royal, eternal reign of God the Creator over his creation, and over Israel, is a highly developed theme in the scriptures, especially in the Pentateuch and in Isaiah.[19] Expressed in poetic fashion, it was central to the Psalms that were chanted in the synagogue, and which Jesus must have known well. In the second book of Samuel, prophet and founder of the monarchy of Israel, it is written that Yahweh sent the prophet Nathan to tell David that his kingdom was given by God, who made him the leader of his people: "Now you shall say to my servant David, 'Thus says Yahweh, Lord of the Sabaoth: I took you from the pasture, from tending the sheep, that you should be prince over my people, Israel'" (2 Sam. 7:8).

This divine, royal lineage of Israel, of which David is essentially the regent or viceroy, and whose posterity is guaranteed by God, is a subtext of the Jewish eschatological vision of the restoration of this royalty at the end of time:

> When your days are fulfilled and you lie down with your fathers, I will raise up your offspring after you, who shall come forth from your body, and I will establish his kingdom. He shall build a house for my name, and I will establish the throne of his kingdom for ever. (2 Sam. 7:12–13)

> My soul blesses the Lord, the great King, for Jerusalem shall be rebuilt, and also his House, for all the ages. (Tobit 13:15–16)

The intertestamental literature of Jesus' time is also replete with references to the reign of God, and to the eschatological expectation of its arrival. One example from the Qumran discoveries is the Psalms of Solomon.[20] These texts, where belief in a human savior has disappeared, proclaim the expectation of a divine, apocalyptic intervention that is very soon to come, when God, the true King of Israel, will send the Messiah, the son of David, to reunite the twelve tribes and reestablish his eternal reign. The Messiah, a viceroy, is the faithful shepherd of the flocks of the Lord. He is without sin, gifted with extraordinary powers, and his words are like those of the angels.

Strictly speaking, therefore, Jesus is not the first to use the words *melukah* and *malkutha,* nor the expression that is translated as "Kingdom of God."[21] But undeniably, even essentially, we acknowledge that he was the first to base his teaching on the theme of the Kingdom of God (or of Heaven, or of the Father) as a contemporary reality. He constantly speaks of this reality, in aphorisms, in beatitudes, and in parables, as well as in his prayers and in the Sayings regarding the miracles he performs. It is important to emphasize that this new mode of expression is attributed almost exclusively to Jesus himself. It would be a fallacy to suppose that these "Kingdom" expressions, like some others, are retrojections from early Christianity. Indeed, though they occur several times in Paul's writings, he never attributes them to himself. Besides, any such argument would be undermined by the fact that they rapidly disappear from the language of the Johannine school, as well as from most of the other writings of the New Testament.

Still, the main question remains: What did Jesus mean when he spoke of the Kingdom? Did he refer to some future event? Was he speaking of something "other worldly"? Or did he mean a Kingdom of the here and now?

What Did Jesus Mean by the "Kingdom of God"?

After twenty centuries of discussion on this subject, we see a striking contrast between the almost unanimous scholarly agreement that the Kingdom Jesus speaks of is central to his teaching and the marked lack of agreement about what he meant by "Kingdom." At first glance, the disagreement appears to stem from the fact that only two passages in the gospels show Jesus accepting the royal title of Messiah (Mark 14:62 and 8:29–30), and their authenticity is contested. Indeed, this title was prolifically applied by the early Church, which would discredit the authenticity of these passages if we apply the criterion of discontinuity.

But another important reason exists for this disagreement about what Jesus meant: The parables were his principal vehicle for speaking of the Kingdom, and they are subject to divergent interpretations.

Thus, the key question is still about what Jesus meant when he used the expression that becomes, translated from Greek into English, "the Kingdom" (". . . of God, of Heaven, of the Father . . ."). We must remember that the chief accusation against Jesus by Roman power, which resulted in his crucifixion, was based on his annunciation of a Kingdom. Some condemned him for planning to establish this Kingdom by having himself proclaimed King of the Jews. If true, this would constitute a direct threat to Roman power, punishable by death.

The words *kingdom* and *king,* as used by his judges when they linked these words to him, to all intents and purposes had nothing to do with what Jesus intended to convey when he spoke of the Kingdom. The Greek word used in the gospels is *basileïa,* usually translated as "kingdom." But the expression Kingdom of God *(balileïa to Théou)* can also mean the "reign of God," as it clearly does in the Lord's Prayer (Matt. 6:10). In English (and in other languages), the word *kingdom* refers to a territory governed by a king. Jesus' notion of the nature of God, as revealed in those synoptic passages whose authenticity is least in doubt, correlates poorly with the image of a kingdom in the worldly meaning of the term. Nevertheless, the notion of divine royalty recurs often in the Jewish scriptures, whether associated with the kingdom of Israel or not.

Historically, this word is associated with a concept of rule and domination in total contradiction to the qualifications referred to by Jesus when he speaks of the Father and the Kingdom. From a reading of the parables that illustrate the nature of the Kingdom, clearly Jesus meant something entirely different when he spoke of it to his disciples and others. The parables are richly varied and typically begin with expressions such as "The Kingdom of God is like . . . " or "To what shall we liken the Kingdom of God?" or again, "What parable shall we use for it?" (Mark 4:30). This demonstrates the difficulty of finding a word or phrase that conveys the full meaning of Kingdom.

When Is the Kingdom of God Coming?

This question is an inevitable corollary to the question of what the Kingdom of God means. The two questions are interdependent, for any answer to one must affect the answer to the other. If we conclude that the meaning of the Kingdom pertains to inner dimensions of reality, then the question of when it will come loses most of its relevance.

Conversely, if we see the Kingdom as pertaining to outer reality, then it becomes important to ask whether it speaks of a historical future or an eschatological one—in other words, whether something is going to happen in the course of history or at the end of time. To get a picture of the various positions scholars take in this debate, we can group them into two general categories.

First, we have the traditional school, which can be characterized as the *eschatological* school, of which E. P. Sanders is a leading proponent.[22] According to these scholars, when Jesus speaks of the Kingdom, he refers to a future event. They hold that his Kingdom will come at the end of time, whether or not that time is near. They base their arguments on the older eschatological tradition that we discussed earlier, and most often cite the following Sayings as evidence:

From that time Jesus began to preach, saying, "Repent, for the kingdom of heaven is at hand." (Matt. 4:17)

I tell you, many will come from east and west to attend the feast of Abraham, Isaac, and Jacob in the Kingdom of Heaven. (Matt. 8:11)

And preach as you go, saying that the Kingdom of Heaven is at hand." (Matt. 10:7)

Then the righteous will shine like the sun in the Kingdom of the Father. Whoever who has ears, let them hear." (Matt. 13:43)

Truly, I say to you, there are some standing here who will not taste death before they see the Son of man coming in his Kingdom. (Matt. 16:28)

So also, when you see these things taking place, you know that the Kingdom of God is near.[23] (Luke 21:31)

The opposing camp can be described as the school of *contemporaneity,*[24] which holds that it is inappropriate to speak of the Kingdom of God in terms of time, because it does not refer to a historical event, future or otherwise. Instead, it is a symbolic expression that Jesus deliberately used to evoke a profound, inner experience.[25]

As we shall see in the following sections, a number of scholars consider it implausible that Jesus would hold a dual vision of the Kingdom: one accessible within every human being and another meta-historical Kingdom coming at the end of time. No doubt this at least partly explains why fewer scholars today support an eschatological view of the Kingdom: It seems incompatible with Jesus' teaching of a Kingdom "within us." In any case, a study of these rival conceptions is important to gain a grasp of the meaning of the Kingdom. A deeper examination of their foundations in biblical tradition will help to clear up misunderstandings on this subject.

Eschatological Interpretations of the Kingdom

Following the early-twentieth-century work of J. Weiss[27] and of Albert Schweitzer,[28] and continuing down to relatively recent times, the eschatological interpretation of the Kingdom was virtually uncontested by most biblical scholars. It was based on a conviction, which Jesus supposedly shared with many of his contemporaries, that the Kingdom of God is not an event in this world, but rather will come at the end of time, at the end of history. Many Jews believed that God had promised to send a savior of the lineage of David at the end of time, one who would reunite the twelve tribes of Israel and establish the Kingdom of Heaven for all eternity. This intervention of the Messiah would happen suddenly and with great violence. This interpretation, an aspect of traditional Judaism, is both eschatological and apocalyptic. It was adopted by disciples and Christians of the early Church, based on a number of biblical verses that gospel redactors had put in the mouth of Jesus.

Supporters of the eschatological and apocalyptic vision often open their arguments by quoting the beginning of the Gospel of Mark: "Now after John was arrested, Jesus went to Galilee, preaching the gospel of

God, and saying, 'The time is fulfilled, and the kingdom of God is at hand; repent, and believe in the Good News'" (Mark 1:14–15).

They also cite the beginning of the Lord's Prayer, the words of Jesus par excellence: "Our Father who art in Heaven, hallowed be thy name; thy Kingdom come'" (Matt. 6:9–10).

They propose that Jesus began his public mission by proclaiming the Kingdom would soon come, continuing the preaching of the Baptist in his own way. In his renowned instructions on how to pray, Jesus apparently says to ask the Father daily for his Kingdom to come. Whatever the nuances of interpretation, one thing is clear: The Kingdom of God has *not yet* come. It must come, "but no one knows the day or the hour. Therefore hold yourselves in readiness, for the Son of Man will come at a time when you do not expect it" (Matt 24:44).

Another major argument in favor of the eschatological interpretation is based on the famous Saying that Mark attributes to Jesus during the Last Supper, when he initiates the disciples in the Eucharist:[29] "Truly, I tell you that I will drink no more of the fruit of the vine until that day when I drink the new wine in the Kingdom of God" (Mark 14:25).

Another previously cited verse is still more explicit. It implies a "meta-historical" vision, where Matthew (or his redactor) has Jesus say: "I tell you, many will come from east and west to attend the feast of Abraham, Isaac, and Jacob in the Kingdom of Heaven, yet the sons of the Kingdom will be thrown into the outer darkness; and there will be weeping, and gnashing of teeth" (Matt. 8:11–12).

A last example may be found in this verse from Matthew: "It is not by saying 'Lord, Lord,' to me that someone shall enter the Kingdom of Heaven, but in doing the will of my Father who is in heaven" (Matt. 7:21).

The message that emerges from these Sayings is that the Kingdom of God is not of this time, nor of this world (in spite of its having existed for all eternity). It is in Heaven, and beyond time, an extratemporal Kingdom that we will know only after death.

However, the passage about the feast, as well as other gospel passages, speaks (implicitly or explicitly) of the establishment of the Kingdom on this earth—at the end of time to be sure, but still within some concept of history.[30] Sanders believes that Jesus never defined precisely what he meant by the Kingdom—a word that can have more than one meaning. However this may be, many authorities agree on one basic assumption: The Kingdom means the reign of God, a "sphere" in which God's power is realized. According to Sanders, the tragic outcome of Jesus' mission does not support the "contemporaneity" interpretation of the Kingdom. He writes: "While maintaining that the Kingdom (in the sense of the power of God) is already active in the world, Jesus also has the expectation of an imminent and direct intervention of God in history, with the elimination of evil and evildoers, the building of a glorious new Temple, and the reunion of the tribes of Israel, in which he and his disciples are to play a decisive role."[31]

This interpretation—which remains an eschatological one, in spite of its subtleties—raises a multifaceted question that some scholars believe has not been answered by proponents such as Sanders: What did Jesus believe to be his own role in the Kingdom? And how did he conceive the relation between the Father and the Son of Man in the Kingdom? A second aspect of this question is: What did believers in the imminence of the Kingdom consider to be Jesus' role in it? Regarding the first aspect, some gospel passages suggest that Jesus was speaking of *his* Kingdom: "You are those who have stayed with me in my trials; and I assign to you, as my Father assigned to me, a Kingdom, that you may eat and drink at my table in my Kingdom, and sit on thrones judging the twelve tribes of Israel" (Luke 22:28–29).

In a parallel passage, Jesus speaks of the throne of the Son of Man: "Jesus said to them, 'Truly, I say to you, in the new world, when the Son of man shall sit on his glorious throne, you who have followed me will also sit on twelve thrones, judging the twelve tribes of Israel'" (Matt. 19:28).

And of course there is this Saying: "Truly, I say to you, there are some standing here who will not taste death before they see the Son of man coming in his kingdom" (Matt. 16:28).

Assuming that the expression Son of Man is Jesus' self-designation, equivalent to saying "I," we might conclude that these two Sayings refer to the same Kingdom as the Saying from Luke 22:26—that is, Jesus was speaking of *his* Kingdom.

But during the Last Supper, he speaks of the Kingdom of God: "Truly, I tell you that I will drink no more of the fruit of the vine until that day when I drink the new wine in the Kingdom of God" (Mark 14:25).

The parallel passage in Luke is essentially the same: ". . . for I tell you that from now on I shall not drink of the fruit of the vine until the Kingdom of God comes" (Luke 22:18).

Sanders claims that "[u]nless he intended to deliberately mislead his disciples, who were constantly hoping for the coming of the Kingdom, Jesus was not speaking symbolically. . . . The vision of Jesus which clearly emerges from the gospel texts is his belief in the restoration of the Kingdom of Israel." But does this refer to a historical restoration? That impression does not emerge from a careful reading of all the gospels. We are faced with two different kinds of Kingdom. This impression of ambiguity may well be a legacy of the gospel writers' own visions.

How did Jesus' disciples understand the meaning of the Kingdom, and what did they consider to be their Master's place in it? "The disciples' vision of the Kingdom must not have been very different from that of the Master, even though his vision had nothing in common with the one which fed the subversive agitation of extremist Zealots."[32] Perhaps like "moderate Zealots," most of the disciples saw Jesus as the Messiah, and hoped that he would return to restore the Kingdom—but on a different plane from that of the actual world. Sanders assumes that when the disciples spoke of the Kingdom with the Master, they meant the Kingdom of which he would be the viceroy. "Even later, the disciples' expectations, which had existed before Jesus' death, and had been transformed by the 'apparitions' of the Christ, would have been incompatible with any political, military, or nationalist agendas."[33]

On the other hand, although some Zealots saw Jesus as a Messiah who would restore the Kingdom on a higher plane than this world, the extreme fundamentalists among them—perhaps including two of his Zealot disciples, Simon and Judas Iscariot—were convinced that Jesus would soon intervene to establish the Kingdom of Israel on earth.[34]

Representing an intermediate ground between these opposed apocalyptic and contemporaneous interpretations of the Kingdom, three scholars' views are worth mentioning inasmuch as they help us to gain a more comprehensive view of the question. First is Perrin, who concludes in his work on the Kingdom that it is inappropriate to speak of the Kingdom of God in terms of "present" or "future," because it has nothing to do with an event in historical time. Instead, it is a symbolic expression that Jesus consciously employed for its rich evocative power.[35] Then we read Scott, whose views are close to Perrin's, who writes that Jesus "used the word 'Kingdom' in a symbolic way, to express his own experience."[36] Finally, Bultmann felt that "the coming of the Kingdom is not an event which can be located in the course of time, nor something which will happen at a given moment, and with respect to which human beings are to either adopt some sort of attitude, or remain indifferent."[37]

The Contemporaneity Thesis

With the work of C. H. Dodd, the first serious cracks began to appear in the eschatological consensus. In his book *Parables of the Kingdom*,[38] he argues that the *eschaton* had already arrived with the coming of Jesus.[39] Following Dodd, Perrot began to write of the "realized eschatology," which both opposed to the "eschatology being realized," favored later by Jeremias.[40] Today, an increasing number of exegetes and scholars accord a fundamental significance to this Saying from Luke: "And above all, let no one say: 'Here it is!' or 'There it is!' For truly, the Kingdom of God is within you"[41] (Luke 17:21).

As Edelmann points out, traditional translations often stated that the Kingdom of God "is among you," or "amidst you." The Greek text reads: *entos hymôn estin*. The primary meaning of the word *entos* is "within" or "inside," but the same word can also mean "among."

Hence the choice of the translator is crucial here. "Either the Kingdom of God is an inner reality, a vertical dimension which concerns one's own being, or else it is a reality centered on the person of Jesus . . . which would give preference to a horizontal dimension."[42] In the first case, the translation is "within," whereas in the second case, it is "among" or "amid." This ambiguity may go back to the Aramaic *legau men,* which also can mean both "within" and "among."[43] Edelmann reminds us, also, that "Middle-Eastern culture made no radical separation between body and mind, between inner and outer." Furthermore—and this fact takes on great importance in this context—whenever Luke wanted to speak specifically of something that was "amidst," he used the Greek word *meso,* not the word *entos.*[44]

Three verses in the Gospel of Thomas speak of the Kingdom in terms that are close to those in Luke. One of the first Sayings in Thomas offers an illustration of this ambiguity of Jesus' native Aramaic:

> If those who guide you say: "Look, the Kingdom is in the Sky," then the birds are closer than you. If they say: "Look, it is in the sea," then the fish already know it. The Kingdom is inside you, and it is outside you. (Gospel of Thomas, Logion 3)

The other two Sayings from Thomas are:

> What you are waiting for has already come, but you do not see it. (Gospel of Thomas, Logion 51)

> The disciples asked him: "When will the Kingdom come?" Jesus answered: "It will not come by watching for it. No one will be saying, 'Look, here it is,' or: 'Look, there it is!' The Kingdom of the Father is spread out over the whole earth, and people do not see it." (Gospel of Thomas, Logion 113)

Authors who advocate, or lean toward, the contemporaneity of the Kingdom emphasize that Jesus spoke of a state of deep, intimate experience, which must be discovered within oneself. They also cite Matthew 12:28 and Luke 11:20 (both from the common Q source), though in this case a temporal dimension can be detected: "If it is through God's finger that I drive out demons, then it is because the Kingdom of God has come unto you."

Edelmann writes that "in the older translations, whether the Pshitta, the Vulgate, or the oldest Latin versions, it says that 'the Kingdom of God is within'; and this was also how Origen and Gregory of Nyssa understood it. This inwardness is not a place or a location, it is a state."

Along with others, the above scholars believe that the eschatological interpretation of the Kingdom is in discord with the general teaching of Jesus and reflects a vision developed by the early Church. Some of them also cite this Saying from Matthew 11:12: "From the days of John the Baptist to the present, the Kingdom of Heaven has suffered violence, and men of violence take it by force." According to them, this passage shows that Jesus was opposed to the establishment of the Kingdom by violence, preached by the most fanatic or zealous. But other authors cite a Saying from Luke that might contradict the one from Matthew: "The law and the prophets were until John; since then, the good news of the kingdom of God is announced, and every one enters it violently" (Luke 16:16).

In spite of the lack of clarity, these two Sayings nevertheless appear to say the same thing: The Kingdom cannot be accomplished through violence. These scholars conclude that the Kingdom of which Jesus speaks is available to us, and not in some indeterminate future, nor at the end of time.

The same scholars also rightly point out that, unlike the views of those who followed Theudas or Judas of Galilee—rebels who were arrested during or after the deaths of their leaders—the actions of Jesus and his disciples would not have been seen by the Romans as a real threat to established order. What irritated them was Jesus' ability to draw crowds and speak to them in a way that his hearers might interpret as a promise to restore the Kingdom of Israel. Pontius Pilate's interrogation of

Jesus furnishes outstanding proof of this.[45] These authors argue convincingly that if the Kingdom of which Jesus spoke was not in itself worrisome to Roman power, this was because it had no political implications. The overall implications of this militate against the eschatological and apocalyptic interpretations of the Kingdom. Hence, in refraining—or ceasing—to speak of a future reign to be expected, Jesus separated his teachings from the beliefs of the Baptist—which, however, were shared by some of his own disciples, as well as by Paul and by the early Church.

Two other types of argument, which seem convincing, exist for the contemporaneity of the Kingdom. First, we have the argument (often used in other contexts) that we cannot make the gospels say more than they do. As we noted in chapter 2, the gospel writers quoted Jesus in Greek, which was not the native language of at least three of the four canonical writers. This has probably been a source of many errors—from translating Aramaic into Greek and from translating Greek into Latin and other languages. We should not underestimate either the importance or the frequency of these errors.[46] The words involved may have several meanings, and different translations can lead to different interpretations.[47]

A good illustration is the prayer in Matthew 6:10 (paralleled by Luke 11:2), in which the Greek word qualifying the Kingdom can be translated as the traditional "thy Kingdom come" but can also be translated as "thy Kingdom be manifest," or "appear."[48] Thus we can conclude that one of the most famous of all Jesus' Sayings, known as the Lord's Prayer, is not necessarily a prayer to God for the realization of his Kingdom in the future. It may be a prayer for the manifestation of the Kingdom here and now. From this point of view, as Perrot points out, it is interesting to compare the words of the Lord's Prayer with those of the ritual blessing of the Kaddish[49]: "May your Name be glorified! . . . May he make his kingdom reign during our lives, in our days, and in the life of the House of Israel; may this be soon, and in a time which is near."

Another argument for contemporaneity is linguistic: Because the future tense does not exist in Aramaic verbs, it follows that Greek and Latin writings, which do have that tense, and have Jesus using it to speak of a Kingdom that will come in the future, are by no means reliable reports of what he really said. Bearing this in mind, André Chouraqui translates Matthew 7:21 literally as, "Not all those who cry 'Yahve, Yahve,' enter the Kingdom of the heavens," and Matthew 19:23 as, "Amen, I tell you: it is difficult for a rich man to enter the Kingdom of the heavens."[50]

Many other Sayings have this same ambiguity, which undermines the credibility of any claim to have found the one, true meaning of Jesus' Kingdom.

Finally, other scholars often refer to this Saying of Jesus, according to Thomas: "Jesus saw some infants being nursed at the breast. He said to his disciples: 'These nursing infants are like those who enter the Kingdom'" (Gospel of Thomas, Logion 22).

The sheer abundance of Sayings about the Kingdom and the variety of sources from which they originate argue in favor of several possible interpretations. However, the hypothesis of contemporaneity has stronger arguments, as well as a greater consistency with other Sayings, including those about justice, as well as the beatitudes. It now appears to be the most favored of the possible meanings of the Kingdom.[51]

The Kingdom in the Parables

In many of Jesus' parables about the meaning of the Kingdom, we find an implication of its presence on earth, here and now. An example is the parable of the yeast: "The Kingdom of Heaven is like yeast which a woman takes, and mixes with three measures of flour, until it all rises" (Matt. 13:33).

This view is supported by a number of Jesus' other parables about the Kingdom. As we noted earlier, he preferred to use parables in his talks to simple people, the "people of the earth." The message he wanted to communicate about the Kingdom was not a simple one. This has been amply demonstrated here. Even the disciples may not have have understood it very well. This is why we find so many Kingdom parables in the synoptic gospels; not all of them are mentioned here, especially those whose authenticity is dubious.[52]

Luke's parables of the lost sheep and the lost coin[53] are allegories intended to illustrate the preceding verses in which Jesus is surrounded by tax collectors and other pariahs. These parables illustrate the importance that the Kingdom of God accords to those who are lost and then found, and the immense joy that is felt on their return.

Luke places the parable of the prodigal son in this same chapter 15, for the same reasons. Jesus wants to convey the vast compassion of the Father, in the Kingdom, for the son who had strayed and whose return is an occasion for extraordinary rejoicing. This is one of the most famous of all parables (along with the story of the good Samaritan). It has inspired an enormous variety of commentaries. But the most common recurring theme is in accord with Luke's message about Jesus' well-attested-to sympathy for outcasts.

The story of the good Samaritan is considered by a majority of specialists to have the highest authenticity rating of all the parables. Luke places it in chapter 10 to illustrate what the notion of "neighbor" should mean for a Galilean, or, rather, a Judaean. The parable is a response to a "legalist" about who *his* neighbor is. Loving one's neighbor as oneself, along with love of God, is one of the two most important of the Mosaic commandments. Note that verse 27 of this chapter speaks of loving one's neighbor as oneself, whereas verse 37 speaks of compassion for others.[54] For today's readers, realize that our word *compassion* has lost much of the power that the original word carried in the Hebrew scriptures. There, the term *divine compassion* is employed as an alternative to *love*.[55] We should bear in mind, also, the animosity and even hatred that existed between Judaeans and Samaritans. Hence the act of compassion described in this parable, associated with a Samaritan who came to the aid of a Judaean left to die in a ditch, one who had been treated with indifference by two members of the priestly class, on the road from Jerusalem to Jericho.[56]

In contrast to the complexity and difficulty that surrounds the question of comtemporaneity vs. eschatology, these few parables provide clear teachings about the nature of the Kingdom: love of one's neighbor, the importance of the return of those who are lost, and the compassion and love of the Father. A still deeper aspect of the meaning of the Kingdom is conveyed in the well-known passages on the beatitudes. According to the Evangelists, Jesus proclaimed them during a sermon on the flanks of a mountain where a crowd had come to listen to him.[57] Here, we quote three of the beatitudes given by Luke, which are considered to be the most authentic:[58] "You who are poor, rejoice, for the Kingdom of God is yours. Rejoice, you who are now hungry, for you shall be fed. Rejoice, you who now weep, for you will laugh" (Luke 6:20–21).

Luke has appended four curses, or condemnations, to these beatitudes.[59] One school of critical exegesis holds that neither the form nor the content of these condemnations corresponds with Jesus' style, nor with the philosophy of his teaching, which avoids harsh judgments, to say nothing of condemnations. But others feel that these condemnations were necessary to create an ethical balance with the blessings of the beatitudes. They are especially directed against the rich, which is a recurrent theme in the gospels. Nevertheless, the majority opinion among scholars is that long speeches were not typical of Jesus, and if some of the beatitudes reflect authentically the teaching or philosophy of the Master, they were likely spoken by him on several different occasions.

Access to the Kingdom

Edelmann[60] points out that for Jesus, access to the Kingdom is gained through a radical inner transformation (a turnaround, the literal meaning of *repentance*). Everyone is invited to its feast[61] and no one is excluded. But the universality of this access does not mean it is unconditional: "*If* someone keeps my word, then he or she will never taste death." The "if" is definitely present. The Gospel of Thomas begins with these words: "Jesus said: 'Whoever lives the interpretation of these words will no longer taste death'" (Gospel of Thomas, Logion 1). And Logion 28 contains these surprising words:

> Jesus said: "I stood in the midst of the world, and revealed myself
> to them in the flesh. I found them all intoxicated. Not one of them
> was thirsty, and my soul grieved for the children of humanity, for

they are blind in their hearts. They do not see. They came naked into the world, and naked they will leave it. At this time, they are intoxicated. When they have vomited their wine, they will return to themselves."

Not everyone answers the call of Jesus. Many abandon it. The way of radical turnaround is an arduous one, full of obstacles and dangers. Says Edelmann, "The occasions for distraction are plentiful, as are rationalizations for leaving the way. Most often, a long period of asceticism is necessary in order to arrive at such a result."[62]

For judgment I came into this world . . .[63] (John 9:39)

Whoever admits to being blind but can and does make the effort will see. The degree of demand made on each person is according to his capacity, as the parable of the talents reminds us.[64] "From those who have much received, much will be demanded."

THE MESSAGE OF LOVE

The reader may well wonder why, in a study of Jesus and his teaching, we have taken this long to broach the subject of love. Is not Love the very core of Jesus' message? Is it not the most recurrent word in Catholic prayers and liturgy? It is inseparable from the Kingdom, and is in a sense the theme of it. But curiously, the word *love* (whether as noun or verb) appears relatively rarely in the Sayings of Jesus. It is as if he intended to be sparing in his use of the word. A careful reading of the Bible, including both Old and New Testaments, shows how difficult it is to understand the meaning accorded to this word. A striking fact is that *love* occurs as a noun only nine times in the Sayings of the canonical gospels. In the synoptic Sayings, the word (*agape* in Greek) occurs only three times, once in Matthew 24:12 and twice in Luke.[65] It occurs six times in John—interestingly, the latter uses the word *kingdom* only three times.[66] This provides a significant contrast with the previously mentioned frequency of the word *kingdom,* which occurs 111 times in the canonical gospels.

As for the verb form *(agapaw),* it appears eighteen times in the canonical gospels, seven of which are in the famous Saying about the precept/commandment about love, which is repeated, in more or less the same terms, by all four gospels.[67]

The Gospel of John contains three Sayings on this subject.[68] The authenticity of the first is suspect, since love of one's neighbor is a major precept of the Hebrew scriptures. The love of which John has Jesus speak almost always involves the Father.

Would Jesus himself have preferred the word *compassion?* No, because this word never appears in the Sayings. We do find the adjective *compassionate,* but only twice, and both are in the same verse from Luke.[69] But *to love* . . . is this not the very culmination of the way of the Kingdom?

JESUS DID NOT PLACE HIMSELF AT THE CENTER OF HIS TEACHING

In the decidedly Christocentric Gospel of John, we should not be surprised to find almost a hundred references to the Father, mostly in association with the Son.

I and the Father are one. (John 10:30)

"The Father loves the Son, and has given all things into his hand." (John 3:35)

In this gospel, Jesus speaks of "*my*[70] Father," often followed by "who is in heaven." It is important to note here that in the Sayings that come from the oldest sources, Jesus never uses such language—he never speaks of the Father in terms of the first-person possessive pronoun. Indeed, as we have already seen, in the least contested Sayings, Jesus does not present himself as the central theme of any teaching or event.

He never offers himself as someone to be venerated, as the Son of the Almighty, and still less as God incarnate. This is a major point, and a conclusion that the most recent historical research insists upon.

All the themes regarding the divine nature of the Messiah, so often repeated in the Johannine and Pauline traditions, are absent in the synoptic gospels. The Good News that Jesus came to announce to the poor, the forsaken, and the outcast is clearly centered on the Father. It implies a self-effacing humility on the part of Jesus, a servant of the Most High, of "the Father of us all." In contrast with the Johannine gospel, the synoptics clearly present a Jesus who refuses to become an object of worship. As he rebuked the devil on the occasion of his temptation in the desert: "It is written: You shall worship the Lord your God, and him only shall you serve" (Luke 4:8 and Matt. 4:1).

In other multiply attested Sayings, Jesus speaks of "*your* Father" and sometimes says "Father." These expressions dispel any impression of exclusivity in his relationship with God:

> All things have been delivered to me by *my* Father; and no one knows who the Son is except the Father, or who the Father is except the Son and any one to whom the Son chooses to reveal him. (Luke 10:22)

> Whoever has seen me has seen *the* Father. (John 14:9)

> For *the* Father loves the Son, and shows him all that he himself is doing; and greater works than these will he show him, that you may marvel. For as *the* Father raises the dead and gives them life, so also the Son gives life to whom he will. (John 5:20–21)

> Be compassionate, as *your* Father is compassionate. (Luke 6:36)

> *Your* Father knows well what you need, before you ask it of him. (Matt. 6:8)

WAS JESUS THE MESSIAH, THE SON OF GOD?

Exegetical research has established that the Aramaic expression translated as "Son of Man" signifies an attitude of modesty, and is often the rough equivalent of saying "I" in modern languages. Moreover, many scholars note that this expression occurs most frequently in Sayings with a strong apocalyptic content, whose authenticity is doubtful.

True, on several occasions in the canonical gospels, the disciples, especially Simon-Peter, accord Jesus the titles Messiah and Son of God.[71] The words attributed to Jesus regarding such exaltations do not always tell us whether or not he accepted them. Perhaps these responses should be classed along with other retrojections or creations of the early Church. By contrast, the authenticity of the Sayings in which Jesus ascribes a divine ancestry to all human beings, including himself, has not been impugned. In the Bible, such an ancestry was attributed to the people of Israel, and to all righteous people.

Another important consensus among scholars is that in the Sayings that have multiple attestations, or an otherwise high degree of authenticity, we find no evidence that would lead us to conclude, without ambiguity of language, that Jesus proclaimed himself the Messiah or the Son of God.[72] Some authors have observed that the Passion narratives contain Sayings in which he did proclaim himself as such. We shall examine these in detail in the next chapter, but we can already assert that none of them constitutes historical evidence that he actually said this.

The preceding conclusions are not presented as "proof" that Jesus was *not* the Messiah, nor the Son of God, nor that he refused to be recognized as such. What they demonstrate is that scholarship has not found convincing historical evidence for the proposition that Jesus proclaimed himself the Messiah (Mashiah in Hebrew, Christos in Greek), or as the Son of God. But, along with Perrot,[73] we can confirm that some of the earliest Judeo-Christians—including Paul, on several occasions—gave him the title of Christ and the Son of God. Even so, did not Jesus himself say that we are all sons of God?[74]

8

The Arrest and
Execution of Jesus

Here we arrive at the gospel sections that stand on the shakiest historical ground[1] because the narratives that comprise them, known as the Passion, are not based on sufficiently reliable sources. As we have already pointed out, the main events of the Passion were not witnessed by any of Jesus' disciples, who, according to the synoptic gospels, had fled for their lives.[2] With the exception of Judas, who is said to have committed suicide, they did not meet again until some weeks afterward.

Several exegetes have chosen to ignore this serious gap, however, and confer the same authenticity to Passion narratives as to other gospel narratives that have multiple attestations.[3] To bolster their arguments, they mention the presence of women who were said to have witnessed Jesus' walk up Calvary (Golgotha) hill, to the place where the cross was planted. Others base their arguments on the passages in the Gospel of John referring to the presence of Peter, accompanied by another disciple near the place where Jesus was judged, when he denied knowing his Master. John 19:26 also mentions the presence of the "disciple he [Jesus] loved" at Golgotha, next to the mother of Jesus, at the moment of his death.[4] Other than these sources (which have no outside support), there is no mention of any of these people's presence at the trial. Yet this trial constitutes the historical key to the entire Passion story, as we shall see.

Before taking a look at what different authors have said about the arrest and death of Jesus, let us get a sense of the historical context of these events to help us better understand the attitudes of the characters in the story, including the civil and religious authorities.

After the death of Herod the Great, in 4 B.C.E., a period of turmoil erupted in Judaea, brought about partly by internal struggles related to the royal succession. During this period, agitators appeared, attracting dissidents and fomenting armed uprisings of varying severity. Roman clumsiness (for example, the ostentatious presence of their troops beside the holy places) seems to have triggered riots in Jerusalem, especially during the Passover or Pentecost (or Shabuoth, the Jewish festival), which attracted huge crowds to the city. Varus was summoned from Syria, with three legions and auxiliary troops. He reestablished order in typical Roman fashion. During this time, there were several rival pretenders to the throne.

Josephus offers details about the three outstanding agitators of the period. The first was Judas, son of Ezekiel,[5] whom Herod had put to death. Judas was known for a brutal attempt to claim the throne for himself at Sephoris, commanding a large number of rebels.[6] Sephoris was burned by the Romans and its inhabitants enslaved. The second Messianic pretender was Simon, a slave of Herod, who led an army of brigands in Perea. He burned the royal palace of Jericho, sacked other royal residences, and claimed the title of king without the approval of Caesar.[8] The third was Athrongaeus, a shepherd of huge size and Herculean power. He also led a band of armed men, aided by four brothers, and claimed the title king of Judaea. Since no one challenged him at first, he managed to keep the title for a time.[9] The careers of these three agitators were obviously brief and tragic. How was Jesus viewed, given this climate of latent insurrection? It is likely he could only have been viewed with suspicion by the authorities, whether Roman or Jewish, for the mere fact that he attracted large crowds.

THE DRAMA APPROACHES

When Was Jesus Arrested?

A primary task for researchers is to determine as precisely as possible the dates of the episodes that immediately preceded Jesus' arrest, including the Last Supper. There is no consensus about the details of these events. What we do know with a high degree of certainty is that, according to various overlapping sources, some of which are independent of Christian texts, Jesus probably died during the reign of Tiberius (14–37 C.E.), when Caiaphas was high priest (18–36 C.E.). Now, the Gospel of Luke sets the beginning of the Baptist's ministry in the fifteenth year of the reign of Tiberius.[10] This would mean that Jesus' ministry began shortly afterward, when he was just over thirty years old.[11] Since we do not know exactly how long his public ministry lasted (eighteen months according to the synoptics and three years according to John), we can deduce that the death of Jesus occurred sometime between 29 and 33 C.E., based on chronological information from the life of Paul.

Given this much, several contradictory hypotheses have been advanced, all of them based on astronomy. Their disagreement is a reflection of that existing within the gospel tradition itself. We know that the synoptics and John all state that Jesus died on the day of Preparation, the eve of the Sabbath, a Friday.

> Since it was the day of Preparation, in order to prevent the bodies from remaining on the cross on the Sabbath (for that Sabbath was a high day), the Jews asked Pilate that their legs might be broken and that they might be taken away. So the soldiers came and broke the legs of the first, and of the second who had been crucified with him; but when they came to Jesus and saw that he was already dead, they did not break his legs. (John 19:31)

Now, according to the Johannine tradition, Jesus died in the afternoon of the fourteenth day of Nissan,[12] a day when sheep were immolated at the Temple.[13] In contradiction to this, the synoptics say that Jesus took the Passover meal at the Last Supper, after the appearance of the first star, which would have been the fifteenth day of Nissan.[14] In any case, this means that he would have been crucified and died some-time during the Passover festival. It is difficult to believe that the authorities would have waited until the festival had begun to arrest, condemn, and crucify Jesus, a man who had great influence among the crowds gathered in Jerusalem. Also, Mark says that the chief priests and scribes, fearing a popular reaction, did not want him to be arrested during the festival: "It was then two days before the Passover and the festival of Unleavened Bread. And the chief priests and the scribes were seeking how to arrest him by stealth, and kill him; and they said, "'Not during the festival, lest there be tumult among the people'" (Mark 14:1–2).

Like many other historians, Perrot gives preference to the Johannine chronology because, according to astronomical calculations, Jesus' death would have taken place on April 7, 30 C.E.,[15] a date that would be in more accord with the chronology of his life. If we accept the fifteenth of Nissan date, on the other hand, the astronomical calcu-lation yields the date of April 27, 31 C.E. Whatever the case may be, we have reason to believe that both the synoptic and the Johannine tradi-tions were influenced by theological vision more than by a concern for precise dating. It is no small problem to establish a precise chronology based on the random inconsistencies of the Hebrew calendar, whose correspondence with astronomy can be uncertain, also. According to Perrot, the most significant fact in this controversy, of which we can be fairly certain, is that the symbolism of Passover during the Last Supper dominates the synoptic narratives, whereas in the Johannine tradition, it is the symbolism of salvation from the sacrifice of the lamb, associ-ated with Jesus' death.

In the Gospel of John, the meal before Passover[16] is not described as a Passover meal, properly speaking. "Now, before the feast of the Passover, when Jesus knew that his hour had come to depart from this world to the Father, having loved his own who were in the world, he loved them to the end. And during supper, when the devil had already put it into the heart of Judas Iscariot, Simon's son, to betray him . . . " (John 13:1–2).

The gospel writer, however, has the death of Jesus, "the Passover Lamb," coincide with the immolation of the sheep on the day of Preparation.[17]

The Last Supper

So we see that this meal is also a subject of much controversy. What is uncontested is that it was a meal of farewell. The synoptics agree on this, having Jesus say, when taking the cup and inviting his disciples to drink wine: "Truly, I tell you that I will drink no more of the fruit of the vine until that day when I drink the new wine in the Kingdom of God" (Mark 14:25).

Matthew relies on the same source,[18] whereas Luke replaces the last phrase with this one: ". . . until the Kingdom of God has come" (Luke 22:17).

It appears that these three Sayings express the same premonition of death by Jesus. According to some authors, they could imply either that God will resurrect Jesus at the time of the restoration of the Kingdom or that Jesus will restore the Kingdom before his death.[19]

What happened during the Last Supper? According to the synoptics, by sharing bread and wine during this meal, Jesus symbolized the sacrifice of his life that was to happen the following day. The most sober text, that of Mark, says: "And as they were eating, he took the bread, blessed it, broke it, and gave it to them, and said, 'Take this: this is my body.' And he took a cup, and when he had given thanks, he gave it to them, and they all drank of it. And he said to them, 'This is my blood of the covenant, which shall be poured out for a multitude' " (Mark 14:22–24).

Matthew and Luke add some words that amplify the sense of sacrifice. In the former, the symbolism is centered on "remission of sins."[20] In the latter, the body is "given for you," just as the blood is "poured out for you." And he adds this sentence, which the Church interpreted as the institution of the Eucharist: "Do this in remembrance of me."

What else happened? Not that much, according to the synoptics. In Luke, Jesus speaks of the one who will betray him without naming him. But the supposition is that he is speaking of Judas.[21] He also speaks of Peter, who will deny him three times before the cock crows, confronted by those who accuse him of being a disciple of Jesus.[22] All of this takes up only a few verses.

By contrast, the Gospel of John has Jesus proclaim a long testimonial speech that takes up four chapters. Many scholars believe this was a creation of the gospel author (perhaps making use of certain Sayings of Jesus), considering its dense theological content and its Johannine style. But the fact that no such theologically oriented Sayings are to be found in the synoptics would argue in favor of a total creation by the author, or perhaps by some later redactor.

According to Vermès and others, some specific questions must be posed regarding the Last Supper.[23] For example, was it at that moment, or at some other time, that Jesus would have conceived of founding a lasting Church which would contradict his eschatological vision? Even more, the imagery of "who eats my body," and even especially of "who drinks my blood," is something that has no echo in any religious or cultural tradition of Jewish Palestine. According to Vermès, the taboos related to blood would have made this shocking to most Jews.

The Treachery of Judas: Reality or Legend?

The tradition of the New Testament is that Judas, one of the Twelve, betrayed Jesus and delivered him to the Jewish authorities. There are no fewer than twenty-one mentions of Judas in the canonical gospels and two in the Acts of the Apostles, all implying his guilt in the betrayal of Jesus, as well as his decisive role in Jesus' arrest. Who was this Judas? How did the gospel writers view him?

He is given the surname Iscariot. Three hypotheses are proposed for the etymology of this name: first, the Hebrew word *ishqarya,* which means "the false"; second, the composite Hebrew word *ish-Qeriyyot,* which means "the man from Kerioth" (a town in Judaea); and finally, a Hebraizing of the Latin word *sicarii,* meaning "men of the dagger," a term often applied to the Zealots.[25] The latter was a nationalist sect that, as we noted in chapter 4, struggled against the Roman occupation and was led in a military confrontation by another Judas, also mentioned earlier. A recent work by Abécassis offers much well-documented material about Judas Iscariot.[26] Its findings suggest that the second and third etymologies are the most likely, and are perhaps both true. The second hypothesis implies that Judas was a Judaean (the only one among the apostles). The third implies that he was a Zealot extremist. Abécassis presents us with a Judas who was very close to Jesus, who must have appreciated his disciple's keen intelligence about political and religious affairs—being a Judaean, Judas was probably the only one of the disciples with important connections in Jerusalem. Abécassis sees him as a radical who was deeply disappointed by Jesus when the Master did not meet the expectations of the Zealot movement.[27] He offers a convincing argument for the fact that, contrary to accusations against him in the New Testament, Judas had no interest in betraying his Master. Instead, with Jesus' consent, Judas delivered him into the hands of the Jewish authorities, hoping to provoke the greatly desired event of the restoration of the Kingdom.

Was There a Plot?

The synoptics speak of a plot several times. The first mention is after the healing of a man with a withered hand, on the Sabbath and in the synagogue. Mark indicates that this took place in the presence of Pharisees and allies of Herod, and Matthew and Luke say: "When they left, the Pharisees held counsel against him, planning to do away with him" (Matt. 12:14). "But they were filled with rage, and discussed how to do away with Jesus" (Luke 6:11).

Then the idea of a plot begins to take shape. The synoptics allude to it again during the parable of the murderous winegrowers. Luke has the Pharisees aligned with both the scribes and the chief priests, and Matthew has them aligned only with the latter. According to Mark: "And they tried to arrest him, but feared the crowds, for they perceived that he had told the parable against them; so they left him and went away. And they sent to him some of the Pharisees and some of the Herodians, to entrap him in his talk" (Mark 12:12–13).[28]

In the beginning, the plotters feared the people's reaction and lacked sufficient evidence for an arrest. They needed a strategy that would furnish them with charges serious enough to bring Jesus before the Roman governor, who alone was empowered to sentence him to death. Later, the synoptics have the Elders joining in the discussion as to the best strategy. At this point, it is obvious that they are plotting to kill Jesus: "Then the chief priests and the elders of the people gathered in the palace of the high priest, who was called Caiaphas, and took counsel together in order to arrest Jesus by stealth and kill him. But they said, 'Not during the festival, lest there be a tumult among the people' " (Matt. 26:3–5).

No specific charges have yet been mentioned, but what emerges clearly is that the accusers were worried mainly about the popularity of Jesus' teaching—especially among the outcasts—and that this was becoming intolerable to the religious authorities. Certain scholars read the following passage as implying an assassination attempt in the Temple itself: "He came daily to teach in the Temple, and the chief priests and scribes, along with prominent men of the people, sought to destroy him" (Luke 19:47).[29]

By now the danger that Jesus represented to the authorities is clearly established: If more and more people come to believe in him through his miracles, he would constitute a threat that the Romans might use as a pretext to destroy the Temple and the nation. The high priest then expresses what is on all their minds: Better for one to die than many! Thus we have the moral justification for his death. The decision is made: Jesus must be arrested before the Passover festival, a time that was always subject to turmoil.

All four canonical gospels clearly state that Jesus was put to death by the Romans, primarily on charges that he was a pretender to the throne. But how did these authors reconcile this with the events of the previous day, which revealed that he had no political ambition? And what about his disciples' belief that he was the Messiah, but that his Kingdom was not of this world? Moreover, nothing in the texts indicates that Jesus or his disciples constituted a threat for the civil, political, or military authorities. True, Jesus spoke often of a Kingdom, which must have aroused hopes in the minds of his listeners. And indeed, his miracles, plus his reputation as a healer and exorcist, drew crowds. All this could not have failed to attract attention and feed the belief that Jesus was gifted with extraordinary power and authority.

Sanders has no doubt that "a man who spoke of a kingdom, and against the Temple and its hierarchy, was destined for execution." The fact that he was said to be executed as "King of the Jews," whereas his disciples were allowed to go free, would be strong evidence that although the Romans knew he was not a military leader, they considered him suspect because he aroused people's expectations. However, still according to Sanders, this explanation is incomplete. After the death of Jesus, his disciples launched an apolitical movement, and it remained apolitical. In spite of this, they were sporadically persecuted by Jewish authorities and not by the Romans, who tolerated them. What the explanation lacks must be related to the tension that existed between Jesus and the politico-religious institutions of Israel. There can be little doubt that his teaching about sinners, his threats against the Temple, and his preaching in general would have been seen as defiance of religious authority.

THE LAST ACT

The Arrest

It began outside Jerusalem, in a garden located on a hill known as the Mount of Olives. Luke gives the fullest account:

> And he left the city, and went, as was his custom, to the Mount of Olives; and the disciples followed him . . .
>
> While he was still speaking, there came a crowd, and the man called Judas, one of the twelve, was leading them. He drew near to

Jesus to kiss him; but Jesus said to him, "Judas, would you betray the Son of Man with a kiss?" And when those who were there saw what was happening, they said, "Lord, shall we strike with the sword?" And one of them struck the slave of the high priest and cut off his right ear. But Jesus said, "No more of this!" And he touched his ear and healed him. Then Jesus said to the chief priests and officers of the temple and elders, who had come out against him, "Have you come out as against a robber, with swords and clubs? When I was with you day after day in the temple, you did not lay hands on me. But this is your hour, and that of the power of Darkness." (Luke 22:39; 47–53)

Both Matthew and Mark tell us that "the disciples all abandoned him, and fled."[30] Mark adds this intriguing detail: "A young man followed him, wearing only a simple cloth. They seized him, but he fled naked, leaving the cloth behind."[31]

The Trial

What happened after the arrest?

And they led Jesus to the high priest; and all the chief priests and the elders and the scribes were assembled. . . . Now the chief priests and the whole council sought testimony against Jesus, so as to condemn him to death; but they found none. For many bore false witness against him, and their testimonies did not agree. Some stood up and bore false witness against him, saying, "We heard him say, 'I will destroy this temple that is made with hands, and in three days I will build another, not made with hands.'" Yet even on this, their testimony did not agree. (Mark 14:53, 55–59)

We recall that all the disciples had fled and dispersed. Only Peter "followed him from afar, to the courtyard of the high priest" (Mark 15:54). Was there one trial, two trials, or none at all? Had the Sanhedrin been convened in a formal council?[32] What prosecutor was finally in charge? We may never know the answers to these questions.

Sanders believes that the Passion narratives are essentially a recon-struction from bits of information gathered and pasted together with passages from the Hebrew scriptures—for the apostles believed that the latter had prophesied the events of the Passion and they were trans-posed into the gospels. Some scholars have advanced the hypothesis that these narratives had a common source, developed by the early Church for use in the liturgy and the celebration of the Eucharist. But, as we have seen, the texts have too many points of variance and con-tradiction, many of which contain incongruities.[33] Mark and Matthew say that the appearance of Jesus before the Sanhedrin took place dur-ing the night before Passover eve. Some specialists point out that this is an implausible scenario.[34] We note also that Luke has the interrogation taking place after sunrise, but it is still the eve of a major festival.

The synoptics speak of at least two trials: first, before the high priest Caiaphas, along with the scribes and Elders;[35] second, before Pilate, the Roman prefect. Luke adds an appearance before Herod Antipas, which Pilate judged as necessary because Jesus was Galilean and under the jurisdiction of the tetrarch of that country. Apparently nothing was gained from the latter interrogation. Jesus remained silent, in spite of the violent attitude of Herod, who sent him back to Pilate. In the Gospel of John, the two trials are preceded by a visit to Annas, the father-in-law of Caiaphas. After a fruitless interrogation of Jesus about his "disciples and his doctrine," he is sent to the high priest. Here is all that Annas can obtain from him: "Jesus answered him, 'I have spoken openly to the world. I have always taught in synagogues and in the temple, where all Jews come together; I have said nothing secretly. Why do you question me? Ask those who have heard me, what I said to them; they know what I said'" (John 18:20–21).

This caused him to be struck by one of the guards. As noted before, the priests and scribes still had not produced solid evidence against Jesus because the witnesses contradicted each other. It must have been the high priest himself who interrogated Jesus, asking if he was the Messiah. Mark has him give this answer: "And Jesus said, 'I am! And you will see the Son of man seated at the right hand of Power, and coming surrounded by clouds of heaven.' And the high priest rent his own garments, and said, 'Why do we still need witnesses? You have heard his blasphemy! What is your decision?' And they all condemned him as deserving death" (Mark 14:62–64).

This version leaves no doubt that Jesus believed himself to be the Messiah. However, many scholars observe that this declaration departs from Jesus' typical style of speaking. This Saying, then, is probably a creation of the redactor, or of the early Church.

According to Luke 22:67, the challenge "If you are the Christ, tell us so!" draws this response from Jesus: "If I told you, you would not believe me." Then he is brought before the Roman prefect, Pontius Pilate, who asks him: "Are you the king of the Jews?" Jesus answers him, "You say it" (Mark 15:2).

Matthew, however, has Jesus give this response to the high priest:

> . . . And the high priest said to him, "I implore you by the living God, tell us if you are the Christ, the Son of God." Jesus said to him, "You have said so . . . ".[36] Then the high priest tore his robes, and said, "He has spoken blasphemy! Why do we still need witnesses? You have now heard his blasphemy. What is your judgment?" They answered, "He deserves death." (Matt. 26:63–66)

Thus the gospels according to Luke and Matthew have Jesus answer the high priest's question in an indirect manner, with a deliberate ambiguity. This conforms to Jesus' style better than Mark's version. If true, it would reflect his distaste, expressed in other gospel passages, for speaking of himself, for proclaiming himself the Christ, and even more for proclaiming himself the Son of God. Jesus had never claimed any of these titles previously, though others may have done so for him.

Sanders is among those who point out that the high priest's question is expressed in a form that is unprecedented in the synoptic gospels. Until this Passion narrative, we find nothing in any words attributed to Jesus that could explain why the high priest would use such language.

Assuming it was asked in this way, was the question a trap laid by his detractors to create an excuse to arrest him? Or was it a real interrogation, a question his judges truly wanted answered?

In the absence of witnesses to these events, we shall never know. Sanders thinks it is strange that the corresponding passage in John does not have the Sanhedrin ask Jesus this question, whereas John had written in a previous chapter: "Thus the Jews sought even more to kill him, because not only did he violate the Sabbath, he spoke of God as his own Father, making himself equal to God" (John 5:18).

Curiously, the accusations against Jesus fail to include threats against the Temple. Perhaps this was simply because the testimonies were contradictory, as Mark wrote. However, they reappear at Calvary in the form of taunts by onlookers insulting Jesus: "The onlookers insulted him, wagging their heads and saying: 'You, who would destroy the Temple, and rebuild it in three days—if you are the Son of God, then save yourself, and come down from the cross!'" (Matt. 27:39–40)

But these threats against the Temple constituted a primary charge against Jesus, which could have held. They are repeated during the trial of Stephen before the Sanhedrin: "We have heard that Jesus, this Nazarene, will destroy this holy place and change the customs which Moses gave us" (Acts 6:14).

There can be no doubt that speaking any threat concerning the Temple was a punishable offense in Jewish society. This is why Jeremiah was threatened with death for having (at Yahweh's command) spoken threats of destruction of the Temple and of the city of Jerusalem (Jer. 26: 8–19). Also, Josephus tells of a man who was punished by the citizens of Jerusalem and flogged by the Romans for shouting against the city and the Sanctuary.[37] In neither of these cases were the guilty put to death, but they had no following and represented no serious threat. By contrast, Jesus had a significant following and his violence inside the Temple could have been seen by the Roman authorities as a seditious act. This would be enough to explain his arrest and execution as a rebel. Josephus also recounts the story of Theudas, a magician who tried to attract crowds to join him in crossing the Jordan as he separated the waters (recalling the miracle of Moses leading the Jews through the Red Sea). The Romans beheaded him. Because he had too many followers, they interpreted his actions as a serious threat of revolt.[38]

But what apparently mattered most to Jesus' accusers was his declaration that he was the Christ and the Son of God. His responses to those crucial questions allowed them to condemn him for blasphemy. We have already noted that the language of these charges agrees with later Christian terminology. Their authenticity is doubly suspect to some scholars. Even if such charges had been made, there is a solid objection that, based on the literature of Jesus' time, these two appellations would not have been judged as blasphemy. Sanders reminds us that others before Jesus claimed the title of Messiah and were not punished. As to his claim to be the Son of God (which has not been proved), there is no doubt that Judaic tradition would allow any son of Israel to do so.

We could therefore agree with Sanders, that the primary charge of blasphemy made by the high priest against Jesus has no support in Jewish tradition and therefore little credibility.

Afterward, Jesus is taken before Pilate, who (as we have just quoted from Mark 15:2) asks him if he is the king of the Jews, only to have the question turned back upon him by Jesus.

To this same question, John has Jesus make the following speech:

Jesus answered, "Do you say this of your own accord, or did others tell you this about me?" Pilate answered, "Am I a Jew? Your own nation and the chief priests have handed you over to me. What have you done?" Jesus answered, "My kingdom is not of this world; if my kingdom were of this world, my servants would fight, that I might not be handed over to the Jews; but my kingdom is not from the world." Pilate said to him, "So you are a king?" Jesus answered, "You say it: I am a king . . . " (John 18:34–37)

In order to be seen as a serious threat to Roman power, Jesus would need many followers. How many were there? In his first Letter to the Corinthians, Paul speaks of five hundred brothers in Christ to whom Jesus appeared after his death. What do the gospels say? Speaking of the triumphant entry into Jerusalem, Mark writes:

> And they brought the young donkey to Jesus, and threw their garments on it; and he sat upon it. And many spread their garments on the road, and others spread leafy branches which they had cut in the fields. And those who went before and those who followed cried out, "Hosanna! Blessed is he who comes in the name of the Lord! Blessed is the Kingdom of our father David that is coming! Hosanna in the highest heaven!" (Mark 11:7–8)

Matthew (21:8) mentions a very large crowd. But in Luke (19:35–37), the crowd has shrunk to just a group of Jesus' disciples who have come to celebrate his arrival. John (12:12–13), on the other hand, also claims the presence of a large crowd.

What is more significant than the number of people is the unanimity of the gospels concerning their praises, which invoke terms such as the Kingdom, Son of David, the King of Israel (daughter of Zion). For many scholars, we can say at least that this entry of Jesus into Jerusalem, however triumphal it may or may not have been, was anything but discreet. It must have been a highly visible, public demonstration of enthusiasm for Jesus by the people and disciples gathered there, whatever their actual numbers. To onlookers, their exclamations must have made an impression of royal praise. Moreover, the young donkey he rode reinforced this scriptural symbol of a royal procession. "Rejoice greatly, O daughter of Zion! Shout aloud, O daughter of Jerusalem! See, your king comes to you; triumphant, victorious, yet humble, and riding on a donkey, on the colt of a donkey" (Zech. 9:9).

Many scholars point out that the authors of the canonical gospels wanted the Jews to appear more guilty and the Romans less. The later interpretations of the Church of Rome did nothing to dispel this impression, and the historical consequences have been disastrous for the Jewish people. But let us recall that Pilate's rationale for a death sentence had nothing to do with the blasphemy charges supposedly brought by the Jewish authorities, but rather with the charge that Jesus pretended to the title of king. So the story appears to be that the Romans, having consulted the Sanhedrin (formally or informally) about religious charges brought against Jesus, tried and executed him on totally different charges relating to sedition. "Pilate said to him: 'So, you are a king?' Jesus answered, 'You say it: I am a king' " (John 18:37).

Thus Jesus does not answer the question directly. The expression "You say it" could be interpreted as "It is you who say it." Pilate seems unconvinced of Jesus' guilt and wants to let him go. He would never have entertained this possibility if he thought Jesus had really made a claim to royalty before him and the other Roman officials.

> . . . [B]ut the Jews cried out, "If you release this man, you are not Caesar's friend. Anyone who makes himself a king sets himself against Caesar!" When Pilate heard these words, he brought Jesus out and sat upon the judgment seat at a place called The Pavement, and in Hebrew, Gabbatha. Now it was the day of Preparation of the Passover; it was about the sixth hour. He said to the Jews, "Behold your King!"[39] They cried out, "Away with him, away with him, crucify him!" Pilate said to them, "Shall I crucify your King?" The chief priests answered, "We have no king but Caesar." Then he handed him over to them to be crucified. (John 19:12–16)

It is true that for a representative of Roman power, anything would be preferable to displeasing Caesar, even sending an innocent man to his death. But instead of being returned to the Jews to be stoned as a blasphemer (as Stephen later was), Jesus received the appalling sentence of crucifixion, a punishment the Romans reserved for rebels. John's claim, then, that Pilate delivered Jesus to be crucified by the Jews cannot be true. Jesus could have been crucified only by the Romans—the only authority empowered to execute the sentence.

Following another line of reasoning, based on the views of

C. Moule,[40] Sanders concludes that "[t]he evidence at our disposal indicates that Jesus . . . did not seek death. He had not come to Jerusalem to die. But he followed, with unwavering devotion, a path of truth which inevitably led to a death which he did not attempt to escape."

Crucifixion and Death

Jesus was hung on the cross at a place named Golgotha, which means "skull." Then:

> And when the sixth hour had come, there was darkness over the whole land until the ninth hour. And at the ninth hour Jesus cried with a loud voice, "*Eloi, Eloi, lama sabachthani?*"[41] which means, "My God, my God, why hast thou forsaken me?" And some of the bystanders hearing it said, "Listen, he is calling Elijah." And one of them ran and, filling a sponge full of vinegar, put it on a reed pole, and gave it to him to drink, saying, "Wait! Let us see whether Elijah will come to take him down." And Jesus uttered a loud cry, and breathed his last. (Mark 15:33–37)

Many scholars have wondered: Was this loud cry at such a tragic moment (a quotation from the first verse of Psalm 22) simply a cry of despair? Or was it rather an expression of the mixture of suffering and hope that this psalm evokes when read in its entirety? Our inclination would be toward the latter interpretation, more in keeping with the greatness of a man who, at the hour of his death, is inspired by one of the most beautiful poems ever written about the relation of humanity to God.[42]

But this does not exclude the hypothesis that Jesus, having seen many disciples leave him, lived the last months of his life feeling the failure of his mission. But what might *failure* have meant to him? Is it conceivable that he had despaired of his fellow human beings? Was it not the patience of love that animated him?

Did he expect such a death? He had referred to the lapidation of the prophets. Like the author of the twenty-second Psalm, he must have felt hunted down by enemies. "Be not far, for trouble is near me, and no help!" Jesus must have known this psalm by heart. He would have followed this prayer and placed his trust in God, as does the speaker in the psalm: After the lines before verse 22, which lament his persecution, God receives the lament ("He has heard me!"). And then a change occurs in the heart of him who has received the sign from God, and he begins to sing praises to him.[43]

Whatever the case may be, the psalm was surely the inspiration for relevant passages of the Passion narratives in all four canonical gospels. As in other Passion events where direct witnesses are lacking, the writers drew their inspiration from the Bible:[44] "For food, they have given me poison, and for my thirst, vinegar" (Psalms 69:22).

Other parts of the Passion narrative that draw on the Bible include the incident where Roman soldiers broke the legs of the two thieves but not those of Jesus. This has been interpreted as a reference to the Jewish prescription given in Exodus concerning the preparation of the Passover lamb: "You shall eat it in one house, and you shall ensure that no piece of meat leaves that house. You shall break none of its bones" (Exod 12:46). And: "For it so happened that not one of his bones was broken, so that the Scripture was fulfilled" (John 19:36).

The Passion narratives were surely inspired also by this passage from Zechariah 12:10: "[W]hen they look on him whom they have pierced, they shall mourn for him, as one mourns for an only child, and weep bitterly over him, as one weeps over a firstborn."

Because no previous tradition existed that spoke of a suffering and dying Messiah[45]—at any rate, we have no evidence for the existence of such a tradition—the disciples of Jesus (and the first Christians) must have been deeply disturbed by his death, and by its brutally sudden and ignominious character.[46] The gospel writers would have searched the Bible for a symbol that made sense of this death. Thus they would have identified Jesus with the scapegoat of Leviticus 16:10,[47] which was spat upon,[48] pierced in its side, and made to bear all the sins of the world.

AFTER THE CROSS

The Burial

Scholars disagree as to whether Jesus was buried in a private tomb or his body thrown into a communal pit. The hypothesis of the private tomb seems more likely, given that Jesus had many friends and followers who would have made an effort to retrieve his body, especially if the crucifixion took place on the eve of the Sabbath. But others believe that, on the contrary, given Jesus' low social status, and his having died in a manner normally reserved for criminals, bandits, and lower-class political troublemakers, the common pit is the more plausible hypothesis.[49] Still other historians point out that it was also common practice to leave the bodies hanging on the cross to be devoured by vultures and other carrion eaters. The latter arguments support the idea that, like most condemned men, Jesus' body would not have been placed in a tomb. But we know nothing for certain, and the references to the empty tomb tip the balance toward the first hypothesis.[50]

The Empty Tomb and the Apparitions

The gospels do speak of an empty tomb, but recent studies of the symbol of the empty tomb suggest that "the belief preceded the tomb."[51] For many believers, the story of the empty tomb was a necessity, a proof that Jesus was still alive. Mark ends his narrative, in the final chapter, as follows:

> And when the Sabbath was past, Mary Magdalene, and Mary the mother of James, and Salome, purchased aromatic oils, so that they might go and anoint him. And very early on the first day of the week they went to the tomb after sunrise. And they said to one another, "Who will roll away the stone for us from the entrance of the tomb?" And looking up, they saw that the stone was rolled back—it was very large. And entering the tomb, they saw a young man sitting on the right side, dressed in a white robe; and they were amazed. And he said to them, "Do not be amazed; you seek

Jesus of Nazareth, who was crucified. He has risen, he is not here. See, there is the place where they laid him. But go, tell his disciples and Peter that he is going before you to Galilee; there you will see him, as he told you." And they went out and fled from the tomb; for trembling and wonder had come over them; and they said nothing to anyone, for they were afraid. (Mark 16:1–8)

The gospel contains twelve verses after this, but the contemporary scholarly consensus is that these are not from Mark, but are instead later additions.[53]

A number of exegetes mention the interesting fact that it is women who arrive first and experience the sight of the empty tomb. It was not technically empty, because they saw a young man seated there, dressed in a white robe.[54] What is striking is that these women, who have just been privileged with an important message, decide not to speak about it "for they were afraid." And it is on this note that the Gospel of Mark closes, with an ellipsis.

In Luke's version, the women do not remain silent. On the contrary, they tell the whole story to the apostles:

On their return from the tomb, they reported the whole matter to the eleven, and to all the other disciples. It was Mary of Magdala, and Joanna, and Mary the mother of James. Other women were with them, and they told these things to the apostles. But their account appeared to them as idle tales; they did not believe them. Peter, however, arose and ran to the tomb; and stooping down, saw nothing there but some linen. And he went away, wondering with amazement about what had happened. (Luke 24:9–12)

Basing his argument on a thesis of Schillebeeckx, Shorto[55] maintains that the synoptics mixed two traditions in their narratives of the death of Jesus. One tradition is the tale of the empty tomb and the other is of the apparitions of the resurrected Christ. As we have just seen, the primitive version of Mark contains no narrative of apparitions. In contrast, the other three canonical gospels, the Acts of the Apostles, as well as Paul, speak at length of personal or group experiences of visions of Jesus after his death.

But let us return to the theme of the tomb. In the last chapter of Matthew, with a dramatic scene including an earthquake, an apparition of an angel appears dressed in white. The angel tells the women that Jesus has returned from the dead and that he has gone to Galilee. On their way from the tomb, Matthew adds: "And behold, Jesus met them and said, 'Rejoice!' And they came up and prostrated themselves, embracing his feet. Then Jesus said to them, 'Do not be afraid; go and tell my brothers to go to Galilee, and there they will see me'" (Matt. 28:9).

After the narrative about the pilgrims of Emmaus, Luke tells of the apparition of the Lord to the eleven:

> But they were startled and frightened, and thought that they were seeing a ghost. And he said to them, "Why are you troubled, and why do doubts arise in your hearts? See my hands and my feet, for it is I myself. Touch me, and see; for a ghost has not flesh and bones, as you see that I have." And he showed them his hands and his feet. While they were still overcome, wondering for joy, he said to them, "Have you anything here to eat?" They gave him a piece of broiled fish, and he took it and ate before them.[56] (Luke 24:37–43)

Two accounts of the apparition of the Lord appear in John. One is before the disciples, inside a room in Jerusalem. There, he breathes upon them, saying: "Receive the Holy Spirit! If you forgive the sins of others, they will be forgiven. If you retain their sins, they will be retained" (John 20:22–23). The other incident takes place at Lake Tiberiad, where Jesus also breaks bread with his disciples: "None of the disciples dared ask him 'Who are you?' knowing that it was the Lord. Jesus came, took the bread and the fish, and gave each of them some. This was the third time that Jesus had shown himself to the disciples after his resurrection from the dead" (John 21:1–14).

The apparition narratives are interesting for other reasons. Historians of the early Church have observed that underlying all the stories of appearances of the resurrected Christ and in proportion to the information given in them, there is an implicit issue of apostolic authority and succession.[57] Indeed, the apostles would have a primary claim to a personal apparition of the Master. Another point that many scholars make is that the resurrection of Jesus does not necessarily mean his physical body was resurrected. These scholars consider Mark's legend of the empty tomb to be more recent than those of the apparitions. Paul never refers to it, and no mention of it occurs in Q or in Thomas. Apparently, all such narratives could have become a major theme in Christological tradition only several decades after Jesus' death. Like many other Pharisees, Paul believed in the resurrection of the dead—but in a spiritual form, not a physical resurrection of the body. Only in the year 34 or 35 C.E.—that is, three or four years after the death of Jesus—did Paul experience his vision of the resurrected and glorified Christ.[58]

Conclusion

In this final section, I offer some reflections and conclusions of my own, which go beyond the framework of a historical study. After all, I've kept my promise not to "theologize."

The early Christian Church was founded long after the death of Jesus,[1] and not without inglorious machinations and fratricidal struggles. The men who built it claimed for themselves the authority of apostolic succession, and also the exclusive right to interpret scriptures and formulate dogmas. Was this the best way to advance toward higher truth in exploring the meaning of the open teaching that Jesus wanted to transmit to posterity?

At the risk of oversimplification, it is true that from the time of Albert the Great and Thomas Aquinas, the Church explicitly allowed the use of human reason—a God-given faculty—to help understand the meaning of the faith. After all, the latter must be expressed with the help of human concepts. But it was also made clear that in any conflict between reason and revelation, it is revelation—as interpreted by the Church—that must prevail. Does this represent progress? This persistent bias turned out to be a wide-open door for the arbitrary powers of the Inquisition.

My own inclination is toward the view of Averroës.[2] It is my belief that neither rabbis, nor priests, nor theologians have a monopoly on Bible interpretation. It seems to me that Jesus himself would have respected the capacity in each of us to contribute—according to our ability and our level—toward the evolution of an oral and written sacred tradition: in other words, toward a kind of midrashic collective work, similar to the process developed (and that continues today) by the Jews, our brothers in religion.

In this study, we never lost sight of both the importance of and the difficulty involved in using the tools of contemporary scholarship regarding the historical Jesus—his life, his mission, his teaching, and his tragic end. Now, at the conclusion of this work of research (which has been massive, and at times arduous), I find myself among those who are convinced that Jesus was a fully human being.[3] I believe that his existence was inscribed in a story belonging to the human condition: beginning with sexual conception, pregnancy, birth, and continuing through a childhood and an adolescence about which we know virtually nothing. His father was more or less known, he had brothers and sisters and neighbors, lived in a village, had a kind of education, learned a trade, and lived in a sociocultural environment whose reality he discovered but about whose real nature he sometimes had doubts, hesitations, lack of knowledge, and tears of lamentation.

Whether one accepts or rejects the belief that he was really the Christ and the Son of God, there is no denying the humanity of Jesus. I have tried to present the richness and vividness of his humanity through this study of the historical literature. Naturally, I am aware of the enormous difficulties of such an enterprise, and of the impossibility of fully realizing it.

However, I made an effort to sift the Sayings and narratives of Jesus through the filter of the history of his era and of the life of a devout Jew from Nazareth, influenced by a messianic and eschatological religious environment, convinced of his own intimate relation with the Most High, impressed by the teachings of the Baptist, continually in search of self-knowledge—a man who took to the road with his companions to proclaim the Good News to those who wanted to hear it.

A first conclusion that imposes itself is that this Nazarene, Yeshua ben Yosef, ultimately has little in common with the Messiah that Paul,

John, and other theologians call "Jesus Christ, Lord and Savior." There is no longer any doubt that many of the words and deeds claimed in the canonical gospels were not those of Jesus. They are creations of the authors or redactors of the gospels, and sometimes interpolations by the early Church. In the absence of multiple attestations—one of the primary criteria that we defined in chapter 2—the major reason for doubting the authenticity of many of these Sayings of Jesus is that they are in disharmony with the personality and deep convictions of their supposed author. This turns out to be the case for almost all the Sayings expressed in the first person. In those Sayings that are least in doubt, Jesus never places himself at the center of the message he wants to communicate. This has been one of the most interesting discoveries that have emerged from our study: Jesus was a teacher who wanted to efface his own personality behind the message of the Good News.

Although the most thorough historical research still yields very little information about the man himself, we can nevertheless take comfort in its evidence that Jesus shares with other great sages of the past an abhorrence for the personality cult. Like the Buddha and the philosopher Socrates, Jesus wrote nothing himself and made no provisions for the transmission of his life and teaching through written testimonials. It is as if he did not want his living experience to be put into written form, did not want his teaching to be frozen in immutable texts—as if he placed the highest importance on leaving to each human being the task of pursuing contemplation, reflection, and continuing to spread the Good News, "creating" the Kingdom themselves, in the light of a message that is always in expansion.

In any case, it seems that the Sayings and deeds of Jesus that have received the highest ratings of authenticity by scholarly consensus are essentially the fruit of his own insight, inspired and fertilized by a keen understanding of the Torah and of the prophets.

The historical and sociocultural contexts indicate that the public teaching of Jesus of Nazareth could hardly have spread beyond the borders of Palestine during his own life. His disciples, disappointed and confused in their messianic hopes, would take years to begin to see the depth and universality of his teaching—and this does not imply any disdain for their capacity of understanding. In any case, when the first attempts at a Judaic preaching of the Good News were poorly received by the "Gentiles," the Hellenization of the teaching facilitated its spread and a progressive deification of the Christ. The drama of the scandalous death of the Master was unacceptable without his subsequent resurrection. Yet it was thereby also depleted of its human substance.

Today, no one can any longer contest the roles of Paul of Tarsus and John the Evangelist as the founders of Christianity as we know it. They are the pillars of its theology of salvation, the initiators of the vision of the eternal Logos made flesh, and the source of the doctrines of grace and the holy Trinity.

But where is Jesus in all this? Coming from a Jew imbued with the teachings of the Hebrew scriptures, his Sayings demonstrate that he never lost sight of the basic promise of Genesis—to restore to humanity, male and female, its role as co-creator, beloved of God their Father, and called to share in his glory.

What other lessons are to be learned from this study? We have found that this subject involves a threefold difficulty: retracing the biblical roots of Jesus' faith; assessing his contemporaries' reactions to his teaching; and establishing an unequivocal causal sequence linking his ministry to his death, in historical context. There have been many scholars, ill informed about the subtleties of the Judaism of Jesus' time,[4] who have published erroneous interpretations. Their consequences have been serious.

I would also add a reflection regarding those who willfully ignore the historical research or who consider the historical Jesus unimportant. Does such an attitude not reflect a strange contempt for humanity? Are we not creatures who are still evolving, still in the process of realizing our potential? Is not the human story of Jesus therefore *essential* to his "advent"? Even if we believe that Jesus realized his "divine sonship" before all other human beings, that would be all the more reason to try to understand the meaning of his biography, his words, and his actions. After all, these are still somewhat accessible to our reason. What a strange life, and what a strange message it would be, if its ultimate meaning were centered on discarnate being. This tendency to privilege the divine nature of Christ to such an extent that the historical Jesus is avoided is a denial of his incarnation. And is not this "incarnation" one of the most distinctive characteristics of Christianity as a religion? In this sense, attempting to discover all we can about the historical Jesus cannot be considered hostile to Christianity.

But beyond all the questions raised by the historical quest for Jesus (whose answers can only be provisional), what meaning can we find in the teaching of Jesus? His message to his "lost sheep," who were especially his own people, can be expressed like this: *Wake up! Arise, and go forth! Go toward your true self! Accept others in their differences, within the vision of the Father's love!*[5] In essence, this is to remember the teaching (expressed in mythic language) of the first chapters of Genesis.[6] The founding myths tell us that this work of self-realization began, and was made possible, by the transgression of Adam and Eve, who ate the forbidden fruit of the tree of knowledge of Good and Evil. Like Jacob wrestling with the angel (Gen. 25:26), do not we human beings become truly ourselves through an inescapable struggle with the divine? Is not this the condition for realizing the potential for freedom and love that is within us?

And we must ask this question: Did Jesus, who died abandoned on the cross, want to appear as more than a messenger, an inspired man, a prophet, a man of God, in the terms of his time and culture? Did he aspire to something beyond his dignity as a son of God, like his fellow human beings, with faith in the Most High of the Bible? As we have seen, this is a question that cannot be answered with certainty by any possible reading of the canonical gospels.

In a letter to the Corinthians, Paul writes: "But if Christ is not risen, then empty is our message, and empty also our faith" (1 Cor. 15:12). But do we really have to believe in the resurrection of Jesus, in the terms employed by Peter and Paul, to have a chance of success in practicing the new Way that Jesus taught, and which he wanted us to understand while he was still alive? If faith in his resurrection is held to be a pre-condition to access to the Kingdom, is this not proof of an extreme pessimism as to the true power of the teaching of Jesus of Nazareth? Is it not a reversal of the Master's own practice? Did he not, from the very beginning of his ministry, and before any talk of death and resurrection, call his disciples to abandon everything and join him in the way of radical turnaround, which would lead them to an awakening and to true life?

The resurrection of Jesus as "Christ, the Savior," a sign of his glorification by God, is proclaimed in the accounts of apparitions in three of the canonical gospels. Is this not simply a mythic narrative, progressively imposed as a belief among the disciples, for whom the mission of their Lord Jesus, the Messiah and son of David, would otherwise lose its meaning? Is this type of question merely a trap to test the faith of those who have doubts? Maybe. But it is also their task to meet this challenge and to extricate themselves from the danger of falling into a sleep that could become deadly.

This return to the Jesus of history, and to his original words, should not serve as a pretext for ignoring all the testimonies of those who built the Church. Even though many of them may have betrayed the message of the Master, or concocted fables to be believed as truth, their experience remains an essential part of history, along with the texts that relate them. And we should not forget that Paul, Peter, Andrew, and many others died heroically because of their faith in the resurrected Christ.

Many people today still ask whether Jesus represents the ultimate divine intervention before the advent of the Kingdom of God; or whether, on the contrary, he represents a prototype of the fully realized human being, the Son of Man. The latter would be a "sketch" of what might be the fulfillment of the great divine plan announced in Genesis: the way to salvation by the progressive realization of the Kingdom in ourselves, the way of our freedom and our dignity.

One of the major metaphysical reflections that marked the end of the nineteenth century seems to have been the claim (if not the observation) that the God of our fathers is dead. This represented a victory of man over his own destiny, according to Dostoyevsky, Nietzsche, and Freud, to mention only a few. But for Nietzsche, this God who had died was the old God. And he added: "Now you say that God is in the process of rotting, but this is only an appearance: he is only shedding his skin of morality. And soon you will find him again—beyond Good and Evil."[7]

Certainly such reflections do not plumb the depths of the Good News of the man from Nazareth. After all, "[t]here are many mansions in my Father's house." But do they not at least offer us a point of view radically different from the naive promise of divine, otherworldly intervention, a meta-historic apocalypse of final judgment that will arrive to set things right, abolishing a botched creation in favor of an eternal felicity, where at last the good are always rewarded and the bad always punished—as if this paternal yet liberating God would separate the good beings and set them apart from the bad ones? Are we not all both good and bad?

Are we humans, created in the image of God, who make mistakes, who have the power of choice, and who had to leave our earthly paradise for it, capable of understanding our divine origin? Are we capable of standing upright and realizing ourselves?

If so, we must not forget that our dimension of freedom also includes a capacity for final judgment, both apocalyptic and destructive, for without this dangerous freedom—the freedom to love, and also the freedom to destroy—there is no human being.

Appendix 1

The Nag Hammadi Papyri

The thirteen books (codices) found at Nag Hammadi in 1945 contain the following material:* (Texts marked with a † existed in more than one version within the codices.)

Codex 1 (also known as the Jung Codex)
The Prayer of the Apostle Paul
The Apocryphon of James
The Gospel of Truth†
The Treatise on the Resurrection
The Tripartite Tractate [a veritable compendium of gnostic theology]

Codex 2
The Apocryphon of John (long version)†
The Gospel of Thomas
The Gospel of Philip
The Hypostasis of the Archons (a very special interpretation of the
    first six chapters of Genesis)

---

* [This English summary is based on the translation of titles established by Robinson, *The Nag Hammadi Library* (San Francisco: Harper, rev. 1990). —*Trans.*]

On the Origin of the World (thought to be No. 40 of the Symphonia of Heresies from the Panarion by Ephiphanes)[†]

The Exegesis on the Soul

The Book of Thomas the Contender

Codex 3

The Apocryphon of John (short version)[†]

The Gospel of the Egyptians[†]

Eugnostos the Blessed[†]

The Sophia of Jesus Christ

The Dialogue of the Savior (Jesus' dialogue with his disciples on typical themes from cosmogony and eschatology)

Codex 4

The Apocryphon of John (long version)[†]

The Gospel of the Egyptians[†]

Codex 5

Eugnostos the Blessed[†]

The Apocalypse of Paul

The (First) Apocalypse of James

The (Second) Apocalypse of James

The Apocalypse of Adam (revelation of Adam to his son Seth regarding the consequences of the Fall)

Codex 6

The Acts of Peter and the Twelve Apostles

The Thunder, Perfect Mind (a revelation in the first person by a feminine divinity, embracing all opposites within herself; of unknown origin, though perhaps related to Isis-inspired religions)

Authoritative Teaching (the recurrent theme of the soul deprived of gnosis)

The Concept of Our Great Power (end-of-the-world apocalypse)

Plato, *The Republic* 588A-589B

The Discourse on the Ogdoad and the Ennead
The Prayer of Thanksgiving
Asclepius 21–29

Codex 7

The Paraphrase of Shem (fragment)
The Second Treatise of the Great Seth
The Apocalypse of Peter
The Teachings of Silvanus
The Three Steles of Seth (prayers dedicated by Dositheos to Seth, addressed as the Father)

Codex 8

Zostrianos (a specifically "gnostic" treatise, with a series of revelations on celestial powers)
The Letter of Peter to Philip

Codex 9

Melchizedek
The Thought of Norea
The Testimony of Truth (a homily on themes as various as the relation of Truth to Law, purity vs. pollution, and a polemic against the Christian Church, but also against certain "gnostics")

Codex 10

Marsanes

Codex 11

The Interpretation of Knowledge
A Valentinian Exposition
  • On the Anointing
  • On the Baptism A
  • On the Baptism B
  • On the Eucharist A

• On the Eucharist B
Allogenes
Hypsiphrone

Codex 12

The Sentences of Sextus [a collection of moral dicta already known
  in Greek and Latin and influenced by extreme asceticism]
The Gospel of Truth
Fragments

Codex 13

Trimorphic Protennoia
On the Origin of the World[†]

Appendix 2

The Earliest Source
of the Gospels[*]

There was nothing innovative in Nautin's method for demonstrating the existence of a source text that predated the hypothetical canonical gospel, or about the name he gave to it: Source. It begins with a close comparison of the texts of Mark and Luke. Their structures show not only that Luke follows Mark faithfully—this had already been observed—but also that two portions of Luke show a discontinuity with the rest of the gospel attributed to him. Nautin analyzed these as interpolations, which are of special interest for any historical study of Jesus. The first interpolation in Luke comprises seventy-two verses and occurs after the narrative of the selection of the Twelve (also related in Mark 3:13–19). The second is much longer, covering a little over eight chapters. It is woven into the narrative taken from Mark, between chapters 9 and 10. Nautin convincingly demonstrates that these interpolations do not originate with Luke himself, but rather are from a text or texts that he took from an older source, which he calls the "primitive Gospel" [*l'Évangile primitif* = EP].

---

*This is a succinct, and no doubt incomplete, summary of P. Nautin's thesis in his work *L'Évangile retrouvé*.

His argument centers on two primary deviations from Mark. In the first verses of his gospel, Luke notifies the reader that his goal is to follow the earlier gospels, which he believes to be well documented and based on reliable witnesses (some even firsthand), and to represent them in what he considers the proper order. This is exactly how he proceeds when, after the narrative of Jesus' childhood (chapters 1 and 2),* he takes up Mark's narrative again in the third chapter. But unlike Mark, who tells of the three missionary journeys of Jesus,† with an abundance of miracles and wonder, Luke's main concern becomes more oriented toward theology. This is how he strives to weave the story of Jesus into the continuity of the history of Israel, placing Jesus' deeds and his message of salvation at the heart of a universal story. This does not prevent him from amplifying the already marvelous aspects of Mark's story, multiplying the number of the most extravagant miracles, and even adding a resurrection of the dead. Nevertheless, he introduces accounts whose tone of reserve and moderation are in marked contrast to Mark's as a whole. Luke's content emphasizes Jesus' teaching and relegates the marvelous aspect to a lesser status.

The second interpolation deviating from Mark consists, above all, of the Sayings of Jesus. Here we find certain phrases and groups of words that have a close similarity to those of the Gospel of Mark. Nautin considers this evidence that these interpolations did not originate with Luke, and that both gospel writers knew and made use of texts from the same source, which therefore had to be earlier.

Matthew also follows Mark's account very closely, and the same analysis of his text shows that he also had knowledge of this earlier source, from which he often borrowed. Since his major preoccupation was to complete Mark's account, a point that Nautin emphasizes, he added Sayings of Jesus that Mark had neglected to include. But instead of grouping them together, Luke inserts them into passages of his gospel

---

*A narrative of little historical interest, given its undeniably legendary origin.

†First in Galilee, then in neighboring countries, in Perea and in Judaea, as far as Jerusalem.

whose theme is relevant to the Saying in question. The outcome of this comparative study is clear: There existed a common source of Sayings, which Nautin calls the EP (or primitive gospel).

Once the existence of this source was demonstrated, Nautin highlighted the contradictions that appear between certain verses within the same chapter. Following this, Nautin examines the hypothesis that these contradictions imply that the presumed author of the *Évangile primitif* made use of a still older source—a source that the author faithfully reproduces. And whenever the meaning of one of its Sayings poses a problem, this author of the EP adds an interpretation based on a theological vision of his own or of his community. Nautin then strives to sift out the material that ultimately comes from the Source of the EP, from the additions of its presumed author. He notes that the Sayings that pose problems in Luke's text, because they contradict each other, are most often juxtaposed, and that those that can be attributed to the author of the EP, because of their characteristic theological orientation and style—by the manner in which the same subject is dealt with, and by the repeated use of similar words—show that they are dependent on the Source.

In conclusion, what we learn from Nautin's considerable exegetical research, and what seems to me to be of primary importance in advancing our understanding of the historical Jesus, are the following points: (1) The moderation of miraculous aspects, compared to the synoptics, strongly suggests that the EP was probably composed at a date relatively close to the death of Jesus. (2) When the EP author quotes Sayings of Jesus whose theology does not accord well with his own vision, he nevertheless scrupulously respects the original text, thereby demonstrating his veneration for this Source. (3) The image of Jesus that emerges from the Sayings of this Source, in contrast to the image that is promulgated by the EP author, is that of someone who "preaches the reign of God, without making any claims for himself." This strongly suggests that these Sayings are not creations of the disciples, but instead come from the historical Jesus.

Notes

Introduction

1. Christ (*christos*, in Greek) means the same as *messiah* (*mashiah* in Hebrew), the "anointed of God" announced by the prophets, the one who will return to this world to establish the Kingdom of God.
2. In our use of the term *the human*, we are also referring to the first chapter of Genesis, in which Adam, "made of clay" is created by Elohim on the sixth day.
3. This is a term used by Marie Balmary in *La Divine Origine* (Paris: B. Grasset, 1993).
4. The canonical New Testament writings comprise the four gospels, the Acts of the Apostles, the Letters of Paul and the other apostles, and the Apocalypse, better known as the Book of Revelation.
5. A more rigorous terminology would distinguish between the Hebrew Bible and the Bible that includes the New Testament, to which "Old Testament" Christians have added a dozen or so deuterocanonical [second canon] texts.
6. In reality, the original word in Genesis, so often translated as "sin," means something closer to "error in judgment." Cf. chapter 6 in this book.
7. Mostly these are Catholic professors of theology.
8. These writers also claim to be proponents of critical historical analysis.
9. Cf. C. Perrot, *Jésus et l'histoire* (Paris: Desclée de Brouwer, 1993), 14, 25.
10. In writing these lines, I am irresistibly drawn to the following

quotation (which some may consider impertinent or simplistic) from one of the most creative modern philosophers who has lately come back into fashion:

> This is why a philosophical, exegetic theology, linked to a sacred scripture which one is not allowed to question, and which must at all costs be defended by intellectual exercises, often demonstrating incomparable subtlety, and sometimes advancing extremely fertile arguments and approaches, is incapable of asking the ultimate question: What if the revelation is not a revelation, but a text like all the others? This is the forbidden question.

Cornelius Castoradis, *Sujet et vérité dans le monde social-historique* (Paris: Le Seuil, 2002).

11. Ernest Renan, *Vie de Jésus* (1867), Arléa, Paris, 1992; also *Histoire du peuple d'Israël* (1893).
12. Albert Lagrange, the author of many influential historical works of Christian inspiration, was the founder of the *École Archéologique Française de Jérusalem* in 1921.
13. The world-famous Protestant theologian whose thesis of 1902 bears the English title *The Mystery of the Kingdom of God: The Secret of Jesus' Messiahship and Passion* (Amherst, N.Y.: Prometheus Books, 1985).
14. John P. Meier, *A Marginal Jew* (New York: Doubleday, 1991–2001). (Still incomplete, with three volumes published at this date and a fourth on the way.)
15. Meier thinks that historical research can serve theological interests in three ways: by giving a richer and more colorful depth to faith; by offering a more concrete humanity of the resurrected Jesus; and by emphasizing his nonconformist aspects.
16. Cf. bibliography.
17. For anyone who doubts the endurance of this "teaching," it will suffice to attend a Sunday Catholic service, where the faithful of the twenty-first century continue to recite a number of such prayers, often incomprehensible, that are still retained in the text of the Mass.

Chapter 1: The Sources

1. The Church did not complete the official list of canonical writings until the second century. These were writings judged to be authentic enough

to have doctrinal value. Later, we will examine this question further, as well as that of the precise definition of these terms.

2. This is the real danger of a system that accords or denies "canonicity" to a text. If critical historical research shows that a canonical text is not "reliable," or there are serious doubts as to the Sayings that it reports, or perhaps that certain non-canonical texts show evidence of greater historical authenticity of Sayings than canonical ones, historians will, of course, draw the logical conclusions, for canonicity is not their problem. Readers who take the trouble to study the conclusions of different exegeses of this material can draw their own conclusions.

3. A definition of this language is given in the next chapter.

4. G. Mordillat and J. Prieur, *Jésus contre Jésus* (Paris: Le Seuil, 1999). The authors of this excellent work are also producers of the documentary television series *Corpus Christi*, which elicited much public interest and was broadcast several times on the French/ German channel ARTE.

5. We shall capitalize "Sayings" in order to single out ancient phrases, sentences, passages, or entire texts that claim to be direct quotations of Jesus' words. In this, we follow the consensus of contemporary scholarship in according special importance to Sayings texts, especially when they are free of narration or theology.

6. Tertullian speaks of the Hebrew scriptures and the New Testament as *Vetus et Novum Instrumentum*.

7. Patriarch of Alexandria, circa 293–circa 373 C.E.

8. [The Hebrew word *besorah,* the Greek word *euangelion,* and the English word *gospel* all mean "good news." —*Trans.*]

9. See especially the posthumous work by P. Nautin, *L'Évangile retrouvé* (Paris:: Éditions Beauchesne, 1998).

10. When comparing the synoptics with each other, an important feature to bear in mind about Luke is that unlike Matthew, he makes an effort not to mix the two sources.

11. Acts 12:25 and 15:37 and 2 Tim. 4:11.

12. The apostle John was the son of Zebedee and brother of James, called the Elder. He was believed to be the husband of Salome, one of the saintly women who followed Jesus and were present at the crucifixion.

13. According to Irenaeus, bishop of Lyons, writing in 180 C.E., Ignatius, bishop of Antioch, also mentioned this presence in a letter to the Ephesians dated 110 C.E.

14. This is how Mark informs us that Jesus gave nicknames to some of his

closest disciples. For example, he called James and John "the sons of thunder." When he prayed, Jesus spoke to God with affectionate familiarity, calling him "Abba," an intimate word for "Father."

15. See Luke 2:30–32 and 24:47.

16. Luke 22:69. This is how Luke returns to the first part of the Saying attributed to Jesus when answering the high priest, found also in Mark and in Matthew: "You will see the Son of Man taking his seat to the right of the Power of God, *and arriving surrounded by heavenly clouds* . . . " Yet Luke omits the italicized portion.

17. In John, only chapter 6 takes place in Galilee. Even then, Jesus returns to Judaea and to Jerusalem at least four times, as compared to only once in the synoptics.

18. Cf. John 2:11, 2:23, 3:2, 4:48, 4:54, 6:2, 6:14, 7:31, 9:16, 11:47, 12:8, 12:37, 20:30.

19. During a secret nocturnal visit to Jesus by Nicodemus, a prominent Pharisee.

20. See chapter 7, "The Good News."

21. The word *kingdom* occurs fifty-one times in Matthew, most often as "the Kingdom of Heaven." It occurs eighteen times in Mark and thirty-nine times in John, most often as "the Kingdom of God."

22. In a part of chapter 16, which many scholars consider to be a later addition from a source different from Mark.

23. Acts 2:22–36.

24. G. Vermès, *The Changing Faces of Jesus* (New York: Viking Compass, 2000). [Quotations from Vermès in this book may vary slightly from the English originals since they are retro-translations from the author's French translations. —*Trans.*]

25. According to the *Oxford Dictionary of the Christian Church*. However, one must not neglect the important influence of John's theological vision.

26. With the exception of the seven Letters mentioned earlier.

27. Opinions differ on this point. A. N. Wilson (in *Paul: The Mind of the Apostle*) claims that Paul, a tent maker whose Jewish name was Saul, belonged to the police of the Jerusalem Temple during the life of Jesus, presumably when he witnessed the stoning of Stephen and was charged with guarding the clothes of the executioners (Acts 7:58). The claim that Paul was a Temple policeman is challenged by others. Many specialists do agree that between 20 and 30 C.E., Saul was a young man living in Jerusalem, where (according to Acts, though Paul himself does

not mention it in his Letters) he probably was educated by Rabbi Gamaliel. It is therefore not impossible that Paul met Jesus during the last part of the latter's public ministry.

28. In Greek, the word for resurrection is *egerté,* which has several meanings: to awaken; to enlighten; to set up, to erect, to stand; and to revive.

29. Vermès notes that Paul was quite capable of twisting the interpretation of the scriptures in question to fit his demonstration. The same is true of his argument that the Jews are descendants of Hagar, Abraham's concubine, whereas Christians are descended from Sarah, via Isaac (Gal. 4:21–31).

30. 2 Gal. 1:13.

31. From the Greek *apocruphos,* meaning "kept secret," "hidden," or "kept under."

32. Norman Golb, *Who Wrote the Dead Sea Scrolls?* (New York: Scribner, 1995).

33. Ibid.

34. Cf. chapter 5, "Was Jesus a Disciple of John the Baptist?"

35. Such as J. A. T. Robinson, J. Fitzmeyer, and Jean Daniélou.

36. Crossan, *The Cross That Spoke: The Origins of the Passion Narrative* (San Francisco: Harper and Row, 1988). Meier rejects Crossan's hypothesis as unfounded on valid historical proof. [*The Gospel of the Cross* can be a misleading term. Most often, at least in English exegetical literature, it refers to a kind of narrative and theological core implicit in the canon, not to a separate gospel, nor to an older source, such as Q. —*Trans.*]

37. In fact, along with the four canonical gospels plus Thomas (discussed later), we could speak of at least eight gospels if we include the Gospel of the Nazarenes, the Gospel of the Ebionites, and the Gospel of Marcion. The first is believed to have been written in Aramaic during approximately the same period as the Gospel of Matthew. The Ebionite text is apparently a composite of the synoptics written in Greek and probably used by Jordanian Christians.

38. See the list of codices in appendix 1.

39. The word *gnostic* is the adjective derived from the Greek word *gnosis,* meaning revealed knowledge. This knowledge is related to mysteries of the divine realm and is supposed to teach initiates the secrets of their origins and the way to salvation. [For a definition of *gnosis* that is more applicable to the Gospel of Thomas, see Jean-Yves Leloup, *The*

Gospel of Thomas (Rochester, Vt.: Inner Traditions, 2005). —*Trans.*]

40. C. M. Tuckett, ed., *The Scriptures in the Gospels* (Leuven: Leuven University Press, 1997).

41. Such as Crossan, Cameron, Davies, Jeremias, Ménard, James Robinson, and G. Quispel.

42. For a detailed account of these points of view, see J. Meier, *A Marginal Jew* (New York: Doubleday, 1991), 127.

43. R. Shorto, *Gospel Truth* (New York: Riverhead Books, 1997), 261.

44. E. Linnemann, "Is There a Gospel of Q?" In *Bible Review* (August 1995): 18. Linnemann had endorsed the Q thesis before turning toward more "fundamentalist" views.

45. Cf. S. Patterson, *The Gospel of Thomas and Jesus* (Santa Rosa, Calif.: Polebridge Press, 1993).

46. It would be more accurate to speak of "Judaisms," because of the rich diversity of Jewish thought and belief during this period.

47. Generally included in this (incomplete) list are the Mishnah (oral tradition), the Palestinian and Babylonian Talmuds (including the Gemara, which are commentaries on the Mishnah), the Tosefta (added sayings that are not in the Mishnah), the Targums (Aramaic translations and paraphrases of the scriptures), and the Midrashim, which are rabbinical commentaries comprising a deeper exegesis of the scriptures, dealing with legal matters (Halakah) or with historical and ethical matters (Haggadah).

48. J. Klausner, *Jesus of Nazareth: His Life, Times, and Teaching* (New York: Macmillan, 1925).

49. Among the rare references to Jesus or his family in ancient rabbinical literature, Klausner discusses an account relating to a certain Ben Pandera, a Roman soldier reported to have had illicit relations with a Jewish woman. Origen, discussing a second-century polemicist named Celsus, reports that the latter claimed to have heard a similar story about Mary, the mother of Jesus. Although many scholars see such stories as evidence of gossip fabricated by critics ridiculing the disingenuous legends about the infancy of Jesus related by Matthew and Luke, Klausner considers the Babylonian Talmud's account of a magician, Yeshua, hanged (on the cross?) on the eve of Passover, to be one of the few serious historical references to Jesus in the Babylonian Talmud.

50. Johann Maier, *Jesus von Nazareth im der talmudischen Überlieferung* (Darmstadt: Wissenschaftliche Buchgesellschaft, 1992).

51. In Greek, *Ego eïmi o ous.*

52. Translated from the Greek by W. Whiston, *The Complete Works of Josephus,* Nashville: T. Nelson, 1998.

53. S. Bardet, *Le Testimonium Flavinium* (Paris: Le Cerf, 2002).

54. [The American Heritage dictionary defines *interpolate* as both "to insert into a text" and "to change or falsify a text by introducing new or incorrect material." —*Trans.*]

55. Eusebius, bishop of Caesaria (d. 337), was the first to quote this passage.

56. Over the course of history, a number of eminent Catholic churchmen, as well as Luther among the Protestants, have engaged in dissemination of anti-Semitic propaganda. This has given rise to excesses that we know all too well. Recently, the Vatican issued a proper public apology regarding this.

57. *Vie des douze Césars, Claudius,* XXV. Roman power of the time saw the Christians as a Jewish sect.

58. Ibid., *Nero XIX.* In that era, "superstition" referred to any belief other than those officially sanctioned.

59. The Letters of Paul, whose redactions are older than the canonical gospels, the Acts of the Apostles, and any other New Testament writings. This also applies to certain apocryphal texts, which constitute important historical source documents, though they are of less importance for this essay, because they contain very few elements that bear directly on historical research about Jesus.

Chapter 2: Exegetical Studies of the Sources

1. Because the linguistic and cultural environment was dominated by Hellenism during the whole era of the New Testament writings.

2. As André Chouraqui (translator of a highly regarded, scholarly French version of the Hebrew scriptures and New Testament that is deliberately literal) notes in his introduction to the Gospel of John: "It would also be an error to insist on too sharp a distinction between Hebrew and the Aramaic spoken by Jesus' contemporaries. The latter is full of Hebrew words . . . In fact, the two languages had become like twin sisters by the first centuries of the Christian era."

3. Cf. Perrot, *Jésus et l'histoire,* 14.

4. Hence the importance of each community's interpretation. Well-established investigations have shown that a fact or an event is never identically reported by every witness. For a community, interpretation is all

the more relative, varying according to emotional, psychological, cultural, and social factors.

5. In contrast to Mark's laconic account of Jesus' baptism, in Matthew, John the Baptist avows that he is not worthy of baptizing such a lofty being. In Luke, however, John was in prison before Jesus' baptism, so no one knows who performed it. As for John, the baptism is simply deleted, probably because it was a cause of dispute between the disciples of Jesus and those of John the Baptist.

6. Cf. Psalm 22:1, Matt. 27:46, Mark 15:34.

7. Mark 2:18–22, 10:2–12.

8. As we shall see, this criterion will prove extremely useful when discussing the attribution to Jesus of the Sayings about the Kingdom of God.

9. Cf. Vermès, *The Religion of Jesus the Jew* (Minneapolis: Fortress Press, 1993).

10. These two sources must not be confused with the Q source mentioned above.

11. See further on. [It is unclear what the exact relationship is between the better-known hypothesis of the Q gospel and Nautin's linked concepts of *Évangile primitif* (EP). See appendix 2 for a fuller discussion of Nautin's thesis. —*Trans.*]

12. That is, satisfying both the criterion of embarrassment and that of multiple attestation.

13. Here, the term Son of Man refers specifically to Jesus. A discussion of changes in the meaning of this term can be found in chapter 4.

14. "It mattered little to him what people thought or said about him personally. Only one thing really concerned him: the refusal to hear his message with a sincere heart, for this message came from a source higher than himself—it came from the Spirit of God. Pierre Nautin, *L'Évangile retrouvé*, 164.

15. E. P. Sanders, *Jesus and Judaism* (Philadelphia: Fortress Press, 1985).

16. Edelmann, *Jésus parlait aramén* (Paris: Éditions du Relié, 2000), 307.

17. With the exception of Luke.

18. See chapter 6 for a fuller discussion of them.

19. [Although all biblical scholars seem to agree with the first part of this sentence, it is not clear that they would fully concur with its last clause. For example, the meaning of the Greek word *hamartia* appears close to that of the Hiphil form of the root *khata,* its probable Hebrew predecessor. Both Hebrew and Greek thus appear to agree on something like

"missing the mark," a meaning that is indeed far from the heavy connotations of the English word *sin* or the French word *péché*. Cf. chapter 6 here, the author's discussion under the heading Publicans and Sinners. Cf. also Leloup, *The Gospel of Mary Magdalene* (Rochester, Vt.: Inner Traditions, 2002). —*Trans.*]

20. For example, consider the passage of Luke 3:7–9, which is clearly a reproduction of Matt. 3:7–12; likewise, Luke 3:16–17 reproduces the Matthew passage.

21. A researcher at the prestigious French C.N.R.S., Pierre Nautin devoted much of his life to answering this question of a primary source. His premature death interrupted this work but the main substance was achieved. A fuller study of his results is given in appendix 2.

Chapter 3: Jesus and His Environment

1. The creation of a mythic narrative of Jesus' childhood, as in Matthew and Luke, is not simply intended to exalt the founder of the religion. It also reflects the need for a theological mediation between the mysteries of the Visitation and the Incarnation. Although these narratives are historically untrustworthy, it is an error to interpret them as if we were judging historical claims. In any case, a mythological exegesis is beyond the scope of this book.

2. Matthew writes that shortly after Jesus' birth, while the family was still exiled in Egypt, Herod died. The date of this death is generally set at 4 B.C.E., about twenty years after Julius Caesar's adopted son Octavius took the name of Augustus, after his military victory over his rival general, Mark Anthony.

3. Jesus has been variously described as either "Nazarene" (Matt. 2:23), "Nazarean," or "from Nazareth." We shall explore the implications of this later. [Though Matthew uses the Greek word Nazoraios, which has traditionally been translated in English as "Nazarene," Mark refers to Jesus as Nazarenos; in English this has traditionally been translated as "of Nazareth"; however, because the correct Greek form for "of Nazareth" would be Nazarethenos or Nazarethaios, many modern translators prefer to use simply Nazarene. —*Trans.*]

4. "In spite of appearances, and the ambiguous account of Josephus, Judaea did not have the status of a full province, administered by a procurator. Instead, it was attached to the province of Syria, and administered by a prefect." Maurice Sartre, *D'Alexandre à Zenobie* (Paris: Fayard, 2001), 472. In the footnotes, the author adds that "an

inscription from Maritime Caesaria in honor of Pontius Pilate designates him precisely as *praefectus*."

5. The disciples' proclamations were also expressed in different ways, which has undoubtedly added to the confusion.

6. The content of this section is based especially on the studies by Sanders (*The Historical Figure of Jesus* [London: Penguin, 1993]); Vermès (*The Changing Faces of Jesus* [New York: Viking Compass, 2000]); and Baron (*Histoire d'Israël*, vols. 1–2 [Paris: Presses Universitaires Françaises, 1956]).

7. After Alexander's death, two of his generals divided the empire he had won: Ptolemy took Egypt and surroundings and Seleukos took Persia and surroundings. The Ptolemaic dynasty dated from 305 to 30 B.C.E. and the Seleucid dynasty from 305 to 84 B.C.E.

8. The Hasmonean dynasty was founded by descendants of Hasmoneus. They were originally from Modin, a village northeast of Jerusalem. This family was also the origin of the Maccabees, who became prominent after a religious uprising against Antiochos IV, a Seleucid king who aggressively Hellenized Palestine and profaned the Temple of Jerusalem. The Maccabees ruled over Judaea from 42 to 40 B.C.E.

9. The Idumeans, also known as Edomites, were descendants of Esau. They invaded southern Judaea in the seventh century B.C.E., as well as northern Arabia, which took the name Idumea.

10. Herod had many children from a number of wives, six of them known to us. He assassinated three of his sons, one of his wives, and a mother-in-law.

11. Also known as Lake Genesareth and Lake Tiberiad.

12. A supreme council and tribunal called the Sanhedrin was founded by the Hasmoneans. The council was appointed, not elected, and comprised seventy-one elders presided over by the high priest (according to Josephus and to the New Testament) or by a Pharisee rabbi (according to Talmudic literature).

13. Baron, *Histoire d'Israël*, 226.

14. Baron points out, however, that the main cities along the Mediterranean coast and in Transjordan, were still Greek-administered cities where Jews were not always well treated. Samaria formed a very different religious group, which Josephus designated by the term *ethnos*, meaning "foreigners."

15. Not to be confused with Caesaria, where the prefect resided.

16. In 5 B.C.E., Sephoris was burned by Varus, proconsul of Asia. The city

of Sephoris is also known as the place where Juda ha Nasi, Judaean patriarch, son of Simeon ben Gamaliel and redactor of the Mishnah, spent the last part of his life.

17. Only six miles apart.

18. S.-W. Baron, *Histoire d'Israël,* vol. 1, 372–73.

19. "When [Galilee] was directly incorporated into the Empire in 6 C.E., the administration imposed tributes of crops, hard labor, direct and indirect taxes, tolls, and customs duties, in order to maintain Roman soldiers and functionaries. This must have made Palestinian farmers' lives extremely difficult." S. -W. Baron, *Histoire d'Israël,* 374.

20. Whenever we refer to gospel authors Luke, Matthew, Mark, and John, it must be recalled that these are traditional, convenient attributions that do not correspond to the collective authors of each gospel, who are unknown.

21. "Bethlehem, land of Juda, you are anything but the least of the clans of Juda, for from you will spring a leader who will serve as shepherd of my people of Israel" (Matt. 2:6, citing Micah 5:2).

22. "But, learning that Archelaus ruled over Judaea in the place of Herod, his father, he feared to return there. Warned in a dream, he retreated to the land of Galilee and settled in a town called Nazareth. This was so that the prophecy would be fulfilled: thus he was called Nazarene" (Matt. 2:22–23).

23. From Luke 2:1–5:

> In those days a decree went out from Caesar Augustus that all the world should be enrolled. This was the first enrollment, when Quirinius was governor of Syria. And all went to be enrolled, each to his own city. And Joseph also went up from Galilee, from the city of Nazareth, to Judaea, to the city of David, which is called Bethlehem, because he was of the house and lineage of David, to be enrolled with Mary, his betrothed, who was with child.

24. Herod died in 4 B.C.E.

25. "Now, the birth of Jesus Christ took place in this way. When his mother Mary had been betrothed to Joseph, before they came together she was found to be with child of the Holy Spirit; and her husband Joseph, being a just man and unwilling to put her to shame, resolved to divorce her quietly" (Matt. 1:18–19).

26. There is definitely a counter-tradition about Jesus as an illegitimate

child. This story, which emerges clearly only in sources from the mid-second century, originates in a polemical pamphlet whose object was to attack the early Christians' belief in Mary's virginity. Of course the latter is totally unverifiable.

27. Niddah, 1:6.

28. From the Encyclopedia Universalis:

> Also called the Credo, the Symbol of the Apostles is the annunciation of Christian faith. It is used in the Catholic Church, the Anglican Church, and in many Protestant churches. It is not officially recognized by the Orthodox Church. One tradition claims that it was written by the twelve apostles, but it really derives from questionnaires used in early Christian times by bishops who wished to assess the faith of subjects during catechisms. A model of these "questionnaires" has been conserved in Hippolytus. The bishop begins with the question: "Do you believe in God the Almighty Father?" Then the major truths of Christian faith are listed. Put in the form of affirmations, these questions have become credos, also known as "professions of baptismal faith." The text of the current Symbol repeats that of a profession of baptismal faith used in the Church of Rome in the third–fourth centuries. It has acquired its definitive form, eclipsing the other forms, and was recognized as the official Credo of the Western Church under Pope Innocent III (d. 1216).

29. The dogma proclaimed by Pope Pius IX in 1854. It is noteworthy that this conception was not unanimously accepted previously. For example, Thomas Aquinas, one of the greatest theologians, had refused this sort of "privileged" Immaculate Conception to Mary.

30. Luke 2:7.

31. From Mark 3:31–35:

> And his mother and his brothers came; and standing outside they sent to him and called him. And a crowd was sitting about him; and they said to him, "Your mother and your brothers are outside, asking for you." And he replied, "Who are my mother and my brothers?" And looking around on those who sat about him, he said, "Here are my mother and my brothers! Whoever does the will of God is my brother, and sister, and mother."

From Matt. 12:46–49:

> While he was still speaking to the people, behold, his mother and his brothers stood outside, asking to speak to him. But he replied to the man who told him, "Who is my mother, and who are my brothers?" And stretching out his hand toward his disciples, he said, "Here are my mother and my brothers!" Then his mother and his brothers came to him, but they could not reach him for the crowd.

From Luke 8:19–21:

> And he was told, "Your mother and your brothers are standing outside, desiring to see you." But he said to them, "My mother and my brothers are those who hear the word of God and do it."

32. *Le Monde,* October 23, 2002. The article discusses an inscription on a tomb, discovered by André Lamaire, that mentions the existence of these brothers.

33. From Luke 4:25–29:

> But in truth, I tell you, there were many widows in Israel in the days of Elijah, when the heaven was shut up three years and six months, when there came a great famine over all the land; and Elijah was sent to none of them but only to Zarephath, in the land of Sidon, to a woman who was a widow. And there were many lepers in Israel in the time of the prophet Elisha; and none of them was cleansed, but only Naaman the Syrian." When they heard this, all in the synagogue were filled with wrath. And they rose up and put him out of the city, and led him to the brow of the hill on which their city was built, that they might throw him down headlong.

34. "After three days they found him in the temple, sitting among the teachers, listening to them and asking them questions; and all who heard him were amazed at his understanding and his answers" (Luke 2:46–47).

35. John 7:15.

36. Mark 6:8, Matt. 13:55.

37. Meier, *A Marginal Jew,* vol. 1.

Chapter 4: The Judaism of Jesus

1. The Torah is a separate book from the Prophets.

2. "Do not believe that I have come to abolish the Law or the Prophets: I have not come to abolish, but to fulfill" (Matt 5:17).

3. "I have only been sent to the lost sheep of the house of Israel." (Matt. 15:24).

4. See especially 2 Sam.: 10–13.

5. A tradition that speaks of the end of days, or the end of time.

6. The term *reign of God* is used here, in preference to *kingdom* (*melukhah* or *malkhut*, in Hebrew). According to Vermès, the word for *reign* is more abstract than that for *kingdom,* and is used only six times in the Hebrew Bible.

7. P. André and J. Hadot, extracted from a commentary in the Encyclopaedia Universalis article on this subject (www .universalis.fr).

8. This term refers to a group of books written during the four centuries preceding the birth of Jesus that are not included in either the Jewish or the Christian canonical Bibles. They have been classified by scholars as either "apocrypha" (from Greek *apocruphos,* "hidden") or "pseudepigraphical," of unknown authorship. In the Catholic Bible, they are listed under the heading of "deuterocanonical" books.

9. Books whose authorship has not been authenticated.

10. Meier, *A Marginal Jew,* vol. 2 (New York: Doubleday, 1994), 26.

11. The two authors then refer to the moment in the book of Enoch when the heavenly high priest Enoch enters the Holy of Holies. This is the place of manifestation of "the royal theophany of the cosmic God, seated on his throne of glory, surrounded by silence. Even the angels, transfigured priests, are excluded from this extremely sacred place, just as ordinary earthly priests were. Here we have the ideal model of apocalyptic representations of the Temple, which one can detect in many apocalyptic writings about the end of the Second Temple, and it is in the very wake of Ezekiel."

12. In the history of Israel, King Solomon rejected Abiathar, the high priest who had been appointed by his father, King David. In his place, he named Zadok, whose descendants were to inherit this office.

13. "Probably thus called because of their extreme piety or ritual purity." S. -W. Baron, *Histoire d'Israël,* vol. 2, 614.

14. For a description of this movement, see Josephus, *The History of the War of the Jews and Romans,* 2:129.

15. This "characteristic" was also a part of the Baptist movement.

16. Josephus writes that he had lived for three years with an ascetic of the Essene sect—a certain Bannos. He quotes a number of rules: In the oath of entry into the sect, the postulant swore "to practice piety toward God; to practice justice toward his neighbor; not to harm another, either on his own, nor at the instigation of others; . . . to show himself loyal, . . . especially toward his superiors, since no leader receives his position except through divine will; . . . to always love truth and expose liars; to keep all community matters secret; etc."

17. Speaking of sects, Josephus describes them as groups of distinct ideologies. He uses the word *philosophy* for a consistent and total vision of the world. Whereas he designates the three first philosophical groups by the well-known names Sadducees, Pharisees, and Essenes, the fourth philosophy remains unnamed. However, it is clear that for Josephus, the latter category groups all the fundamentalist extremists sharing the same convictions and a common enemy. The Zealots and Sicarii are included here.

18. A. Abécassis identifies at least two of them: Simon and Judas Iscariot. The latter's surname apparently means "of the Sicarii" (cf., *Judas et Jésus,* 104). However, as Abécassis points out, there is another interpretation: The Hebrew form of Iscariot (ICH QeRiYot) would indicate an inhabitant of QeRiYoT, a town in Judaea. If this is true, Judas would be the only apostle from Judaea.

19. A pagan philosopher who lived in the second century and converted to Christianity. He wrote two books: *Apologies* and *Dialogue with Tryphon.*

20. A second-century Christian writer, the author of *Memoirs* and *Apostolic Constitutions.*

21. Epiphanes, a fourth-century bishop of Cypress, writes in his Panarion against the Arianists, and distinguishes the *nazaraïoi* Baptists from the Christian Nazarenes.

22. The religious community known as the Mandeans, located in Mesopotamia, are descended from the Baptist movement of John, according to some scholars.

23. See Stephen's speech in Acts 7:1–54.

24. The fact that the synoptic gospels speak of instructions given by Jesus to his disciples for preparation of the Passover ritual would alone provide sufficient proof.

25. The canonical gospels contain ample testimony of this when they speak

of the annual trips of Joseph and Mary to Jerusalem, of the purification rite after Jesus' birth, and of the sacrifice of two doves in the Temple.

26. The Greek word for repentance *(metanoia)* means "change of mind."

27. This is the source of the famous prescription "an eye for an eye, a tooth for a tooth" (Exod. 21:24). What this means is that the transgressor must pay an indemnity, set by "arbiters," that is in proportion to the gravity of the injury. The context makes it clear that this is a formula for reparation, not vengeance.

28. But it was not until the middle, or even the end, of the second century B.C.E. that we find a detailed code of Sabbath rules—in the book of Jubilees and in the Mishnah.

29. Stephen was a Hellenized disciple of the Way (one of the first Judeo-Christian sects). His speech is part of his plea before the Sanhedrin after his arrest for "subversion," only hours before he was stoned to death.

30. Sanders, *The Historical Figure of Jesus* (London: Penguin, 1993), 239.

31. Abba is an Aramaic word that is properly left untranslated. It literally means "little Father," but there is no exact translation for the term, both intimate and respectful. "Daddy" would lack the respect, and "Father" lacks the intimacy.

32. It began to be called the Golden Rule in the sixteenth century.

33. We should also recall the famous aphorism attributed in the Talmud to Hillel (bShab.31a): "Do not do to your neighbor what is abhorrent to you." Hillel adds (in words remarkably similar to those attributed to Jesus): "This is the whole of the Torah, the rest is just interpretation. Now, go and study!"

34. The interpretation of these verses and those that precede it is difficult, since the original text on which these verses are based is not known. Matthew and Luke seem to have reversed the order of the sentences in the Q gospel source.

35. But this does not exclude inner spirituality, nor a concern for ritual or cultural purity.

36. Vermès, *The Religion of Jesus the Jew*, 204. The power of this love comes from God. This shows a deepening of Jesus' faith as he centered it on the act of love, rather than on the act of obedience to Mosaic law.

37. "Why do your disciples violate the tradition of the elders? Indeed, they do not wash their hands at mealtimes" (Matt. 15:2).

38. And they saw some of his disciples eat their meal with impure

(unwashed) hands—for the Pharisees, and indeed all the Jews, did not eat without washing their hands and arms up to the elbows, in accordance with the tradition of the elders" (Mark 7:2).

39. See especially E. Drewermann, *L'Amour et la réconciliation* (Paris: Le Cerf, 1992), 74.

40. The Hebrew original in this passage of Genesis in fact means "male and female" and not "man and woman," as it is often translated. The implication, according to M. Balmary, is that YHWH created male and female humans whose task was then to become man and woman through their own efforts. (Cf. M. Balmary, *La Divine Origine*.)

41. Vermès, *The Religion of Jesus the Jew,* 44–45.

42. This is an evocation of *sanctification*.

43. Vermès, *The Religion of Jesus the Jew,* 25. The part of Matthew that speaks of the mouth should dispel any remaining doubt: "Do you not know that everything that enters your mouth descends into the stomach and is afterwards expelled? But what comes out of the mouth comes from the heart, and it is that which pollutes a man" (Matt. 15:17–18). Matthew's version of this Saying does not include the dubious sentence about Jesus making all food pure.

44. The position of Jesus regarding the Temple is examined from another perspective in chapter 7.

45. Similar to this text of the Acts 6:13–14: "[They] set up false witnesses who said, 'This man never ceases to speak words against this holy place and the law; for we have heard him say that this Jesus of Nazareth will destroy this place, and will change the customs which Moses gave to us.'"

Cf. also this text from Mark 15:58–59: "We heard him say, 'I will destroy this temple that is made with hands, and in three days I will build another, not made with hands.'" Yet even with this, their testimonies were not in accord.

46. Referring to mockeries shouted by passersby at Jesus as he was hanging on the cross.

47. From John 2:13–19:

> The Passover of the Jews was at hand, and Jesus went up to Jerusalem. In the temple he found those who were selling oxen and sheep and pigeons, and the money changers at their business. And making a whip of cords, he drove them all, with the sheep and oxen, out of the temple; and he poured out the coins

of the money changers and overturned their tables. And he told those who sold the pigeons, "Take these things away; you shall not make my Father's house a house of trade." His disciples remembered that it was written, "Zeal for your house will consume me." The Jews then said to him, "What sign have you to show us for acting in this way?" Jesus answered them, "Destroy this temple, and in three days I will raise it up."

48. This was also a belief of the Zealots, the most famous of whom was Judas. Abécassis stresses this point, which he considers an explanation of the frustration of this apostle with his master, when he realized that Jesus did not want to pursue this "mission" to its conclusion.
49. Chapter 1 of Leviticus and Deuteronomy 12:5–6.
50. Mark 13:2, Matt. 24:1, Luke 21:6.

Chapter 5: Was Jesus a Disciple of John the Baptist?

1. P. Johnson, *A History of Christianity* (New York: Simon and Shuster, 1976), 21.
2. Referring to John, known as the Baptist.
3. Referring to the Pharisees, as the gospel makes clear.
4. Rom. 2:11.
5. "Thus I will send you Elijah, the prophet . . ." (Ma.l 4:5).
6. In answer to a question asked by his disciples about the coming of Elijah, the writer of Matthew has Jesus say: "Yes, Elijah must come, and put all things in order. But I tell you, Elijah has already come, and they did not recognize him, but treated him as they pleased. And the Son of Man will likewise suffer from them." Then Matthew adds that the disciples understood that "Elijah" meant John the Baptist (17:11–13). Some authors think this passage was a later redaction, either by the gospel writer or by the early Church.
7. This famous quotation is a slightly inaccurate translation of the ancient text. Translated literally, the verse John refers to says: "A voice cries: Prepare a way for Yahweh in the wilderness" (Isa. 40:3). The synoptics repeat the error in speaking of "a voice crying in the wilderness" (Mark 1:3, Matt. 3:3, Luke 3:4). The quotation originates in the Septuagint, where the voice is implicitly that of Yahweh, calling to the prophet. The Evangelists transformed it into the voice of John, precursor to the Messiah. [The author quotes primarily the Jerusalem Bible, whereas we more often use others. As in all versions

in French, the word *désert* appears in the above passage. But the English word *wilderness* is closer to the original Hebrew, which includes both arid desert and wild forestland. In general, when the author deliberately resorts to literal translations of Bible passages, we have chosen to translate from André Chouraqui's highly acclaimed, scrupulously literal translation in French: *La Bible* (Paris: Bayard, 2001). —*Trans.*]

8. Note that Matthew speaks of the Baptist in chapter 3, after the genealogy of chapter 1 and the infancy narrative of chapter 2.

9. Mark 1:1–13.

10. [The American Heritage Dictionary defines *teleology* as "the use of ultimate purpose, design, or final cause, as a means of explaining phenomena or history." —*Trans.*]

11. Some of the later developments here owe much to Meier's exhaustive study of John the Baptist and Jesus in *A Marginal Jew*, vol. 2; and to C. Perrot, *Jésus et l'histoire,* 87–118.

12. The most common explanation is that John's baptism of Jesus would have raised the issue of their hierarchical status for Luke. Given his belief in Jesus' supremacy, the contradiction would have been untenable.

13. Luke 1:26–27, 31.

14. This annunciation of a miracle is followed by another. Six months after the miraculous conception of John, the same angel, Gabriel, appeared to Mary in Nazareth. She was the fiancée of Joseph, a carpenter descended from the royal line of David. The angel said: "And behold, you will conceive in your womb and bear a son, and you shall name him Jesus. He will be great, and will be called the Son of the Most High; and the Lord God will give to him the throne of his father David, and he will reign over the house of Jacob for ever; and of his kingdom there will be no end" (Luke 1:31–33).

15. Book XVIII, chapter 5.

16. The war between Herod Antipas and Aretas IV, Nabatean king of Petra and Damascus. One probable cause was Herod's divorce from a daughter of Aretas and his remarriage to Herodia, the daughter of Antipas's brother Aristobulus and sister of Herod Agrippa, the Great.

17. A liberal translation by the author. A reference to Jesus is in chapter 3 of this same Book XVIII.

18. Josephus, *Antiquities,* XVIII, 2. According to Mark, although John the Baptist was beheaded because he publicly opposed Herod's marriage to

Herodia, the beheading was decreed when Herod, enchanted by the dance of Herodia's daughter Salome, offered the girl anything she desired. Instigated by her mother, Salome demanded the Baptist's head on a platter.

19. The first part of the phrase is from Mark 1:4 and the second from Matthew 3:2. A better translation from the Greek of the Septuagint, from which these texts are extracted, is: "The conversion of those who are in error." Translations that use the word *repent* convey a harsher connotation than *convert*. Apparently, the Baptist's message was an exhortation to turnaround, a radical change of life, which is more faithful to the Greek word *metanoia*.

20. See chapter 7 for more on the Kingdom.

21. Mark writes that Herod imprisoned him for this reason, but Josephus says it was because he feared John's growing popularity.

22. Cf. Perrot, *Jésus et l'histoire*, 108.

23. Cf. Funk, et al., and the Jesus Seminar, *The Five Gospels* (San Francisco: HarperCollins, 1993), 41.

24. In the Saying that follows here, as well as in Luke 13:5, 15:7, 24:47.

25. Sanders notes that although the great themes of collective repentance and divine forgiveness (frequently linked with restoration of the Kingdom of Israel and conversion of the Gentiles) figure prominently in parts of the Hebrew scriptures, as well as in intertestamental texts, few Sayings of Jesus in the New Testament demonstrate such a link, except for the four discussed in the preceding paragraph.

26. 1 Heb 25:3 ff.

27. Bultmann identified fourteen occasions when the word *judgment* occurs, but the authenticity of virtually all of them is doubtful.

28. See Mark 9:42–48 and Matt. 10:28.

29. People do not change without reason—and in any case, change has a cost. Thousands of examples illustrate this. Consider, to overcome certain addictions, one must confront the reasons behind the enslavement. This implies a painful process. (Unless, of course, one admits "miraculous" conversions . . .) How could it be easy to abandon the secondary benefits of a neurosis? This may explain a tendency to refuse healing.

30. A voice cries: "In the wilderness, clear a road for Yahweh; in the steppe, make straight a way for our God" (Isa. 40:3).

31. The most recent studies (Golb, Guyénot, and others) raise doubts that John the Baptist was linked to Qumran. [In late 2004, major new

archaeological discoveries by Itzhak Magen and Yuval Peleg provide impressive support for the studies the author mentions, further discrediting what Golb calls the "Qumran myth." They imply that Qumran was never the site of an Essene community; it probably never was a monastic community at all; and the Dead Sea Scrolls were collected from a number of Jewish sects and do not constitute an "Essene library." Neither the scrolls nor the Qumran site appears to have any connection with the Baptist. —*Trans.*] Cf. the *University of Chicago Chronicle* online: http://chronicle.uchicago.edu/041104/scrolls.shtml

32. Perrot, *Jésus et l'histoire.*

33. Meier, *A Marginal Jew,* 2:26.

34. Chouraqui translates this as: "A stronger one than me comes after me. I have immersed you in water; he will immerse you in the holy breath" ("breath"—that is, *pneuma,* spirit).

35. Among scholars who have studied the relationship between John the Baptist and Jesus, we note the work of Laurent Guyénot, *Jésus et Jean Baptiste* (Chambéry: Imago-Exergue, 1999). This exhaustive and rigorous study questions several accepted ideas about the person and role of the Baptist. Guyénot's work is invaluable to gain a comprehensive view of the Baptist and the way his image was "exploited" by the early Church. Guyénot believes that John was the leader of a baptist sect.

36. For these disciples, it was critical to recognize Jesus' superiority. Thus he should have baptized John, and not the reverse.

37. Meier, *A Marginal Jew,* 2: 20–22.

38. In contrast with Mark's laconic account of Jesus' baptism, Matthew has John confess that he is not worthy to baptize one who is so much greater than he. In Luke, Jesus is baptized after the Baptist is imprisoned and it is not stated who baptizes him. As for John, the entire incident of Jesus' baptism is omitted, probably because it was a source of controversy between the disciples of Jesus and John the Baptist.

39. The available sources on this issue predate the canonical gospels and are independent of them, as exemplified by Paul's reference to the coming of the Christ (1 Thess. 4:15–17). The authors of the canonical gospels would not have had access to Paul's letters, which were doubtless written before these gospels but published afterward.

40. In Aramaic, the root is *tab(aran),* and in Hebrew the word used is *teshubah,* which means "a complete turnaround" or "change of direction." In Greek, it is *metamelomaï* (the root *meler,* signifying "wholehearted"), which means a "wholehearted change."

41. This may also be translated as "is approaching" or "approaches."

42. Which does not mean it is a unique category in itself. In fact, the category of literature known as "apocalyptic" includes many similar texts, some of which are far older than Revelation. An example is the Book of Daniel, which apparently dates from the early Maccabean dynasty; others are attributed to later Christian authors, such as those who use the pseudonyms Peter, Paul, and Thomas. Given the differences in style, the grammatical errors, and the underlying theology, most scholars believe Revelation and the Gospel of John were written by different authors.

43. The Greek word translated as "repentance" or "penitence" appears fifty times in the canonical texts, of which twenty-five are from Luke (counting the Acts of the Apostles), ten from Matthew, only three from Mark, and none from John.

44. Guyénot bases his argument on the exchange between Jesus and his disciples on the return of Elijah (following the transfiguration), and on Jesus' last words on the cross ("Eli, Eli! Why have you forsaken me?"). [Unlike the French *Elie,* the sound of the English name for the prophet Elijah bears no resemblance to the original Hebrew name Eliyeh, sometimes prounounced E-leeli, rhyming with *belly.* The root of this name is related to the word for "My God," and sounds similar to it. Therefore, Jesus' cry in Aramaic *"Eli, Eli, lama sabakhthani?"*—so Guyénot suggests—could mean "Elijah, Elijah, why have you forsaken me?" instead of the traditional "My God, My God, why have you forsaken me?" —*Trans.*] Guyénot argues that "Jesus represented the return of Elijah, inasmuch as he experienced the presence of Elijah in him, or with him—a presence which he felt had deserted him when he was on the cross." According to Guyénot, this was why Jesus believed himself to be the awaited Messiah. Though this argument is clever, we cannot agree with it. It is based on the assumption that Jesus wanted the people of Israel to see him as the Messiah, and that in order to accomplish this, he needed the support of the most revered prophet of his time, John the Baptist. (The latter would thus have played a role similar to the prophet Samuel's in gaining recognition for Saul's royal lineage.) But the assumption is unfounded, as we shall show in the following chapters.

45. His execution may have taken place in the year 33 C.E., according to the gospels that place his death before that of Jesus. But other sources, such as Josephus, imply the year 36 C.E., when King Aretas IV defied

Herod's troops—an event that, according to Josephus, led to John's arrest and execution.

46. Meier, *A Marginal Jew*, 2:22.

Chapter 6: The Mission of Jesus

1. According to synoptic chronology in the first case or to that of John in the second case. This question will be further examined later in this chapter.

2. The visit of Jesus to Jerusalem where a crowd welcomed him with palm branches (Mark 11:8, Matt. 21:8, John 12:13).

3. "Now, the chief priests and all the Sanhedrin searched for a witness against Jesus so as to have him put to death, but they found none" (Mark 14:55). See also Matt. 26:59.

4. However, one passage that is identical in Matthew and in Luke (the famous Q, their common source) could imply that Jesus went to Jerusalem several times. But its meaning relevant to this point is far from clear: "Jerusalem, Jerusalem, you who murder prophets and stone those who are sent to you, how many times have I wanted to gather your children together, as a hen gathers her chicks under her wings . . . but you did not want it!" (Matt. 23:37, Luke 13:34).

5. "The foxes have their dens, and the birds of the sky have their nests, but the Son of Man has no place to lay his head" (Matt. 8:20, Luke 9:58).

6. Meier devotes an entire chapter of his third volume to this question. Cf. *A Marginal Jew*.

7. On this subject, Meier cites A. Culpepper's study showing that schools consisting of a very restricted circle of disciples were widespread, occurring among Pythagoreans, Platonists, Aristotelians, Epicureans, Stoics, and the disciples of Hillel, of Philo, and so forth. See A. Culpepper, *The Johannine School* (SBLDS 26, 1975).

8. Gen. 49:28, Exod. 24:4, Josh. 3:12, Ezek. 47:13, Esdr. 6:17, 1 Chron. 27:7.

9. Bar. 4:37, 5:5; 2 Macc. 1:27, 2:18.

10. Andrew is the brother of Simon-Peter (Kephas). He had been a disciple of the Baptist, as probably was his brother. Simon the Zealot is also known as the Canaanite (Matthew and Mark) or the Zealot (Luke and Acts). The mother of James, son of Alpheus (also called James the Younger in Matthew, Mark, Luke, and Acts) is one of the women present at the crucifixion. Bartholomew is mentioned by Matthew, Mark,

Luke, and the Acts. Thaddeus is mentioned in Matthew and Mark; he is also called Judas, but is not Judas Iscariot.

11. In his Letter to the Galatians, Paul counts James as one of the apostles (Gal. 1:19).

12. Strangely, Matthew does not give the name of the mother of James and John, the sons of Zebedee, friends of Simon and close disciples of Jesus. Matthew is the only gospel that speaks of this holy woman (Matt. 20:20, 27:56).

13. Joanna and Susanna were reputed to be daughters of wealthy families who helped Jesus financially (Luke 8:3).

14. Salome and Miriam of Magdala (a.k.a. Mary Magdalene) had followed Jesus in Galilee, and were present under the cross when he died. They were the first to go to his tomb. There they found, not the body of the Master, but a young man dressed in white (Mark 16:1, 27:56). Luke mentions Jesus healing these women of illness and of demonic spirits (Luke 8:2).

15. The sister of Lazarus and of Martha, "It was Mary who anointed the Lord with perfumed oil, and wiped his feet with her hair" (John 11:2).

16. The exact Hebrew term, as quoted by Baron in his *Histoire d'Israël*, 373, is *am ha-ars*. In the Talmud (Pesaim, 49b), we finds statements like: "A Jew must not marry a daughter of *am ha-ars*, because they are impure animals and their wives are unclean reptiles." Baron also quotes R. Eléazar, who said: "One can chop up one of the *am ha-ars* even when the day of Expiations falls on a Sabbath [that is, when any sort of work is doubly forbidden]." His disciples asked, "But Master, why not say 'slaughter' instead of 'chop up'?" But he replied: "Slaughter requires a blessing, but not chopping up."

17. Vermès, *The Religion of Jesus the Jew*, 205–206.

18. Luke 7: 36–38:

> One of the Pharisees asked him to eat with him, and he went into the Pharisee's house, and took his place at table. And behold, a woman of the city, who was a sinner, learned that he was at table in the Pharisee's house, and brought an alabaster flask of perfumed oil. Standing behind him at his feet, weeping, she began to wet his feet with her tears, and wiped them with the hair of her head, and kissed his feet, and anointed them with the perfumed oil.

19. Mark tells the story like this:

> And as he sat at table in his house, many tax collectors and sinners were sitting with Jesus and his disciples; for there were many who followed him. And the scribes of the Pharisees, when they saw that he was eating with sinners and tax collectors, said to his disciples, "Why does he eat with tax collectors and sinners?" And when Jesus heard it, he said to them, "Those who are well have no need of a physician, but those who are sick; I came not to call the righteous, but sinners." (Mark 2:15–17)

In Luke, it is:

> And the Pharisees and their scribes murmured against his disciples, saying, "Why do you eat and drink with tax collectors and sinners?" And Jesus answered them, "Those who are well have no need of a physician, but those who are sick. I have not come to call the righteous, but the sinners to repentance." (Luke 5:30–32)

20. In this context, Philo is speaking of Capito, charged with collecting Roman taxes in Judaea. Poor when he began, he had amassed a fortune in various forms through cleverness and lies.
21. S. -W. Baron, *Histoire d'Israël,* 1:374.
22. This refers to the lost sheep, to the woman who lost a drachma, and to the prodigal son.
23. [The English word *wicked* is even heavier than *sinner,* suggesting willful malice and depravity. By contrast, *lost* is lighter, suggesting someone who has gone astray. Although "lost" is still a mistranslation of the Greek and Hebrew words, in some contexts it is closer than "sinner," which specifies someone who has transgressed divine law. Unfortunately, most Bibles continue to use the latter term, or the French equivalent, *pécheur.* —Trans.]
24. See chapter 2.
25. This remark is valid for most gospel passages that oppose Jesus to the Pharisees in Galilee. The word "Pharisee" occurs seventy-seven times in the canonical gospels, evidence that early Christians were involved in a vehement dispute with this group.
26. Sanders, *Jesus and Judaism,* 183–87.
27. Cf. the section of his book *Jésus et l'histoire* that deals with the Baptist movement and practices of ritual purity.

28. On this subject, Perrot cites Philo of Alexandria (*Quod Deus sit immutabilis* 8 and *De Plantatione* 162), as well as Josephus (*Contra Apion* 2, 198 and 202).

29. Some of them did not want to observe ritual prescriptions of purity.

30. Perrot notes that the Pharisee sect had central rifts based on the degree of observance of ritual purity.

31. An excellent example of this is found in the Greek Septuagint text on the beatitudes. The first beatitude quoted by Luke reads: "And raising his eyes upon his disciples, he said: 'Blessed are you, the poor *(ptôkoï),* for the Kingdom of God is yours'" (Luke 6:20).

32. This is attested to in many synoptic gospel passages, such as Mark 5:43, Matt. 8:4, Matt. 9:28–30, Matt. 11:38.

33. Luke says exactly the same thing, except he adds: ". . . to repentance."

34. The French word *sain* has the same root. [As does the narrower English word *sane,* and more obviously the word *soteriology.* Presumably the root the author refers to is a common Indo-European root for Latin *sanus* and Greek *saos.* —*Trans.*]

35. We recall that in eschatological tradition, the arrival of the Messiah puts an end to the powers of Evil (see chapter 4).

36. Matt. 8:28–32; see also Luke 8:27–32

37. Luke 4:34–37

38. Luke 9:38–43; see also Matt. 17:14–18

39. Luke 11:14–20; see also Matt. 9:32–34

40. Matt. 15:22–28

41. Including Matthew's version of the healing of the centurion's servant.

42. L is the scholarly abbreviation that refers to materials and sources unique to Luke.

43. Let us recall that Q is an abbreviation of the German word *Quelle,* meaning "source." This refers to a hypothetical vanished source, common to Matthew and Luke, that contains the collection of Jesus' Sayings upon which they drew (see chapter 1).

44. See Meier, *A Marginal Jew,* vol. 2, 251.

45. Whereas Mark would restrict the phrase Son of Adam to mean Jesus himself, Matthew adds an explanatory note: "When the crowd saw this, they were filled with trembling, and glorified God, who had given such power to human beings."

46. See especially Sanders, *The Historical Figure of Jesus,* 170.

47. John presents the resurrection of Lazarus as the immediate cause of the arrest and execution of Jesus:

> So the chief priests and the Pharisees convened the council, and said, "What are we to do? For this man performs many signs. If we let him go on like this, everyone will believe in him, and the Romans will come and destroy both our holy place and our nation." But one of them, Caiaphas, who was high priest that year, said to them, "You know nothing at all; you do not even realize that it is expedient for you that one man should die for the people, and that the whole nation should not perish." (John 11:47–50)

48. John is the only gospel that founds its entire theology on the eternal preexistence of the Son of God, who was made incarnate in the form of Jesus of Nazareth. Martha refers to this in her profession of faith (John 11:27).

49. The other gospel writers already had the stories of the daughter of Jairus and the son of the widow of Nain at their disposal. They had no real need for another resurrection story.

50. John 11:11.

51. There are five accounts of the multiplication of loaves: Mark 6:30–44; Matt. 14:14–23 and 15:32–38; and John 6:5–14.

52. See John 2:1–11.

53. Geza Vermès rules out the possibility that Jesus would have visited Sephoris, where there was at least one theater. His argument is not convincing. It is true that going to a theater was against the rules of Jewish conduct, but the nonconformist Jesus is hardly an example of strict Jewish observance. As for the word *hypocrite* (*upocritès* in Greek), employed by Jesus in the Saying of Matthew 6:16, in this context it means someone who is pretending—it has no theatrical association.

54. We can imagine, as some have, that in some inn of this cosmopolitan center, Jesus had an opportunity to exchange views with Stoics, or even Buddhists. Many other events can be imagined as well. But in a historical study, it is inappropriate to elaborate on hypotheses without documentary foundation.

55. On this subject, see Marcus Borg and Ray Riegert, eds., *Jesus and Buddha: The Parallel Sayings*, (Berkeley, Calif.: Ulysses Press, 1997). Borg discusses the teachings of both regarding "the Way," emphasizing three important common points: (1) a new way of seeing; (2) a process of transformation, requiring a radical turnaround; (3) the supremacy of compassion.

56. *Letters*, 92:3.

57. Matt. 5:48.

58. Perrot defines *midrash* as involving "both research and realization of the revealed word, written or oral, towards a fuller discovery of God's plan for the world" (*Jésus et l'histoire*, 140).

59. See notes 46 and 47, chapter 1.

60. Some count a total of thirty-nine, including Matthew 13:52, which reads, "And he said to them, 'Therefore every scribe who has been trained for the kingdom of heaven is like a householder who selects out of his treasure what is new and what is old.' " But the authenticity of this verse is doubtful, because it does not conform to Jesus' teaching.

61. See Vermès, *The Religion of Jesus the Jew*, chapter 4, section 3, which was the inspiration for the paragraphs that follow here.

62. The authenticity of the following parables is in doubt: the fig tree (Mark 13:28–31, Matt. 24:32–36, Luke 21:29–33); the two sons (Matt. 21:28–32); the ruthless debtor (Matt. 18:23–35); the destitute Lazarus and the heartless rich man (Luke 16:19–31); the last judgment (Matt. 25:31–46); and the narrow gate (Luke 13:25–26). Vermès also has doubts about certain passages in the prodigal son parable, as well as that of the good Samaritan, neither of which has multiple attestations.

63. Vermès's hypothesis comprises the following parables: the weeds (Matt. 13:24–30); the murderous winegrowers (Mark 12:1–12, Matt. 21:33–56, Luke 20:9–19); the disloyal steward (Luke 16:1–8); the renunciation of all possessions (Luke 14:28–33); vigilance so as to avoid surprise (Matt. 24:43–44, Luke 12:39–40); and the ten virgins (Matt. 25:1–13).

64. For example, see Jeremias, J., *Les Paraboles de Jésu* (Paris: Le Seuil, 1984); Neusner, J., "Types and Forms in Ancient Jewish Literature," in Moore, et al., *History of Religions* (London: T and T Clark Books, 1972).

65. In his *Antiquities*, Josephus claims that Solomon had composed three thousand books of parables and aphorisms.

66. Apart from the parable of the sower, which is followed by a lengthy explanation; but verses 11–20 have been questioned by members of the Jesus Seminar, who see them as invented by Mark or, more likely, by the early Church.

67. With the exceptions of the parable of the murderous winegrowers (3), which refers to Isaiah and concludes with a quotation from Psalm 118,

and that of the good Samaritan (26), which is an illustration of the precept to love of one's neighbor, as stated in Lev. 19:18.

68. Note that in this context, certain authors, such as R. W. Funk, in his book *Honest to Jesus* (San Francisco: HarperCollins, 1996, claim solid evidence shows that the parables and aphorisms included in the canonical gospels were originally formulated in Greek, noting the poetic style characteristic of that language. Hence Jesus may have been fluent in Greek also! This hypothesis supports the notion of esoteric teachings, but it does not fit the hypothesis that Jesus used simple parables above all to be understood by listeners with little education.

69. This last point on the meaning of the Kingdom, which the parables are supposed to illustrate, is examined in detail in chapter 7.

70. Indeed, the word *yeast* had the negative connotation of rottenness. Jesus was alluding to this aspect when he spoke to his disciples before the multiplication of the loaves: "Open your eyes, and beware of the yeast of the Pharisees and Sadducees!" (Matt. 16:6). This also conforms to the prescription of unleavened bread during the Jewish Passover.

71. From Latin *sapientia,* wisdom.

72. Once the biblical canon of Jewish scripture was officially established during the first half of the second century B.C.E., the concept of ultimate authority in religious matters became progressively identified with the written word of God. The Midrash Bible commentaries were still accepted, inasmuch as they were founded on the canon and judged in conformity with its teaching. Meanwhile, after the Babylonian exile, teaching in the form of a judicial compilation evolved, to adapt the ancient laws to new realities. This was part of the Talmud, the oral tradition of the law.

73. Some scholars doubt that these verses are from Jesus.

74. Sanders, *The Historical Figure of Jesus,* 238.

75. Vermès, *The Religion of Jesus the Jew,* 50–67.

76. Luke 13:1–5 offers a good illustration of this attitude.

77. The Saying that John has Jesus announce, which is often cited as a key teaching, is: "I give you a new commandment: love one another; just as I have loved you, love one another" (John 13:34). Yet this is not a new commandment, because it occurs in the Hebrew scriptures. John's formulation of it must be considered in the context of the Last Supper, when Jesus is addressing his disciples. Some authors, including the Jesus Seminar (a group that includes seventy-five eminent scholars), think this Saying is John's own creation. It is intended to mark a depar-

ture from the Mosaic law to love our neighbor—especially because it includes love of our enemies, which was the new teaching given by Jesus. If we must identify a commandment by Jesus, a more plausible one would be the one he applies to himself in this Saying:

> And I have other sheep, that are not of this fold; I must bring them also, and they will heed my voice. So there shall be one flock, and one shepherd. For this reason the Father loves me, because I lay down my life, that I may live again. No one takes it from me, but I lay it down of my own accord. I have power to lay it down, and I have power to take it again; this commandment I have received from my Father. (John 10:16–18)

78. Matt 5:48. The Greek word *teleios,* translated as "perfect" (first in the plural, then in the singular form), has other meanings: "adult," "initiate," and "fully mature."
79. In fact, Luke's version of this Saying is: "He said to another man: 'Follow me.' The man said: 'Allow me first to go and bury my father.' But he said: 'Let the dead bury their dead. As for you, go and announce the Kingdom of God' " (9:59–60).
80. Edelmann, *Jésus parlait araméen,* 220.
81. According to the definition of the Torah.
82. See Mark 2:5, Matt. 9:1 ff., and Luke 5:17 ff.
83. See, for example, Mark 2:6–10 and Luke 5:17–24.
84. Edelmann, *Jésus parlait araméen,* 66 ff.
85. Rom. 3:24, 8:23; 1 Cor. 1:30; Eph. 1:7; Col. 1:14; Heb. 9:12.
86. Isa. 43:14, 44:6, 47:4, 48:17, 49:7, 49:26 and 8:59, 8:20, 60:16, 63:10.
87. Jer. 15:20–21.
88. Micah 4:10.
89. 2 Sam. 7:23.
90. Benoit and Boismard, *Synopse des quatre Évangiles en français* (Paris: Le Cerf, 1972).

Chapter 7: The Good News

1. In the preface to Marie Vidal's book, *Un juif nommé Jésus, une lecture de l'Évangile à la lumière de la Torah* (Paris: Albin Michel, 1996).
2. In fact, one could speak of at least eight gospels, if one includes (besides Thomas and the four canonicals) the Gospel of the Nazarenes, the Gospel of the Ebionites, and the Gospel of Marcion. [Plus the Gospel of

Mary, the Gospel of Philip, and the Gospel of Truth. — *Trans.*]

3. For more information on the Gospel of Thomas, see chapter 1. [Cf. also Jean-Yves Leloup, *The Gospel of Thomas* (Rochester, Vt.: Inner Traditions, 2005). —*Trans.*]

4. Cf. the Gospel of John: "Truly, truly, I tell you, whoever keeps my word will never taste death" (8:51). In contrast with this Saying from John, where keeping the word is enough to confer immortality, the Saying in Thomas 1 requires that one discover the meaning of the words of the Master.

5. See especially Vermès, *The Changing Faces of Jesus*, 167 ff.

6. From Matt. 8:5-10:

> As he entered Capernaum, a centurion came to him, beseeching him and saying, "Lord, my boy is lying paralyzed at home, in terrible distress." And he said to him, "I will go and heal him." But the centurion answered him, "Lord, I am not worthy to have you come under my roof; but only say the word, and my boy will be healed. For I am a man of authority, with soldiers under me; and I say to one, 'Go,' and he goes, and to another, 'Come,' and he comes, and to my slave, 'Do this,' and he does it." When Jesus heard him, he marveled, and said to those who followed him, "Truly, I say to you, not even in Israel have I found such faith."

7. Matt. 15:22–28:

> And then a Canaanite woman arrived from that country, and cried, "Have mercy on me, O Lord, Son of David; my daughter is severely possessed by a demon." But he did not answer her with even a word. And his disciples came and begged him, saying, "Send her away, for she is crying after us." He answered, "I was sent only to the lost sheep of the house of Israel." But she came and knelt before him, saying, "Lord, help me." And he answered, "It is not fair to take the children's bread and throw it to the dogs." She said, "Yes, Lord, yet even the dogs eat the crumbs that fall from their masters' table." Then Jesus answered her, "O woman, great is your faith! Be it done for you as you desire." And her daughter was healed instantly.

8. The forty-eight verses in the fifth chapter of Matthew and the twenty-six final verses of the sixth chapter of Luke.

9. Such as the prodigal son and the good Samaritan. See ff.

10. Jesus responds rather cryptically to the question of the resurrection of the dead: "And as for the dead being raised, have you not read in the book of Moses, in the passage about the bush, how God said to him, 'I am the God of Abraham, and the God of Isaac, and the God of Jacob'? He is not the God of the dead, but of the living; you are quite wrong" (Mark 12:27).

11. The Greek word *entolè* can be translated as "order," "commandment," or "precept." It seems that "precept" is in better accord than "commandment" with the language typical of Jesus.

12. Matt. 4:23, 9:35, 24:14; Luke 4:43, 8:1, 9:60, 10:9, 16:16.

13. Mark and Luke use only the first expression, whereas Matthew prefers Kingdom of Heaven. But these expressions were interchangeable, as shown by their usage in both similar and different contexts.

14. In the conversation with Nicodemus (John 3:3). Then in chapter 18, John has Jesus say to Pilate: "My Kingdom is not of this world."

15. Actually, the expression Kingdom of God occurs only once in the Hebrew scriptures: in the Wisdom of Solomon (10:10), which is used in the Catholic and Orthodox Bibles. In the Hebrew Bible, we find the expression Kingdom of YHWH once in 1 Chronicles 28:5, a late addition to the Hebrew canon.

16. These are books of the Hebrew canon.

17. In Luke 22:30, Jesus also speaks of the Kingdom that God has bestowed upon him, and that he bestows in turn upon his apostles.

18. For the word *melukah,* see Abdias, verse 21, and Psalms 22:29; for the Aramaic word *malkutha,* see Dan. 4:31.

19. For example "Yahweh will rule forever and ever" (Exod. 15:18).

20. This is a collection of eighteen poems written by a group of Jerusalem Pharisees after the capture of the Temple by Pompey's troops in 63 B.C.E.

21. Contrary to a widespread opinion, Jesus was not the first to preach the Kingdom of God. The Gospels of Mark and Matthew clearly state that the Baptist preached conversion, "for the Kingdom of God is at hand" (Mark 1:15, Matt. 3:2). Besides, the Greek text of Luke uses the word *apo* in relation to John, meaning "from John on." The transitive form of the Greek verb *biaxô* is translated by "constrain" or "force." In its intransitive form, it means "to be violated" or "obtained by force." As Nautin says, this was because John the Baptist did not preach a moral lesson only, but the imminence of the

Kingdom where the righteous would be welcomed, and thus the necessity of conversion. This, plus his influence over large crowds, made the authorities suspicious of him, finally leading to his arrest and execution. Jesus, who may have been a disciple of the Baptist, probably baptized by him, took up the theme of the arrival of the Kingdom.

22. Although he admits that the reign of God has already begun.

23. We have not reproduced the Sayings transcribed in the Gospel of Luke, which are from the same source.

24. Meier, *A Marginal Jew,* 2: 433, and Perrot, *Jésus et l'histoire,* 196, speak of a realized eschatology. The word *contemporaneity* is probably inappropriate, since it refers to the domain of time, whereas the Kingdom is a vision of timelessness, even though it is both present and from all eternity. [Among some English-speaking New Testament scholars, the word *contemporaneity* is used in the author's sense; but some conservative scholars use it as a condescending reference to contemporary exegesis in general. —*Trans.*]

25. See especially the work of Perrin on the Kingdom, *Jesus and the Language of the Kingdom* (London and Philadelphia: Fortress Press, 1980). B. Scott, who agrees with Perrin on this, says that Jesus "used the word 'Kingdom' as a symbol, to express his experience." Cf. his *Symbol-Maker for the Kingdom,* (Philadelphia: Fortress Press, 1983).

26. From my own research, I am convinced that a choice between these two visions is unavoidable. No compromise is possible, unless—and this cannot be entirely excluded—we assume that Jesus' thinking on this evolved, distancing itself progressively from the Baptist's eschatology, toward an affirmation of the Good News: "The Kingdom is within you."

27. J. Weiss, *Jesus' Proclamation of the Kingdom of God* (Minneapolis: Fortress Press, 1971).

28. Albert Schweitzer, *The Quest of the Historical Jesus* (Philadelphia: Fortress Press, 2001).

29. An anachronism in this context, which will only be used again later by the early Church.

30. This refers to Sayings with an apocalyptic content—that is, that God will establish his Kingdom at the end of time.

31. E. P. Sanders, *Jesus and Judaism,* 152.

32. Ibid.

33. Ibid. He presents this as evidence that the disciples had nothing to fear

from Roman power just after Jesus' death, and that they could set to work founding a movement distinct from Judaism.

34. See chapter 4.
35. Perrin, *Jesus and the Language of the Kingdom.*
36. Scott, *Symbol-Maker for the Kingdom.*
37. R. Bultmann, *Jesus and the World* (New York: ET, 1958).
38. (London: 1st ed., 1935; revised ed., 1961).
39. The "last days" or the "last times," from the Greek *escaton.*
40. *Les Paraboles de Jésus* (Le Puy: Xavier Mappus, 1962).
41. The Septuagint text reads: "Idou gar è basileia tou theou entos hymôn estin." There is no parallel to this in Mark or in Matthew. However, Mark does contain a verse that says, "My children, how difficult it is to enter the Kingdom of God!" But this is in the present tense, with no implication of a future event.
42. Edelmann, *Jésus parlait araméen,* 308.
43. Doublas-Klotz, *The Hidden Gospel: Decoding the Spiritual Message of the Aramaic Jesus* (Wheaton, Ill.: Quest Books, 1999).
44. See Luke 2:46, 3:22, 8:7, 27:24, 27:36.
45. If we take the Passion narrative as having historical content.
46. A commonly quoted example to illustrate this challenge is the frequent use of the word *kai* in Greek, which is usually translated as "and," whereas it can also mean "then," "at this moment," "but," "however," "nevertheless," and "also."
47. In fact, the gospels are written not in classical Greek, but in a simplified language (the *koinè*) commonly spoken by non-Greeks in the first century, and sometimes containing Semiticisms from the Jewish Diaspora.
48. The Jesus Seminar's translation is "impose your imperial rule." *The Five Gospels,* 148, 325.
49. The Kaddish is the Jewish prayer for the dead, invoking the Holy Name of the Lord.
50. The Greek verb *eiselaô,* "enter," is conjugated in the same tense: *eiseleusetaï.*
51. But in any case, this is not my opinion.
52. In fact, there are a certain number of parables that are "fabrications." Sometimes they are inspired by sayings and proverbs from Hebrew culture, at other times they are illustrations of a message that a gospel redactor wanted to get across. Many are allegories, often rather long, eschatological, and sometimes apocalyptic.

53. A Greek silver coin.

54. The Septuagint says: *agapèseistov plèsion sou séautov,* whereas the words used in the parable are *éleos met autou.* Some authors see this dissimilarity as evidence that the parable and the dialogue that precedes it are from two independent sources, brought together to serve the cause of the redactor's community.

55. The Hebrew word used by the prophet Hosea for the compassion of Elohim for orphans, is יֶרחם, which Chouraqui translates as "maternal compassion." As he points out, it is also the root of the word for "womb." It occurs in many places in the Hebrew scriptures, and most English Bibles translated it as "compassion," and sometimes "mercy."

56. It is precisely because of this Judaean itinerary that we assume that the wounded man was a Judaean.

57. From Luke: 6:17–19:

> And he came down with them and stood on a level place, with a great crowd of his disciples and a great multitude of people from all Judaea and Jerusalem and the seacoast of Tyre and Sidon, who came to hear him and to be healed of their diseases; and those who were troubled with unclean spirits were cured. And all the crowd sought to touch him, for power came forth from him and healed them all.

58. The fourth beatitude absent from Luke's version says: "Blessed are you, when they hate you, banish you, insult you, and slander your name, for the sake of the Son of Man. Rejoice upon that day, and tremble with happiness, for your reward shall be great in Heaven. Indeed, this is how their fathers treated the prophets." This beatitude is a reflection of the persecutions encountered by the early Church. To these four beatitudes, Matthew adds four more: "Blessed are the pure in heart, for they shall see God. Blessed are the peacemakers, for they shall be called sons of God. Blessed are those persecuted for their righteousness, for theirs is the Kingdom of Heaven. Blessed are you when they slander you, persecute you, and bear every sort of false witness against you, for my sake." As for historical authenticity, the same challenge applies as to the preceding passages. Most authors believe that the first three were derived either from the Psalms or from popular proverbs.

59. These curses are: Woe to you that are rich, for you have received your consolation." "Woe to you that are full now, for you shall hunger."

"Woe to you that laugh now, for you shall mourn and weep." "Woe to you, when all men speak well of you, for so their fathers did to the false prophets."

60. Some of the discussion that follows is inspired by chapter 9 of Edelmann's book *Jésus parlait araméen*. His exegesis offers an antidote for excessively pious interpretations.

61. "Very well! I tell you that many will come from the east and the west to sit at the feast of Abraham, Isaac and Jacob in the Kingdom of Heaven" (Matt. 8:11).

62. "For many are called, but few are chosen" (Matt. 22:14).

63. And Jesus then explains: "So that those who are blind may see, and that those who see may become blind." The Pharisees who heard this asked him: "Are we, then, also blind?" Jesus answered them: "If you were blind you would not be in sin. But you say, 'We see!' So your sin persists." [In the passage from John, the author quotes a French translation that uses *discernement* rather than *jugement*. Virtually all English Bibles use "judgment" here. This seems appropriate, because the Greek word is *krima*, which is closer to "judgment" than to "discernment." —*Trans.*]

64. Matt. 25:15–30.

65. Where, in the first instance (Luke 7:47), it refers to love proffered by a woman of bad reputation, and in the second instance (Luke 11:42), a Saying where Jesus utters imprecations against the Pharisees.

66. In John, the Kingdom is spoken of twice in the third chapter (in the crucial dialogue with Nicodemus) and a third and final time where Jesus says, "My Kingdom is not of this world," during his trial. But the authenticity of the latter is subject to the same doubt as all the other trial narratives.

67. "You shall love the Lord your God with all your heart, with all your soul, and with all your mind. This is the first and greatest commandment. The second is like the first: You shall love your neighbor as yourself" (Matt. 22:37–39; Mark 12:30–33; Luke 10:27).

68. "I give you a new commandment: Love one another; just as I have loved you, love one another" (John 13:34). "If you love me, you will keep my commandments" (John 14:15). "For the Father himself loves you, because you love me, and you believe that I came from the Father" (John 16:27).

69. "Be compassionate, as my Father is compassionate" (Luke 6:36).

70. The italics here and in the following text are the author's. Apparently

he intends the preceding passages as illustrations of contrasting usages attributed to Jesus. He does not state whether the criterion of multiple attestation applies to all of them. —*Trans.*]

71. See especially Matt. 14:33 and 16:16.

72. To quote only one French author who is a specialist on such questions, Perrot writes: "To summarize the consensus, let us say that almost all scholars believe that Jesus never applied the title Son of God to himself, and never used the term." *Jésus et l'histoire*, 238.

73. Ibid., 236.

74. See Matt. 5:9, 5:45, and many other passages that implicitly or explicitly speak of the sons of God.

Chapter 8: The Arrest and Execution of Jesus

1. Along with that of the resurrection and apparitions, but excepting the accounts leading up to and including Jesus' arrest.

2. "And abandoning him, they all fled" (Mark 14:50).

3. Such as Reumann and Harvey, who tend to take the Passion texts literally, even though they question the authenticity of certain words or deeds in their analyses.

4. John 18:25.

5. Not to be confused with Judas the Galilean, the charismatic character mentioned earlier.

6. Josephus, *Antiquities*, XVII.

7. Ibid., II.

8. According to the *Annals* of Tacitus.

9. *Antiquities*, II, XXVII.

10. Sometime around 29 C.E.

11. " . . . And Jesus was thirty years old when he began. And he was believed to be the son of Joseph" (Luke 3:23).

12. The days are counted beginning with the appearance of the first star in the evening. The Jewish Passover festivities lasted for seven days, from the fifteenth to twenty-first of Nissan, the seventh month of the Jewish civil year, and the first month of their sacred year (corresponding to the moon and the vernal equinox, March–April in our calendar).

13. Jewish tradition sets the date as the fourteenth of Nissan: "on the eve of Passover, Jesus the Nazarene was hanged."

14. From Luke 22:8:

> And he sent Peter and John, saying: "Go and prepare the Passover meal for us to eat.

From Mark 14:12:

> The first day of the Azymes, when the Passover lamb was offered, the disciples asked him: "Where do you want us to go make preparations for your Passover meal?"

From Luke 22:7–8:

> The day of the Azymes came, when the Passover lamb was immolated, and he sent Peter and John, saying: {Go prepare the Passover meal for us to eat."

15. According to Perrot, astronomical calculation shows that, in order for the fourteenth of Nissan to fall on a Friday, the corresponding date of our calendar would have to be April 7, 30 C.E. (or April 3, 33 C.E.)

16. In Palestine, Passover (from the Hebrew *hag ha Posakh*, "that God passes over" [that is, over the houses of the children of Israel when he struck the firstborn of the Egyptians in Exod. 12:23]) begins the fifteenth day of Nissan, the first month of the Jewish liturgical calendar year, and continues for seven days. This festival, which in Jesus' time was one of three annual occasions for major pilgrimages to Jerusalem, celebrates the deliverance of Israel from slavery in Egypt. In the Bible, Passover is also designated as the festival of the Azymes (*hag ha massot*: unleavened bread); cf. Exod. 23:15. This was the food that had been eaten during the hasty departure of the Hebrews (Exod. 12:39). The essential rite is the sacrifice of the *korban Pesakh,* or Passover lamb on the fourteenth of Nissan, associated with the escape from Egypt.

17. John 1:29 and 36, Acts 8:32, 1 Peter 1:19. Also, cf. the Book of Revelation, where "lamb" stands for "Christ."

18. Matt. 26:26.

19. "Truly, I tell you that I will drink no more of the fruit of the vine until that day when I drink the new wine in the Kingdom of God" (Mark 14:25).

20. Matt. 26:28.

21. "However, it so happens that the hand of him who will deliver me is with me at this table" (Luke 22:21). It is noteworthy that Jesus does not speak of betrayal here.

22. "I tell you, Peter, the cock will not crow today before you have denied knowing me three times" (Luke 22:24–37). Matthew sets this prophecy after the Last Supper, on the Mount of Olives.

23. Vermès, *The Religion of Jesus the Jew,* 15–16.

24. However, this tradition seems to go far back to the early Church, since Paul cites to the Corinthians what is already being commemorated in the congregations (1 Cor. 11:23–26), and this represents the first statement attributed to Jesus regarding bread and wine.

25. According to Josephus, these were "brigands," followers of Judas the Galilean, who called themselves Zealots.

26. See A. Abécassis, *Judas et Jésus, une liaison dangereuse* (Paris: Édition no. 1, 2001).

27. According to this hypothesis, Judas Iscariot was the second Zealot disciple of Jesus, after Simon the Zealot (not to be confused with Simon-Peter).

28. See also these passages: "When the chief priests and the Pharisees heard his parables, they perceived that he was speaking about them. But when they tried to arrest him, they feared the crowds, because they held him to be a prophet" (Matt. 21:45–46). "The scribes and the chief priests tried to lay hands on him at that very hour, but they feared the people; for they perceived that he had told this parable against them. So they watched him, and sent spies, who pretended to be sincere, that they might report what he said, so as to deliver him to the authority and jurisdiction of the governor" (Luke 20:19–20).

29. Referring to the Temple scandal, Mark writes: "And the chief priests and the scribes heard of it and sought a way to destroy him; for they feared him, because all the multitude was amazed at his teaching" (Mark 11:18). After the resurrection of Lazarus, John says:

> So the chief priests and the Pharisees gathered the council, and said, "What are we to do? For this man performs many signs. If we let him go on like this, everyone will believe in him, and the Romans will come and destroy both our holy place and our nation." But one of them, Caiaphas, who was high priest that year, said to them, "You know nothing at all; you do not understand that it is preferable for you that one man should die for the people, so that the whole nation should not perish." (John 11:47–52)

30. Mark 14:50; Matt. 26:56.

31. Who was this young man? It remains a mystery.

32. The Sanhedrin (from Greek *sunidrion*) designates the supreme religious, judicial, and political authority of Israel. It was a council whose

members were chosen either by the existing members or by political authority. In plenary assembly, the Sanhedrin included seventy-one members, divided into three groups: priests, Pharisees, and aristocrats. Each contained twenty-three members, and was presided over by the Nassi, assisted by a magistrate. Acting as a supreme court, one of the Sanhedrin's powers was to pass judgment on a false prophet, on a high priest, or on an "Elder." In 142 B.C.E., Simon Maccabee was apparently elected by the assembly as ethnarch and high priest (1 Macc. 14:27–49), an allegation confirmed by Demetrios, king of Syria. It appears that the Sanhedrin of the Roman era had its prerogatives limited to religious matters.

33. This is yet another reason to believe that several texts were inspired by a common source.

34. According to the Mishnah, the Sanhedrin met in the Temple, and could hold session only between the two daily sacrifices (between 7:30 A.M. and 3:30 P.M.). In any case, they met neither on the Sabbath nor during festivals, including festival eves. Yet in the synoptic gospels, the trial of Jesus before the Jewish authorities is said to have taken place at night, in the house of the high priest, on Passover eve.

35. Note that the Pharisees are no longer spoken of here.

36. The rest of this extract is: "And I also declare to you: hereafter, you will see the Son of Man sitting at the right hand of the Almighty, and coming wrapped in clouds of heaven." Many authors also see this as an interpolation of the early Church.

37. Josephus, *The History of the War of the Jews and Romans*, VI, 301.

38. Josephus, *Antiquities*, XX, 5.

39. This could also be read as an ironic exclamation: "You—take care of this king!"

40. Moule, C. F. D., *The Origin of Christology* (Cambridge: Cambridge University Press, 1977).

41. Henri Meschonnic, in his new translation of the Psalms (*Gloires: Traduction des Psaumes*, Psalm 22 [Paris: Desclée de Brouwer, 2001], 90), translates this as "Elohim, Elohim, why have you abandoned me?"

42. We cannot subscribe to Guyénot's explanation, which is based on the assumption that Jesus claimed to be the Messiah—a supposition that does not hold up, as we have explained in an earlier chapter.

43. In a provocative but definitely apt remark, Beauchamp says that without the twenty-second Psalm, there would be no Jesus. It expresses the

faith of Israel, challenging God, despised by the nations because of its devotion. Destruction looms before it: "My unique one, save me! " and the outcome: "You have answered me!" Psalm 22 begins as a cry of lament and ends as a song of praise. The implication is that Elohim has responded and intervened, that something has happened.

44. With the exception of the "holy women," whose presence before the cross at Golgotha is affirmed by the synoptics. The Gospel of John adds others: Peter (in the praetorium), Mary, mother of Jesus, and "the disciple Jesus loved," assumed to be John. But the fact is that the authenticity of these passages is often questioned. They lack multiple attestation, and we are virtually certain that none of these people witnessed the trial(s).

45. Vermès, *The Religion of Jesus the Jew,* 210.

46. Since the funerary discoveries at the Giv'artha-Mirtav site in 1968, we have more detailed knowledge about the practice of crucifixion in Jesus' time. Probably the cruelest form of execution, it was reserved for criminals of the lowest social classes. The wrists of the victim were nailed or tied to a beam or log, which was attached to a pole to form a T-shape. Death came through a slow and extremely painful process of suffocation. To draw out the agony farther, the feet of the victim were supported by being nailed or tied to a ledge farther down on the pole. If death had not come by nightfall, the legs were broken, so that the body slumped, resulting in a rapid death by suffocation. In fact, the Jewish law prohibited leaving a dead body on the cross during the Sabbath, which would have begun at nightfall on Friday.

47. "[B]ut the goat on which the lot fell for Azazel shall be presented alive before Yahweh to make atonement over it, that it may be sent away into the wilderness to Azazel" (Lev. 16:10).

48 On the day of Atonement, the high priest laid the sins of Israel on the goat's head before sending it into the desert to die. This is the origin of the concept called *scapegoat* in English.

49. A large number of archaeological digs around Golgotha have yielded the remains of only one crucified man, whose skeleton bears marks of nails through the wrists.

50. As we said previously, many scholars believe that a substantial part of the Passion story is derived from the Hebrew Bible, especially Psalms 22, 69, and 118, and that the Passion narrative was the theme of a ritual of celebration of victory over death. This ritual was mostly chanted in psalms, in a procession representing the road to the cross.

51. Doctoral thesis in philosophy by Ellen Bradshaw Aitken, Harvard Divinity School; J. S. Spong, *Born of a Woman* (San Francisco: HarperCollins, 1992).

52. Certain authors have observed that the presence of the young man in white (in Mark's account) could be interpreted as a sign from God. He tells the women that Jesus is "risen"—not that he himself is risen.

53. Cf. verses 9–20, not reproduced here.

54. Was this the same person as the young man who fled, leaving his robe behind, when Jesus was arrested? Cf. The Arrest of Jesus, in this chapter.

55. Russell Shorto, *Gospel Truth* (New York: Riverhead Books, 1997).

56. Here is John's description of the first apparition:

> . . . [A]nd she saw two angels in white, sitting where the body of Jesus had lain, one at the head and one at the feet. They said to her, "Woman, why are you weeping?" She said to them, "Because they have taken away my Lord, and I do not know where they have laid him." Saying this, she turned round and saw Jesus standing there, but she did not know that it was Jesus. Jesus said to her, "Woman, why are you weeping? Whom do you seek?" Supposing him to be the gardener, she said to him, "Sir, if you have carried him away, tell me where you have laid him, and I will take him away." Jesus said to her, "Miriam." She turned and said to him in Hebrew, "Rabbuni!" (which means Teacher). Jesus said to her, "Do not hold onto me, for I have not yet ascended to the Father. Go instead to my brothers and say to them, I am ascending to my Father and your Father, to my God and your God." (John 20:12–17)

57. Funk, *Honest to Jesus*, 272.

58. Ibid., 259. [In the Gospel of Mary (which the Jesus Seminar dates as contemporaneous with the last redactions of the Gospel of John), it is Mary Magdalene who is first to experience the vision of the (non-physical) resurrected Jesus. There is no mention of the tomb in this gospel. Cf. Leloup, *The Gospel of Mary Magdalene,* and The Jesus Seminar, *The Five Gospels. —Trans.*]

Conclusion

1. There are some who believe that, to the end of his life, Jesus maintained a belief in the imminence of Judgment and the end of time. If so,

then founding a long-lasting church would hardly have been a priority. The choice of the twelve apostles is a subject that has given rise to many divergent, if not contradictory, interpretations.

2. A twelfth-century Muslim philosopher, doctor of law, and commentator on Aristotle, Averroës held that there could be no real contradiction between faith and reason: "Truth cannot contradict truth."

3. This should not be interpreted as denying all theological aspects of Jesus, which are outside the scope of this essay.

4. Obviously this remark does not apply to certain scholars who, either because of their origins or from their own broad experience, have deep knowledge of Judaism. Among them, some of the best known are Abécassis, Ben-Chorin, Perrot, Sanders, Vermès, and Vidal (and no doubt this neglects others just as remarkable). These authors have provided indispensable cultural and religious insights to those who have not had the good fortune of possessing their expertise.

5. Some might say: "Toward the one whom God, our Father, wants you to come."

6. For a reinterpretation of Genesis, see Marie Balmary, *La Divine Origine*.

7. *The Will to Power*, part 2, chapter 407. Rarely have I encountered a thinker who comes so close to the essence of Jesus' teaching: yes, the same Nietzsche who was so viciously attacked by those who saw him as a threat to a dismal and death-oriented world, a world his critics supported, consciously or not.

Bibliography

Abécassis, Armand. *La Pensée juive*. 4 vols. Paris: Librairie Générale Française, 1989.

———. "En Vérité, je vous le dis" in *Une Lecture juive des Évangiles*, Paris, Éditions No. 1, 1999.

———. *Judas et Jésus, une liaison dangereuse*. Paris: Edition No. 1, 2001.

Armstrong, Karen. *A History of God*. New York: Ballantine, 1993.

Aron, Robert, *Les Années obscures de Jésus*. Paris: Desclée de Brouwer, 1995.

Arrien, F. *Manuel d'Epictète*. Paris: Librairie Générale Française, 2000.

Averroës. *L'Islam et la raison*. Paris: GF-Flammarion, 2000.

Balmary, Marie. *Le Sacrifice interdit: Freud et la Bible*. Paris: Grasset, 1986.

———. *La Divine Origine*. Paris: Grasset, 1999.

———. *Abel, ou la traverée d'Eden*. Paris: Grasset, 1999.

———. *Je serai qui je serai*. Exode 3:14. Brussels: Alice, 2001.

Bardet, S. *Le Testimonium Flavinium*. Paris: Le Cerf, 2002.

Baron, S.-W. *Histoire d'Israël*. 2 vols. Paris: PUF, 1956.

Baslez, Marie-Françoise. *Bible et Histoire: judaïsme, hellénisme, christianisme*. Paris: Fayard, 1998.

Baudart, Anne. *Socrate et Jésus*. Paris: Le Pommier-Fayard, 1999.

Ben-Chorin, Schalom. *Mon Frère Jésus*. Paris: Le Seuil, 1983.

Benoit, P., and M. -E. Boismard. *Synopse des quatre Évangiles en français*. Paris: Le Cerf, 1972.

Borg, Marcus. *Meeting Jesus Again for the First Time*. San Francisco: HarperCollins, 1995.

————. *The God We Never Knew.* San Francisco: HarperCollins, 1997.

Borg, Marcus, and Riegert, Ray, ed. *Jesus and Buddha: the Parallel Sayings.* Berkeley: Ulysses Press, 1997.

Bornkamm, Günther. *Jesus of Nazareth.* London: ET, 1960.

————. *Paul.* Minneapolis: Fortress Press, 1995.

Botero, Jean. *Naissance de Dieu.* Paris: Gallimard, 1986.

Botero, Ouaknin, and Moingt. *La plus belle Histoire de Dieu.* Paris: Le Seuil, 1997.

Bowker, J. *Jesus and the Pharisees.* Cambridge: Cambridge University Press, 1973.

Bultmann, R. *Jesus and the World.* New York: ET, 1958.

Cannac, Edith. *Caïn, ou le détournement du sens.* Paris: Plon, 2002.

Cazenave, Michel. *Bible et religion.* Paris: Desclée de Brouwer, 2002.

Changeux, Jean-Pierre. *L'Homme de vérité.* Paris: Odile Jacob, 2002.

Changeux et Connes. *Matière à pensée.* Paris: Odile Jacob, 1989.

Charlesworth, James. *Jesus Within Judaism.* New York: Doubleday, 1988.

Chouraqui, André. *Moïse.* Monaco: Éditions du Rocher, 1995.

————. *Les Dix Commandements aujourd'hui.* Paris: Laffont, 2000.

————. *La Bible* [a literal, scholarly French translation of the Jewish Bible and the New Testament]. Paris: Bayard, 2001.

Crossan, John Dominic. *The Cross That Spoke: The Origins of the Passion Narrative.* San Francisco: Harper and Row, 1988.

————. *The Historical Jesus: The Life of a Mediterranean Peasant.* San Francisco: HarperCollins, 1992.

————. *Jesus: A Revolutionary Biography.* San Francisco: HarperCollins, 1994.

————. *The Birth of Christianity.* San Francisco: HarperCollins, 1998.

Culpepper, A. *The Johannine School.* SBLDS 26, 1975.

Daniélou, Jean. *L'Église des premiers temps.* Paris: Le Seuil, 1985.

Deleuze, Gilles. *Nietzsche et la philosophie.* Paris: Quadrige/PUF, 1997.

Dewermann, Eugen. *Psychanalyse et Éxégèse.* Paris: Le Seuil, 1984, 2000.

————. *Le Mensonge et le suicide.* Paris: Le Cerf, 1992.

————. *De la Naissance des dieux à la naissance du Christ.* Paris: Le Seuil, 1992.

Dibelius, M. *Jesus.* Philadelphia: ET, 1949.

Dodd, C. H. *The Founder of Christianity.* New York: Macmillan, 1971.

Douglas-Klotz, N. *The Hidden Gospel: Decoding the Spiritual Message of the Aramaic Jesus.* Wheaton, Ill.: Quest, 1999.

Dunn, James. *The Evidence for Jesus.* London: SCM Press, 1985.

Edelmann, Eric. *Jésus parlait araméen.* Paris: Éditions du Relié, 2000.

Ehrman, Bart D. *The Orthodox Corruption of Scripture.* New York: Oxford University Press, 1993.

———. *The New Testament: A Historical Introduction to the Early Christian Writings.* Oxford: Oxford University Press, 1997.

———. *Jesus: Apocalyptic Prophet of the New Millenium.* New York: Oxford University Press, 1999.

Evans, C. Stephen. *The Historical Christ and the Jesus of Faith.* Oxford: Clarendon Press, 1996.

Ferry, L. *Qu'est-ce qu'une Vie réussie?* Paris: Grasset, 2002.

Feuerbarch, Ludwig. *L'Essence du christianisme.* Paris: Gallimard, 1968.

———. *Pensées sur la mort et sur l'immortalité.* Paris: Pocket, 1997.

Josephus. *The Complete Works of Josephus.* Trans. A. M. William Whiston. Grand Rapids, Mich.: Kregel Publications, 1981.

Fredriksen, Paula. *De Jésus aux Christs.* Paris: Le Cerf, 1992.

———. *Jesus of Nazareth, King of the Jews.* New York: Knopf, 1999.

Freud, Sigmund. *Moïse et la religion monothéiste.* Paris: Gallimard, 1986.

Friedman, Richard Elliott. *The Disappearance of God: A Divine Mystery.* Boston: Little, Brown and Co., 1995.

Funk, Robert W. *Honest to Jesus.* San Francisco: HarperCollins, 1996.

———, Roy W. Hoover, and the Jesus Seminar. *The Five Gospels.* San Francisco: HarperCollins, 1993.

Geoltrain, Pierre. *Aux Origines du christianisme.* Paris: Gallimard, 2000.

Golb, Norman. *Who Wrote the Dead Sea Scrolls? The Search for the Secret of Qumran.* NewYork: Scribner, 1995.

Goodman, M. *The Roman World.* London: Routledge, 1997.

Grant, Robert M. *Augustus to Constantine: The Emergence of Christianity.* New York: Barnes and Noble Books, 1970.

Guitton, Jean. *Dieu et la science: Entretiens avec Grichka et Igor Bogdanov.* Paris: Grasset, 1991.

Guyénot, Laurent. *Jésus et Jean Baptiste.* Chambéry: Imago-Exergue, 1999.

Hexter, J. H. *The Judeo-Christian Tradition.* New Haven: Yale University Press, 1995.

Israël, Gérard. *La Question chrétienne.* Paris: Payot-Rivages, 1999.

Jeremias, Joachim. *Jerusalem at the Time of Jesus.* Philadelphia: Fortress Press, 1969.

———. *New Testament Theology I: The Proclamation of Jesus.* London and New York: SCM Press, 1971.

———. *Les Paraboles de Jésu.* Paris: Le Seuil, 1984.

Johnson, Paul. *A History of Christianity.* New York: Simon and Schuster, 1976.

Jonas, H., and C. Chalier. *Le Concept de Dieu après Auschwitz.* Paris: Rivages, 1999.

Käsemann, E. "Blind Alleys in the 'Jesus of History' Controversy." In *New Testament Questions of Today.* London: 1969.

Klausner, J. *Jesus of Nazareth: His Life, Times, and Teaching.* New York: Macmillan,1925.

Kümmel, W. G. *Theology of the New Testament.* New York: ET, 1974.

Küng, Hans. *Vingt Propositions de Être chrétien.* Paris: Le Seuil, 1979.

Leloup, Jean-Yves. *The Gospel of Mary Magdalene.* Rochester, Vt.: Inner Traditions, 2002.

———. *The Gospel of Philip.* Rochester, Vt.: Inner Traditions, 2004.

———. *The Gospel of Thomas.* Rochester, Vt.: Inner Traditions, 2005.

Léon-Dufour, Xavier. *Résurrection de Jésus et message pascal.* Paris: Le Seuil, 1971.

Levinas, E. *Difficile Liberté.* Paris: Albin Michel, 1963.

Linnemann, E. *Jesus and the Paraboles.* New York: Harper and Row, 1966.

MacMullen, Ramsey. *Christianisme et paganisme du IV au vnf siècle.* Paris: Les Belles Lettres, 1998.

Mack, Burton. *Who Wrote the New Testament?* San Francisco: Harper, 1996.

Maier, Johann. *Jesus von Nazareth im Der Talmudischenü Berlieferung.* Darmstadt: Wissenschaftliche Büchgesellschaft, 1992.

Mason, Steve. *Josephus and the New Testament.* Peabody, Mass: Hendrickson Publishers, 1992.

Meeks, Wayne A. *The First Urban Christians.* New Haven: Yale University Press, 1983.

Meier, John P. *A Marginal Jew,* vol. 1. New York: Doubleday, 1991.

———. *A Marginal Jew,* vol. 2. New York: Doubleday, 1994.

———. *A Marginal Jew,* vol. 3. New York: Doubleday, 2001.

Meschonnic, Henri. *Gloires: Traduction des Psaumes.* Paris: Desclée de Brouwer, 2001.

Meyer, Ben. *The Aims of Jesus.* London: SCM Press, 1979.

Miles, Jack. *Dieu, une biographie.* Paris: Robert Laffont, 1996.

Mordillat, Gérard, and Jerome Prieur. *Jésus contre Jésus.* Paris: Le Seuil, 1999.

Morin, E. *L'Identité humaine.* Paris: Le Seuil, 2001.

Moule, C. F. D. *The Origin of Christology.* Cambridge: Cambridge University Press, 1977.

Nautin, Pierre. *L'Évangile retrouvé*. Paris: Beauchesne, 1998.

Neusner, Jacob. *Judaism in the Beginning of Christianity*. Philadelphia: Fortress Press, 1984.

———. *Jews and Christians*. Philadelphia: Trinity Press International, 1991.

———. "Types and Forms in Ancient Jewish Literature." in George Foote Moore. *History of religions*, vol. 2. (London: T. and T. Clark Books, 1972).

Nietzsche, Friedrich. *Vie et vérité*. Paris: PUF, 1971.

———. *Beyond Good and Evil*. New York: Vintage, 1989.

———. *The Antichrist*. (Chicago: Independent Publishers Group, 1999).

Pagels, Elaine. *Beyond Belief*. New York: Vintage, 2004.

———. *The Gnostic Gospels*. New York: Vintage, 1989.

Perrier, Pierre. *Évangiles: de l'oral à l'écrit*. Paris: Le Sarment-Fayard, 2000.

Perrin, Norman. *Rediscovering the Teaching of Jesus*. London: Harper and Row, 1967.

———. *Jesus and the Language of the Kingdom*. London and Philadelphia: Fortress Press, 1976.

Perrot, Charles. *Jésus et l'histoire* (2nd edition). Paris: Desclée de Brouwer, 1993.

Pliny the Younger. *The Letters of the Younger Pliny*. IndyPublish.com, 2003.

Renan Ernest. *La Vie de Jésus*. Paris: Arléa, 1992.

———. *Marc Aurèle ou la fin du monde antique*. Livre de Poche, LGF, 1984.

Roman, Yves. *Le Haut-Empire romain*. Paris: Ellipses, 1998.

Rosa, Jean-Pierre. *Jésus-Christ ou la liberté*. Paris: Bayard, 1999.

Sachot, Maurice. *L'Invention du Christ*. Paris: Odile Jacob, 1998.

Sanders, E. P. *Jesus and Judaism*. Philadelphia: Fortress Press, 1985.

———. *Paul*. Oxford: Oxford University Press, 1991.

———. *The Historical Figure of Jesus*. London: Penguin Books, 1993.

Sartre, M. *Le Haut-Empire romain*. Paris: Le Seuil, 1991.

Schlosser, Jacques. *Jésus de Nazareth*. Paris: Noêsis, 1999.

Schopenhauer, Arthur. *Sur la Religion*. Paris: GF-Flammarion, 1996.

Schumann, Hans Wolfgang. *Le Bouddha historique*. Vannes: Éditions Sully, 1999.

Schweitzer, A. *The Quest for the Historical Jesus*. Minneapolis: Fortress Press, 2001.

———. *Le Mystère de la messianité et de la souffrance: Esquisse d'une vie de Jésus*. Tübingen, 1901.

Schweitzer, E. *Jesus*. London and Richmond, Va: ET, 1971.

Scott, B. B. *Symbol-Maker for the Kingdom*. Philadelphia: Fortress Press, 1981.

Segal, Alan F. *Paul the Convert*. New Haven: Yale University Press, 1990.

Shorto, Russell. *Gospel Truth*. New York: Riverhead Books, 1997.

Sibony, Daniel. *Les Trois Monothéismes*. Paris: Le Seuil, 1992.

Simon, Marcel, and Andre Benoît. *Le Judaïsme et le christianisme antique*. Paris: PUF, 1968.

Spinoza, B. *Œuvres III, Ethique*. Paris: GF-Flammarion, 1965.

Suetonius. *The Twelve Caesars*. London: Penguin 2003.

Tacitus. *Annales*. Paris: GF-Flammarion, 1965.

Trocme, Étienne. *L'Enfance du christianisme*. Paris: Hachette, 1997.

———. *Saint Paul*. P.U.F., Collection "Que sais-je?," 2003.

Tuckett, C. M. *The Messianic Secret*. Philadelphia: Fortress Press, 1987.

———, ed. *The Scripture in the Gospels*. Leuven: Leuven University Press, 1997.

Vermès, Geza. *Jesus the Jew*. Philadelphia: Fortress Press, 1981.

———. *The Religion of Jesus the Jew*. Minneapolis: Fortress Press, 1993.

———. *The Complete Dead Sea Scrolls in English*. New York: Alien Lane, Penguin Press, 1998.

———. *The Changing Faces of Jesus*. New York: Viking Compass, 2000.

———. *Enquête sur le Jésus historique, nouvelles interprétations*. Trans. E. Billoteau. Paris: Bayard, 2003.

Vidal, Marie. *Un Juif nommé Jésus*. Paris: Albin Michel, 1996.

Weiss, J. *Jesus' Proclamation of the Kingdom of God*. Philadelphia: Fortress Press, 1971.

Wells, G. A. *The Jesus Myth*. Chicago: Open Court, 1999.

Wénin, André. *L'Homme biblique*. Paris: Le Cerf, 1995.

Wilson, A. N. *Jesus: A Life*. New York: Fawcet Columbine, 1992.

———. *Paul: The Mind of the Apostle*. New York: W. W. Norton and Co., 1997.

Wittgenstein, Ludwig. *Tractatus logico-philosophicus*. Paris: Gallimard, 1961.

Wright, N. T. *The New Testament and the People of God*. Minneapolis: Fortress Press, 1992.

Index